S0-CDN-796

Renovating Your Home for Maximum Profit

How to Order:

Quantity discounts are available from the publisher, Prima Publishing, P.O. Box 1260DLB, Rocklin, CA 95677; telephone (916) 624-5718. On your letterhead include information concerning the intended use of the books and the number of books you wish to purchase.

U.S. Bookstores and Libraries: Please submit all orders to St. Martin's Press, 175 Fifth Avenue, New York, NY 10010; telephone (212) 674-5151.

Renovating Your Home for Maximum Profit

Dan Lieberman
Paul Hoffman

Prima Publishing
P.O. Box 1260DLB
Rocklin, CA 95677
(916) 624-5718

©1991 by Dan Lieberman and Paul Hoffman

All rights reserved. No part of this book may be reproduced or transmitted in any form or by any means, electronic or mechanical, including photocopying, recording, or by any information storage or retrieval system without written permission from Prima Publishing, except for the inclusion of quotations in a review.

Copy Editing by Cheryl Smith
Typography by Miller Freeman Publications
Production by Robin Lockwood, Bookman Productions
Interior design by Judith Levinson
Jacket design by The Dunlavey Studio

Prima Publishing & Communications

Library of Congress Cataloging-in-Publication Data

Lieberman, Dan.
Renovating your home for maximum profit / Dan Lieberman and Paul Hoffman.
p. cm.
Includes index.
ISBN 1-55958-097-6
1. Dwellings—Remodeling. I. Hoffman, Paul. 1957– II. Title.
TH4816.L53 1989
643'.7—dc20 89-3934
CIP

91 92 93 94 RRD 10 9 8 7 6 5 4 3 2 1

Printed in the United States of America

To Miran

Acknowledgments

No book of this type comes out of the experience of a single person. It is a compilation of the experience and teachings of many. I'd like to especially thank the following people:

To my parents, for supporting me on my first venture. To my professors and fellow students in architecture, who introduced me to the world of building. To Tim Kaarto, who unintentionally launched me in a new career. To Avi Weil, Joel Shefflin, and Greg Galli from whom I first learned about real estate. To Barbara Leicht who expanded my knowledge, guided me, and helped put my plans into action. To Marlene Daniels and others whose faith in me sometimes exceeded my own.

To the many people who I met while renovating; contractors, agents, and tenants who all had something to show me. And to the many authors whose books I have read, whose experience I learned from and without whom this book would not be possible.

To Brian Malony, Gerry Cheney, Lauri Paul and others whose thoughts and ideas added to the text.

To Robin Lockwood, Laura Glassover, and the others at Prima Publishing and Bookman Productions without whom this book would not have been possible.

And to all those who learn something of value from me and apply it in their own lives.

Dan Lieberman
July, 1989

Contents

Introduction

THIS BOOK IS ABOUT creating monetary value in your home. Since the mid-1960s, homeownership has been viewed by many not just as shelter but as an investment, and for most Americans it has been the largest investment they've ever made, if not the best. But unlike stocks and bonds, houses are physical structures, of wood and brick and mortar. Houses are homes, the places where people live their lives, raise a family, and often eventually retire. So a house can be viewed in two ways: as a home to live in comfort and as a financial instrument. This book will concentrate on the latter, although they are intertwined.

Just as there are investment guides for stocks and bonds, there should be one for your home. This book answers the key area of the investment—how to add value. To do that, we will have to concentrate on the physical structure as well as the emotional involvement. Many of the items in this book may appear simple, but just as a simple magic trick may appear amazing until the answer is revealed, the results you get from this book's advice may appear out of proportion to the work involved. But don't let that fool you. These are the same tricks developers and professional renovators use to get the maximum price for their buildings.

Although it involves a very large financial decision, home buying is not rational. It is an emotional issue, and it is emotions and people's associations between building form and lifestyle that builders are constantly using when they design new homes. You will be doing the same—affecting people through proper renovation. If you decide to pursue renovating homes as a business, you will become more and more aware of what buyers want and what affects them, or in builder's language, what pushes their hot buttons.

Renovating your home can be a lot of fun and very profitable. It can be an addictive process as you find yourself viewing your home and others' homes with new eyes, the eyes of possibility. This skill you will develop to envision possibilities can be used to buy other properties to renovate, and could become a way to financial independence for you.

People who successfully renovate homes get paid well for the process. But it does take a lot of work and creativity. The nicest part is you get to see the results of your efforts—improving a home and upgrading a neighborhood. You will become sensitive to the needs of your buyers, and because you are giving them what they want, you will reap the rewards.

If you are fortunate enough to own a house, or if you're looking for one, renovating properties is one of the few areas available to make a profit. There was a time not too long ago when just about everything went up in value. As long as you owned some real estate, you'd probably make money. Real estate was talked about at every party and property appreciation was the topic on everybody's lips. In California it was almost considered unrespectable to be earning less than your house did. Now, however, times have changed and creating value, or "forced appreciation" is the name of the game. There are many ways to create value, such as rezoning, change in land use, or building a new structure. But renovating real estate is one of the safest and potentially one of the most lucrative ways to create value. The purpose of this book is to show you, using specific data, what and how to renovate in your home or income property in order to get the maximum profit for your time and money.

Why Renovate?

On average, more than 95 percent of all homes on the market during a given year are resales. Only 5 percent are new homes. Yet those 5 percent seem to sell very quickly despite lacking many of the amenities and conveniences of the older established neighborhoods. That is because they are designed, built, decorated, and marketed professionally with the sole purpose of selling that home.

The average homeowner, on the other hand, decides he wants to move and then proceeds to put his home up for sale, giving little thought to his competition, the impression his home makes on a typical buyer, who his typical buyer even is, or what he could possibly do to get a better price.

The sad part of the story is that the older home is probably better located than the new homes, which are now on the fringes of town; it probably has character and charm that many new homes lack, and it's probably on a larger piece of property. Yet many buyers will look at and buy the new homes because of the way they have been designed and sold for the home buying market.

Perhaps you've just bought a home and would like to maximize its potential for when sale time comes a few years down the road. Knowing which renovations will make you money can save you many headaches later.

Renovating is probably one of the quickest and easiest ways to add value to your home. You will realize a tremendous equity buildup in a very short time through your ingenuity and labor. The equity you build can be a source of tax-free investment funds, since you don't pay any taxes on the increased value of your home until you sell it (and then, only if you don't reinvest the money within two years).

There's also a chance to make great money renovating other homes. In every town or city there are buildings that have been let go, areas that are just on the rebound, and distress situations—all opportunities for a skilled renovator.

Renovation can be fun, it can be a way to learn new skills and become empowered, and it can be highly profitable. Wouldn't you like to get $2, 3, or 4 back for every one you spend, even after paying yourself at full union scale? You can if you're selective about how you spend your money and if you develop the ability to see what others can't see.

Creating Value in Your Home Through Renovation

Would you like to get the best price for your home or investment property? Of course you would. But to do that means providing people with what they want.

Since the first grade, we've heard of the old economic law of supply and demand. Yet most home sellers ignore this very basic law of economics. If you ask the typical seller how she determined the price for her home, you'll probably get some vague answer about it being what she thinks the house is worth. There will be no talk about what the market is currently seeking. Well, what is true with most products is true with most homes: Items in demand command higher prices, while items that are commonplace and in oversupply generate lower prices. Developers and builders spend millions of dollars each year on extensive market research to determine what buyers want. These studies, combined with plain old experience, have taught these professionals how to build their new homes. You can use that same knowledge in preparing your home for sale.

Your house probably has many characteristics that would cause a buyer to want it, including many that a new home would lack. Most likely, it also has some flaws that might turn people off and cause them to continue their search for a home elsewhere. In this book, you will learn techniques to help you redesign your home, accentuating the positives and mitigating or transforming the negatives in order to create the highest sales price, for the effort and investment, that you can get for your home.

Although people may talk of a home being the largest investment they'll ever make, most people view the purchase of their house as a lifestyle investment more than a monetary investment. Most of the people coming to look at your home will be looking for a potential lifestyle more than an expected rate of return on their investment, no matter what they may say.

The features and amenities they want in a home have less to do with financial practicality than with making a statement as to who they are and what their status is in society. It is the rare buyer who will walk into your home with calculator in hand, estimating potential appreciation and rate of return. Most of us want a home, and that's where you'll make your money—selling not a house, but a home containing the features most buyers want to get the lifestyle they need.

Some of the following renovations are major, some are minor. How much you want to do depends on your own needs, temperament, financial resources, and amount of profit you really want. You don't need to maximize your monetary profit to get a good return. There are times when your peace of mind, energy, and time are worth more than the few extra hundreds or thousands you might pick up if you did every renovation possible on your home. Also, some of the renovations will just not be possible in the home you own. There are literally tens of thousands of different home designs built in America. No one book can cover what's right for every one of them. However, you will be given the principles needed to increase your home's value. It is up to you to adapt them to your specific home.

Buying a House for Renovation

Buying a property to renovate can be one of the most profitable undertakings you've ever attempted if you do it right. Not all homes have the upside potential you need to make a renovation practical. The key is to distinguish between those items that add value (known as improvements) and those that just cost you money (known as repairs). Since you will be selling your home in a real estate environment, knowing the market is crucial to your success.

It has been said by many a successful remodeler that you make your profit at the time of purchase and you realize that profit at the time of sale. No amount of skill and wonderful remodeling will make a good investment out of a poor purchase. You must know what a home will be worth after you remodel and subtract out your costs and required profit before you can determine your purchase price. Real estate values are crucial in the planning of your project.

There are many characteristics that make a home desirable to a prospective buyer, and all these factors get figured into the price come time of sale. These include

- Location of the property (in relation to schools, employment, and shopping centers)
- Quality, status, and trends of the neighborhood
- Charm potential of the home
- Condition of the home
- Relation of the home to surrounding homes in the neighborhood.
- Potential of the lot (zoning, drainage, plantings)
- Functionality of the home

We will consider all these topics and others necessary to choose a home or an investment with the best potential for profit.

Getting $2–4 for Every $1 Invested

Where you put your money is crucial in renovations. Stories of cost overruns and overimprovement abound. Beware of getting too emotionally attached to the buildings you examine. You may want to remove those asbestos shingles and restore all the original gingerbread on that lovely 1880s Victorian, but if it is located next door to a new auto garage, chances are you'll never get your money back. Why spend $20,000 renovating to get $10,000 back? You might as well give it away. At least it will save you the effort.

Just as all locations are not alike, all areas of the home are not treated equally by buyers in determining if they want to purchase a particular home. Over the years, most renovators have developed their own unique formulas for adding value. Some only concentrate on kitchens and baths, others emphasize curb appeal or some other aspect of the home. Analyzing what works has shown that there are general rules that are proven in giving excellent returns. These are what we'll be focusing on in detail in this book.

Planning Your Budget and Time

You may be reading this book because you intend to sell your home soon and want to get top dollar. Or perhaps you are not planning to move yet but are contemplating a major renovation and want to know where to concentrate the money for highest return when it does come to resale time. We will talk about budgeting and planning your renovation, phasing it (if you intend to live in the house for a while), and dealing with contractors and subcontractors.

INVESTING LARGER AMOUNTS OF MONEY

It is not necessary to spend large amounts to drastically increase the money you will earn from your home. However, you may decide you want to earn even more and get all you can out of your home or investment. We talk about major rehab projects in this book, too. The same principles apply, though—you should only do what will bring you a return that is significantly higher than your investment of money, time, and energy.

Larger projects have the potential of bringing in larger amounts of money, but there is also significantly more risk. Be careful with your budget.

INVESTING JUST A LITTLE

We also have checklists and reminders of the little things to do that can bring a high return for little or no investment. You can probably add a few thousand dollars to the value of your home just by following these hints.

Get Started

Remodeling your home can be one of the most profitable activities you will undertake. Remodeling is a labor-intensive activity. As much as two-thirds of the cost of remodeling can be labor. As you remodel, you will be increasing your home's value based on appraisal, not what it cost you or what you would have to pay a contractor to do the work. This money is even essentially tax-free until you sell. You can borrow against increased equity (home equity loans) for personal consumption or to finance another renovation.

If you start renovating for profit as an investment vehicle, you will find that you don't have to follow the ups and downs of the real estate market. You will be creating value by making neglected properties attractive to rent or own. Your ability to see what others can't and to renovate economically can mean incredible financial success.

Renovation and remodeling are the keys for making money in real estate in the 1990s. Anyone can do it. You don't need to be a professional. Times change, people's desires change, and uses of buildings change. You can be part of the renaissance of a structure by making it meet the wants and needs of today.

It's easy to renovate your home if your budget is unlimited. There are many books on the subject, full of lavish pictures. In renovating for profit, the key is not to spend so much that you can't recoup your expenses. Many people have tried remodeling, only to find that they overimproved the house for the neighborhood. As you use these tips and techniques, you will soon find yourself having acquired the renovator's eye and the chance to improve buildings and communities and to make a lot of money in the process.

There's an old story about the value of knowing what to do. It seems a man had a problem with the boiler in his apartment building. It kept making horrible noises and he wanted it to stop. The man tried to fix it himself but in desperation finally called a plumber to fix the problem. After looking over the situation, the plumber gave the man a quote of $150 for the job and the man readily agreed. Upon hearing that, the plumber walked over to the boiler, tapped it with a wrench, and the noise ended. The owner, upon seeing this, was outraged and asked for an itemized bill explaining why this 30-second operation was worth $150. A few days later when he got the bill, it read

For tapping pipe	$ 0.50
For knowing where to tap	$149.50

This book will show you where to tap in your renovations so that you may achieve the best price for your home.

CHAPTER ONE

Getting Started

WHAT DO ALL THESE phrases from real estate listings seem to have in common?

- Traditional central floor plan and exquisite detailing
- Large master suite
- Bright and airy living with views of the hills
- Newly remodeled "gourmet kitchen"

These are all clues to what buyers are looking for. Certain items are highly desired by the house-buying public. If you are to receive top dollar for your home, you need to respond to this pent-up want. Phrases from advertisements give you good starting clues. The question then becomes what is reasonable to do to your existing home so as to reap the maximum benefit with the minimum investment.

How to Create High Demand for Your Home

When people are buying a home, emotions usually override the rational mind. Most people like to think home buying is an objective decision—that they've carefully compared the value of the home to others in the area—but in reality, it seems to come down to whether they like the home and the neighborhood or not.

Professional renovators, designers, and real estate agents who know this and use it well consistently sell their homes more quickly, easily, and for a higher price. They've learned that one must appeal to the emotions, to the senses, with light and flowers and music.

CREATE THE ILLUSION OF SPACIOUSNESS

Most buyers are looking for a lot of space—as much space as their money can buy. Even if a buyer has to settle for a small home, he wants it to look as large as possible. In recent years, land and building costs have climbed very high and developers are using architectural tricks to make homes seem more spacious than they are.

The house should seem as big as possible. Varied ceiling heights (volumes), carefully placed sightlines, and shared spaces will enhance this feeling of spaciousness. If you have a small home, you must make up in excitement what the home lacks in size.

CREATE THE ILLUSION OF LIGHT

People like bright homes bathed in natural light. You may not be able to provide the ideal lighting character with the configuration of your current home, but you can improve on what you have. We will explore ways to increase light coming into the home and to direct it to areas of most importance.

CREATE A SENSE OF WARMTH AND HOMINESS

People want to feel comfortable in the home they're about to buy. They need to be able to picture themselves living in and using your home as theirs before they will make an offer to buy it. A sense of retreat and sanctuary is high among buyers' unstated needs. We will show you how to generate those feelings both in the architecture of the home and in the decorating and setting. Make your home so comfortable that the buyer wants to take off her shoes and stay—forever.

CREATE A SENSE OF QUALITY

Most people want to feel like the home they are in is well built. It should feel good as well as look good. Do the drawers drag out of the wall cabinets or glide out smoothly? Does the door sit properly in its frame or do you have to force it out with a little push? These little things can make the difference in people's impressions of your home.

Low maintenance is also a high priority, especially with today's busy two-income couples. Few people want to spend their day off working on the plumbing or mowing the lawn. A home that feels like it won't take too much effort to keep up will sell more easily than one that feels like a handyman's special.

ENHANCE THE CHARACTER OF THE HOME

When planning your renovation, keep in mind a total concept for the home. An underlying theme allows the whole impression to be greater than the sum of the parts. This can be done through as simple a technique as keeping colors consistent between rooms, or it can be in the use of details. A home needs to have a certain character about it. Whether it be English Tudor, ranch, modern, or colonial, the home should be unified—not a jumble of rooms and textures. There should be an unwritten order underlying the plan.

MAKE THE HOUSE FEEL NEW

Even in old homes, people want their homes to feel new. It may sound like a contradiction, but mastering this principle may make you a lot of money. Although intellectually the buyer knows it's a "used" home, on an emotional level he wants it to feel like it was built especially for him. For example, there are colors that are considered "old." Mustard yellows and lime greens were in style at one time but now they date a house. Repainting it in current colors like roses or grays instantly updates it. It's the same with flooring. Replacing a carpet that "smells old" can do wonders for your home's value.

MAKE THE HOUSE INTERESTING

Having eight-foot ceilings throughout the whole house tends to make it dull and uninteresting. But if one of those rooms bursts open into the rafters, it adds excitement and sex appeal to your home. This translates into higher sales prices. Planned contrasts create interest and drama in your buyer's mind and she will remember your house over all the others she's visited that Sunday.

MAKE THE HOUSE A HOME

Home is a quality that the best houses have. It connotes a setting for family gatherings and for parties, for lively conversation and good dinners. But also it is a sanctuary, a very private and special place, full of little pocket-like places that tempt you to linger, morning sunlight shining through the windows, open and airy, yet uncompromisingly private. That's the home you want to create.

The Immutable Laws of Real Estate

Where your home is located and what the other homes nearby look like is crucial in determining how much upside there is to improving your home. There's a tried and true old axiom in real estate that the three most important things in a piece of property are (1) location, (2) location, and (3) location. Tired as this may seem, there's a lot of truth contained within it. If you live in a mansion but it's located in a slum, it's not going to be worth very much, no matter how much time or money you put into it. It may end up being the most expensive home in the neighborhood but it still will be worth less than some two-bedroom bungalow in the best part of town. Know this in the back of your mind as you start to plan your renovation campaign.

You may think to yourself "I can defy the laws of nature. I will improve my home and get more than the market says I will." Don't be fooled, however. Those happenings are rare to say the least. You make the most money in bringing your home up to the level of the better homes in your neighborhood, not in surpassing them. The worst home on the block has a lot more chance to improve substantially than the best.

The first step in upgrading the value of your home is to find out what it is worth and what potential it has based on its size, layout, and location. To do this, we must perform what is known as an appraisal. There are three basic ways professional appraisers value property. One is the replacement value—what it would cost to rebuild your home to the same quality and condition it is today. The second method is the income method (this applies more to rental and commercial properties). This method bases the value on how much rent you can get. The third method is the one used by most real estate and appraisal professionals on single-family homes—the comparable sales method.

The comparable sales method uses recent sales of homes similar to yours in your neighborhood to determine what the value of your home would be. That's how many real estate agents price homes for sale, but it's a very inexact science. In fact, it's more an art than a science, as even professional appraisers rarely get the same value if asked to do the same appraisal. What most people never do on an appraisal is take it a step further to see what your home could sell for given all the possibilities.

The way to start is to get a list of homes sold in your area recently and to see the range of prices received. In addition to the selling price, you need to know as much about the properties as possible: the number of bedrooms, bathrooms, and total rooms; the square footage of the home and of the lot; any special features due to site or structure, such as being on the top of the hill (good) or

Address	List price	Sales price	BD	BA	Features	End Date	Days on market
6031 Farilane Drive	$259,000	$237,000	3	1	DR FR FP	1/5/88	138
6051 Westover Ct.	$425,000	$415,000	4	3	DR FR FP	1/6/88	62
5950 Valley View	$235,000	$211,000	3	1	FP	1/22/88	58
6295 Chambers	$237,000	$237,000	3	1	DR FP	1/23/88	16
2636 Maxwell Avenue	$220,500	$202,000	3	1	FP	1/26/88	68
5551 Brookside	$169,000	$120,000	2	2		1/29/88	122
322 Scenic Avenue	$405,000	$392,000	4	2	DR FP	1/31/88	47
3612 Glenwood	$412,000	$405,500	4	2	DR FR FP	2/5/88	45
4325 Gregory	$130,000	$128,000	1	2		2/6/88	30
2708 Maxwell Avenue	$249,500	$222,500	3	2	FP	2/19/88	53
44 Ridge Drive	$310,000	$285,000	3	2	DR FP	2/23/88	42
453 Scenic Avenue	$350,000	$349,000	4	2	DR FR FP	2/28/88	18
12 Stoneridge Ct.	$240,000	$192,000	3	1		3/1/88	102
6432 Rockridge Drive	$215,000	$214,000	2	2	FR FP	3/2/88	20
2637 Colby St.	$522,000	$499,000	4	3	DR FR FP	3/12/88	58
390 63rd Street	$95,000	$ 70,000	1	1		3/13/88	135
2432 Russell Street	$330,000	$310,000	3	2	DR FP	3/16/88	82
7201 Wood Drive	$186,000	$160,000	2	2	FP	3/25/88	105
245 Scenic Avenue	$290,000	$295,000	3	2	FR FP	3/25/88	5
3115 Maxwell Avenue	$119,500	$113,000	1	1		4/1/88	76
5727 Brookside	$335,000	$324,500	3	2	DR FP	4/17/88	73
4985 Ralston	$195,000	$192,000	2	2	DR FP	4/21/88	86
5482 Shafter Ct.	$126,000	$122,500	1	1		4/23/88	80
345 Glenview	$360,000	$360,000	4	2	DR FP	4/24/88	10
5344 Madrone	$260,000	$249,500	3	2		5/2/88	32
6680 La Salle Avenue	$269,000	$260,000	3	2	FP	5/4/88	26
52 Manzanita	$390,000	$369,000	4	2	DR	5/19/88	45
3725 McGee	$159,000	$159,000	2	1	FP	5/23/88	22

Figure 1.1 *Listing of recent neighborhood home sales*

being on the freeway off ramp (bad). The more information you have, the better you will be able to determine the parameters of your home's current and potential value.

Look at the different homes on your list. What did the most expensive one sell for and what was it? What did the least expensive one sell for and what was it? This helps give you the range of values in your neighborhood. If the highest-priced home sold for $300,000 and the lowest $150,000, and your home is worth $250,000 as is, you should avoid any expensive remodels because the most upside you could expect would be around $50,000 ($300,000 minus your home's $250,000).

Let's look at an example. Figure 1-1 shows a recent sales list. Let's say your home is a three-bedroom, one-bath house in this neighborhood. You see that four homes of the three-bedroom, one-bath variety have sold in the last year. The list shows prices ranging from $192,000 to $237,000, but you know the $192,000 has some problems. So you average the other three which are similar to yours and arrive at a value of approximately $210,000. That's where most real estate agents stop. But not a skilled house renovator. Look at the most expensive home on the list. Notice it's a four-bedroom, three-bath house that went for $499,000. Now notice the lowest-priced sale. It's a one-bedroom shack with no working plumbing and sold for $70,000. So you now see that what is basically a lot is worth $70,000 and the best home in your neighborhood is worth in the range of half a million dollars.

Now look at some of the simplest combinations. What is the average for three-bedroom, two-bath houses? We see the average is $275,000. So it appears that adding a bathroom might substantially increase the value of your home. Let's see what an extra bedroom might do. Well, we see there are no four-bedroom, one-bath homes but there are four-bedroom, two-bath homes selling for an average of $375,000, which is $100,000 more than the 3/2 houses (3/2 means 3 bedrooms, 2 baths). It appears your best bet would be to add an extra bedroom and bath.

But there's more. Many other factors come into play. What is the size of the public rooms (living room, dining room, etc.) in those more expensive homes. They may be substantially different from yours. What other basic structural or floor plan differences are there? There are many elements that come into play and the more you know, the better. However, just on a quick look, we can see that there's more money to be made working on your home than just selling it as is.

But let's suppose you don't want to spend a lot of time or energy or money on a renovation. All you want to do is sell your home and move. There are still many small things you can do to increase the value of your home. Remember that there were other 3/1 houses more valuable than yours. Why is that so? What features do those other houses have that yours doesn't? You might want to analyze these homes. You will be able to add thousands of dollars to your home's value just by following the specific items we talk about in the chapters on room-by-room renovation.

KNOW YOUR BUYER

If you are going to design and present your home for an imagined buyer, you must know who that buyer is going to be. If your home is set up for a family with children, but the schools in the area are horrible, you are going to have to overcome that somehow. (Perhaps convert the home to two apartments.)

Or perhaps you live in a neighborhood with many retired individuals. The type of people looking at homes in your neighborhood is more mature. You would not aim your home at the first-time buyer.

BE OBJECTIVE

We all have emotional attachments to our homes, but in determining value and potential we must detach ourselves and view the house as a design challenge. What can be done to increase value, taking into account the neighborhood value limits, the budget, and the type of buyer we are marketing toward?

Common Mistakes to Avoid and Easy Solutions

The key ideas of profitable renovating have been known for years. If you have to choose where to put your money, it should be where the buyer can see it, touch it, and feel it. But in the past all we had were vague generalizations to go on. Now we will get into specifics, so you can receive top dollar for your home or income property.

The most common mistake people make in renovating is renovating the wrong item. Let's say a person's home is a two-bedroom, one-bath home worth $115,000, located in a neighborhood of three-bedroom, two-bath homes that sell for $150,000. The owner decides he wants a new family room, which costs him $25,000 to build. What's the home worth now? Probably $120,000. The fact is the family room brought him negative return. Why? Because it wasn't what was needed most for that house in that neighborhood. What was needed was another bedroom or bathroom.

The second most common mistake is to overimprove for the neighborhood. This is related to the first one. The old real estate cliche that the three most important elements in determining the value of a home are location, location, location is true. It's like gravity. You can try to work against it but you'll lose every time. If you take the White House and move it to East Oakland, what's it worth? Perhaps $150,000. But, you say, it's the White House. So what. It's overimproved for the neighborhood and the people looking for a house like that will look somewhere else. Few millionaires want to live in slums, even if the homes are nice.

You will find that most home prices don't vary more than 25 percent or so from the median for a particular type of home in a particular neighborhood. If most three-bedroom, two-bath homes are selling for $235,000, improving yours so much that you need $300,000 to break even is economic suicide. Better to shoot for the median or a little above than to try to have the nicest home.

Remember, most people looking for a $300,000 home will be looking in a better neighborhood. They will probably have ruled out your neighborhood without ever setting foot in it. By creating the best house you are severely limiting your potential market of prospective purchasers.

Another major mistake many people make is confusing repairs with improvements. Repairs are broken items you must fix, such as an old roof or cracked foundation. Improvements are items that increase the value of the home, such as adding another bathroom or repainting.

Sometimes there's a fine line between repairs and improvements. Is renovating an old, outdated bathroom into a larger, more desirable one a repair or an improvement? Being able to spot the difference between these two is crucial to your success.

Another major mistake is to make the home too personalized. When a buyer comes looking at your home, she has to be able to picture herself living in the room and enjoying being there. Many people look to homes to give them a lifestyle image they want. If you paint your bedroom purple, put in a sunken waterbed, have incense burning at all hours, and blast Jimi Hendrix from your stereo at top volume, you're going to limit the market appeal of your home.

The more personalized you make your home, the greater the chance you'll have to undo that renovation come sale time. There are endless stories of people who spent thousands of dollars remodeling their homes, only to find they actually lowered the home's value in the process.

Many old homes contain a myriad of small rooms. Although buyers today prefer large rooms, removing walls may be a mistake. Care must be taken in the selection of rooms you intend to enlarge. Many people will take three small bedrooms and combine them to make two nice large bedrooms. This is usually a mistake. Buyers always pay more for three bedrooms than two, no matter how small the three may be or how beautiful the new two bedrooms are.

Departing radically from the neighborhood style is another common mistake. If your home sits amidst wood-shingled craftsman bungalows, re-siding it as a brick Tudor home will not increase its value—it will probably lower it. Just as too large a home or too improved a home never gets what its true value should be, a home that sticks out becomes less appealing than it seems it should be.

Most other mistakes in renovating center around doing the job wrong the first time and having to come back to fix it. This will cost you far more than twice as much. It could cost you an order of magnitude more. Be thorough and do quality work. You don't want to have to tear open a ceiling because your new plumbing leaks or be subject to banging every time someone flushes the toilet because you didn't wrap the pipes before sheetrocking the wall.

Remember to avoid the use of tired looking, dull, cheap looking, or dated materials. Although, as expenses mount, you will be tempted to save money, these can do more harm than good.

Finally, beware of the designer magazine home syndrome. These magazines show you idealized views of homes that are probably unlivable and certainly very, very expensive to create. The average home will just cost too much to do up to the designer magazine level. Use the magazines for inspiration but don't take their ideas too literally.

The typical buyer is very happy with a bright, clean, airy home. Anything extra you give is money out of your pocket. You must gear your level of renovation and design to where the house is located.

Don't be discouraged. There are times when homes should be done decorator perfect. That is in the upper price ranges, where people can afford, and will pay for, such quality and designer touches.

CHAPTER TWO

Do You Really Need to Use a Contractor?

NOW THAT YOU'VE DECIDED to move forward with renovation, you must decide how much of the work you want to do yourself. If you decide to use a contractor, you will avoid many of the hassles of managing the work yourself and hiring subcontractors for the actual labor. If you do not have the time to manage the project effectively, hiring a contractor will probably save you both heartache and money in the long run. However, if you have the time and fortitude to take on the roles of negotiator, manager, and project coordinator, you may be able to increase your financial rewards substantially. The key is to be honest with yourself about how much time and energy you can afford to give the project.

Hiring a General Contractor

A general contractor serves as the coordinator of the work. He hires and directs the subcontractors, orders the materials, and makes sure they get delivered to the site on time. This is mostly a managerial job, although knowing what you're looking at is important if you should happen to deal with an unscrupulous subcontractor. Have you ever gone to an auto mechanic and had him tell you "the carburetor is in the crankshaft with the piston rings blocking the oil" or some other made-up problem? It's possible to have building subs do the same thing. Knowledge is power. But don't be intimidated; a basic understanding of buildings, which can be gained from a single text, is all you'll need.

The primary reason to be your own general contractor is to save money. Many full-service general contractors will mark up costs as much as 30–50 percent. This markup covers profit, overhead, and contingencies, an important consideration since many construction problems are hidden from view until a project is started. So a job that would cost you $40,000 by hiring subcontractors might cost you $52,000–$60,000 if you hired a general contractor. This is, of course, after-tax income. So if you're in the 28-percent bracket, you will have had to earn between approximately $70,000 and $80,000 just to pay for this $40,000 job.

As a general contractor, you will be responsible for the overall project. This includes coordinating your subcontractors, securing any needed insurance, perhaps buying materials, and meeting with inspectors.

It's not so easy. Being a general contractor takes a great deal of time. If you have another full-time job, the time lost in meeting inspectors, solving job-site problems, and paying for materials can eat into your productivity. On the other hand, much of the job can be done in the evenings and on weekends. Tasks such as scheduling contractors and ordering and paying for materials fit this category while others, such as meeting with the city planning commission and obtaining building permits, can usually be done with a day or two off.

It is recommended that you hire a general contractor at some point if you intend to make remodeling your career, full- or part-time. This way you can observe him and learn the tricks of the trade. Also, you just may find it pays to let him do the work.

Make sure you hire only established contractors. Stories abound of shifty contractors running off with a client's money and leaving a job unfinished. You want someone who is dependent on the community to stay in business.

References are always the best source for contractors. If you know someone who's had some remodeling work done and was very pleased, that's a good start. People are rarely pleased with remodeling contractors, so when you get a good report, jump on it.

Another good place to look is professional organizations of builders or remodelers. These people know that remodelers have a bad reputation and will often give you referrals of very good people to counteract that image. The National Association of the Remodeling Industry is located in Arlington, Virginia. You can call them at (703) 276-7600 to get the location of a local chapter, or ask for a list of member contractors.

Banks can be a good source of information, as they often make remodeling loans. Materials suppliers and real estate agents can be good sources, too.

Being a General Contractor Yourself

If you're short on technical skills but have the time, energy, and talent to manage and supervise others, then being your own general contractor can be a rewarding experience in terms of growth and especially in terms of dollars saved. There are three main areas of concern.

INSURANCE

You never know what might happen on a project, and proper insurance coverage is the best way to limit your exposure to liability. If you are using licensed contractors, they should have their own worker's compensation insurance. You must insist on seeing proof of current coverage or you could be liable for any injuries sustained by persons working on your home.

If you are using unlicensed contractors, friends, or family, you should make sure your homeowner's policy has a worker's compensation rider on it. This is usually quite inexpensive and it could save you substantial amounts of money should injury occur.

BONDS

Bonds are used as collateral to ensure against risks of losses due to unfinished or poorly performed work. It's like an insurance policy on the quality of the job. There are many different types of bonds—payment bonds, performance bonds, surety bonds. All of them guarantee that a specific aspect of the project will be done. They tend to add between 1 and 5 percent to the cost of a project, but are valuable insurance should something go wrong.

Bonds are only recommended on larger projects because the costs, paperwork, and delays are not usually worth the headache on smaller jobs.

LIENS

By law, people who do work on your property are entitled to be paid. A legal instrument called a lien may be placed on your property if your contractor fails to get paid. A lien will prevent the sale of your home until the worker is paid and will cloud your title to the property.

Even if you are scrupulous about paying your contractor, if she doesn't pay her subcontractors or material suppliers, they can place liens on your property. You must be certain these people are getting paid, too. Either pay the workers directly or have your contractor supply you with an unconditional lien release, relieving you of responsibility for the payment of subcontractors so long as the contractor is paid.

Locating and Hiring Subcontractors if You Are the General Contractor

Finding good subcontractors is a combination of experience, luck, and diligence. The best way to get a good sub is to ask for references from other people who have had work performed by him. However, if you don't know anyone who has had the appropriate sort of work done satisfactorily, here's a list of some of the places to find subcontractors.

The Yellow Pages. This is hit and miss. You know the business is probably established if the name is here. But they also tend to charge more and you are very uncertain of quality. Stay away from the quarter page or larger ads. Who do you suppose is paying for that advertising?

Job sites. Drive around and see who's remodeling in your area. Ask if you can see the work. If it looks good, you have a potential sub. Get his business card and have him bid on your job.

Around town. Take down phone numbers off of trucks you see driving around town. If a subcontractor is busy, there must be a reason. You want to be wary of someone no one else is hiring.

Classified ads. Many professionals moonlight at nights and on weekends or when times are slow at their companies. You can usually get top quality work at a rate much reduced from the full cost that includes overhead and advertising (maybe $16/hour rather than $45).

Building and trade associations. Membership rosters will give you a lead to go on. These people are concerned about their image and will usually do a good job. But get some references before hiring.

References from other contractors and renovators. Probably the best source. You know they've satisfied others with the same requirements as you—low cost and high quality. Most contractors and subs have worked with others from the different trades and know who's good and who's not. Architects and construction lenders are other good sources of references.

Building supply stores. Many lumberyards, electrical supply houses, and plumbing shops keep bulletin boards where tradespeople can pin their cards. They can also give you recommendations as to who's good or who needs work and can do it cheaply or quickly.

Find out as much as you can about a subcontractor before hiring him. Always get references. You don't want to trust your home to someone you know nothing about.

GETTING BIDS

Some bids include materials, some don't. Make sure you know what you're getting. You probably don't need a set of finished plans to get an accurate bid. Many times just walking the plumber or electrician through the home and explaining what you want will be sufficient. Just get the bid in writing before work starts. There shouldn't be any objection to that.

Remember to get several bids for each job. Three is always the recommended number. Make sure you know what you want. Changes can be disproportionately expensive. If you think you might want something else, run both ideas before your tradesman and get estimates for each. That way you'll know what you're getting yourself into.

When you get your bids, make sure everyone is bidding the same specifications. If the bids come out very different, find out why. Is one really cheaper than the other or is there skimping on materials? Check whether one left out a portion of the job. Always leave an extra

10 to 20 percent for unexpected problems and contingencies.

Be prepared to give your bidding contractors drawings, plans, specifications, and a copy of the contract you intend to use. You should be prepared to help clarify questions and items on the documents.

Evaluate the bids carefully. If all of them are higher than expected, try to locate the reason. If there is a wide range of prices, call to confirm that they are all bidding the same items you requested. If one has a cheaper way and it seems reasonable, go with it.

Call up the contractor you felt was best and see if he can defend his bid against the others. He might even lower it to get the job. You might try having the contractors all work their bids out against the others, justifying their price or the way they plan to do the job.

If the bids do not include materials, getting your own detailed material estimates requires a lot of legwork. You need to make the rounds to various suppliers. The salespeople will usually help you out, as long as you go at off-peak times.

PAYING SUBCONTRACTORS

Absolutely do not pay a subcontractor until you are completely satisfied with the work. Many will give you stories about needing money to pay the rent, etc. You need a substantial holdback to guarantee the work gets done. Once you've paid, the incentive to perform for you is gone. Only the best subs value honor above pay. It is standard to keep 10 percent for two weeks after the work is done to protect yourself from some problem showing up.

Pay your subs proportionally to the work done. Most people really do need the money and they can only go so long without some. However, make sure the work is always ahead of the pay. For example, if the work is 80 percent complete, you could reasonably pay 50 percent of the amount to the contractor. All payment schedules should be worked out ahead of time in writing.

Try to get bids from all workers. Paying by the hour almost always ensures cost overruns, sometimes substantial ones. If you're hiring some local kids to do the work, you should estimate the time you think it will take, the amount you're willing to pay per hour, and multiply. Then offer that amount to your worker to do the complete job. Period. Deviating from this procedure will only cost you.

SCHEDULING

It is your responsibility to schedule the job efficiently and effectively. Most tradesmen like to complete their portion of the work in one uninterrupted block of time. They don't like to have to stop because some part of the job, that was someone else's responsibility, is missing. If your electrician has to stop in the middle of his job because of some mistake of yours, you may have a hard time getting him back to finish the job when you need him. You'll have to fit his schedule.

CHANGES

Many times items will come up that require deviation from the established plans. Perhaps there is wiring in a wall where it was thought there was none. Perhaps there's now a better way to run the plumbing. Your subcontractors may request they be allowed to make these changes. Trust their advice, especially if it costs you nothing. They are experts in their fields and you are not. If costs will increase because of the change, scrutinize it more carefully. You want to know the reason is truly valid. It's good to have a professional you can call with questions like these. Perhaps hire a home inspector on a retainer and have her bill you hourly for her advice.

LICENSES

Depending on who does your work and the type of work they are performing, you may or may not require them to have a license. Just be aware that you are more liable if they don't. Usually if they are doing major work like electrical or plumbing, or if they're installing major components such as a new heating system, it pays to go with a licensed professional. Insurance is a key issue. Make sure they carry it, or you could have a big headache if something should happen. If you still insist on hiring labor without insurance, make sure you have it on the property. It's a standard item with most insurance companies and it doesn't cost very much.

NEGOTIATIONS

Many quotes will not be the best price you can get. Different subs use different strategies to get jobs. Some quote high and hope that a sucker takes their full bid. Others quote low to get the job and then constantly try to add things to the bill or start doing inferior work. Or they bid low and go out of business. You want them to be around later if a call back is necessary. Others bid correctly, giving you a fair price but also allowing them to make a reasonable profit. Negotiating is an art. The best way to get good is by practicing. The money you save can be substantial over the long haul. When you get their "final price," ask them how much lower they'll go if you pay them all cash. If it drops a bit, there's room in the price.

Especially in remodeling work, some contractors prey on the novice homeowner or renovator. Be alert and check around.

SUPERVISION

If you decide to take on the role of a general contractor, be warned it will be time-consuming. You need to be on call to receive deliveries, solve minor problems, and be ready for general emergencies.

A practical alternative to devoting all your time to the job site is to hire a carpenter to act in your place as supervisor. It's important to have someone you can trust overseeing the work. A good carpenter can do this and should be compensated. Since carpentry is one of the main trades on a building and is there from start to finish, your carpenter will most likely have something to do the whole time he's not solving problems.

CONTRACTS

You want everything in writing in order to cover you if problems arise. You don't want to find, in the middle of a job, that a contractor has substituted cheap materials for the ones you wanted, and not have any legal recourse. Starting and completion dates should be spelled out and the schedule of payments should be clear.

Remember that you're not just paying for the work. You have mortgage obligations and other "time is money" commitments. So if you can't get contractors to lower their price, you might be able to get them to start the job sooner or convince them to work weekends to speed up the project.

Questions to Ask a Contractor

Contractors are used to making bids. They can turn anywhere from one in three to one in ten inquiries into paying clients. At this stage of the process, your goal is to see how imaginative the contractor is, if he can do the job, if you think you'll get along with him, and how soon he can start.

Ask if he's done similar jobs and if you can take a look at the work. Also see what type of priority your job gets. If it's at the bottom of the list, look somewhere else. You don't want his workers only coming to your job site when other jobs slow down.

After your interview, you should do some background checking on your potential contractor. See if he just works out of his home. This may not be bad, but it is riskier than someone with an office. Does he have a license and carry workmen's compensation insurance?

Call the Better Business Bureau or your state Contractor's License Board to see if any complaints have been lodged against this contractor.

You might also ask the contractor what projects he is currently working on and go visit the job site. There you can talk to the homeowner and see how happy she is with the work. Also, you can get an idea of the quality of the workmanship and of how professional an organization is. Many contractors will want to show you their showroom, but you want to see actual jobs, not sales tools.

Find out if the contractor is actually going to work on your home or just have one of his staff be foreman. Ask how long he expects the job to take and then check previous jobs to see if his time frames are accurate. A great question to ask is "why would we be better off dealing with you than another contractor?"

Remember, you will be entrusting your most valuable asset, your home, to someone you have never met and giving that person a sizable percentage of your savings. So be careful who you choose. No matter where you find a contractor, check his background. Have any complaints been filed against him? Is he licensed? How long has he been in business? And the ultimate question: "Would you hire him again and why or why not?"

Doing the Labor Yourself

When your plumber bills you at $50/hour and your electrician at $65 and your architect charges $100, it's easy to imagine going broke within the week and the temptation is there to attempt to do the work yourself. But be honest—do you really have the time or skill to do the work? What else would you be doing with your time? Many jobs you shouldn't even consider doing. They require a certain expertise to achieve professional results. Other jobs (such as asbestos removal) can be hazardous to your health and should be hired out.

However, many jobs can be done by the homeowner or novice remodeler and many times with a level of skill near that of a professional. In the chapters on renovation, we'll talk about which jobs to do and which to avoid.

You may be able to find a contractor who will work with you. With the recent emergence of owner-builder centers and of people wanting to renovate their own homes, some contractors have carved themselves a niche in the market by offering to work with the homeowner. This helps reduce the costs and, especially if this is your first project and you intend to do more, it allows you to view a professional in action without being an annoyance or getting in the way.

If you do intend to work with a contractor to save some money, keep your commitment to finish your share of the work on time. It's easy to get bogged down in paperwork or other tasks and ignore some of the basics. Also, you may end up paying for his time if he has to wait around for you.

Open up charge accounts, too. Most contractor accounts get 30 days to pay. You get the float and save the interest.

Beware of being overly concerned with costs. Many people become penny-wise and pound-foolish. Labor usually accounts for between 60 and 75 percent of a job's total costs, materials being the rest. So cutting back on quality of materials is usually false economy. Proportionally, labor is the big ticket.

This isn't to say don't be concerned about prices. On the contrary, look for the best price and choose a quality that is appropriate. You don't need a $5000 professional stove in a two-bedroom bungalow. The $279 model should be just fine. But many people will buy the stock cabinets sold at many home improvement centers just because they seem to be half the price of custom cabinets. Look again. What materials have gone into them? Do they look and feel like particleboard? Do the drawers open smoothly on side guides or are they being dragged across a center wooden track. Your buyers can feel the difference.

In general, beware of the two extremes—top of the line and bottom of the line. There's usually a middle ground that has a low cost-per-quality factor.

You may not have the time to work on your home but you may have family members, friends, or others that do. They can be a cheap source of labor, especially if they have any construction experience or are detail oriented. However, the usual precautions apply when getting involved in a business relationship with family and friends—namely, that you might get your house remodeled but at the cost of the friendship.

If you haven't done much remodeling work in the past, or the work you've done has never come out the way you hoped, remember it will take you substantially longer than a professional to do the task and if the results don't look good, you may actually be decreasing rather than increasing the value of your home. You can't just decide to start the project and "see how it goes." You are committed to the end. Few contractors like to come in at the middle of a job and finish it. The ones that do charge a premium.

Professionals have special tools and know tricks to get the job done quickly and looking good. Think about the price of learning as you look at the price of hiring.

Certain tasks, such as demolition, painting, and cleanup are easily done by the amateur remodeler. Others require expertise.

Materials

Material costs can add up on a project. The money you save here is more profit in your pocket at time of resale. In order to obtain the best prices, you will have to do a lot of calling around to different suppliers. This may sound time-consuming, but it is the same method professionals use, and it can save you hundreds or thousands of dollars depending on the scope of your remodeling.

The method is simple. You list all the materials you will need based on your plans and call around to several suppliers, seeing who will offer you the best price. Check for quantity discounts. Obviously, your time is worth much and this method should only be used on the more costly items such as windows, lumber, plumbing, etc. Don't start pricing the cost of doorknobs if you only need two. But, on substantial items, even a single call can save you a hundred or more dollars.

Attempt to get discounts from materials suppliers. Many don't really offer contractor discounts, they offer discounts to those that they view as volume customers or repeat clientele. You may qualify. The key word is ask. If you are doing your renovation over a period of time and you want to look like a regular to get a discount, every time you need something, go to the same supplier and purchase it. Let's say you need plumbing. If you need a valve, go to the plumbing supply. A week later if you need a new faucet, get it at the same plumbing supply house. Initially only purchase the small items. Talk to the people at the checkout stand. Soon they'll recognize your face. You'll become "a regular." When you finally do purchase the big order, such as all your supply and drain lines, walk up to the cashier and ask for your discount. She will probably assume you're a volume customer since she's seen you all the time. If she does ask for a license, tell her you are a property owner and do many renovations. Many suppliers give discounts to owners, too.

Where you shop is crucial, too. You don't want to always pay retail. There are many levels to the distribution process, from the manufacturer down to the retail building supply shop open to the general public. Depending on the quantities you're buying, you may be able to purchase directly from the manufacturer or the local distributor. The farther up the chain you are, the better price you will get, as you don't have to pay for several levels of profit. Consider these hints when you are preparing to buy materials.

Shop by phone if possible. It will save you countless hours.

If you can get free delivery, do. If not, pick the materials up yourself. This can be a great savings over the course of the project. If you are getting delivery, see if you can order over the phone and pay the driver upon delivery. This saves you two trips down to the materials supplier, time you could be working on your home.

Check different policies among different suppliers. How do they handle returns? Do they give refunds or just credits? Make sure you can live with their policies.

Use retail showrooms, home improvement stores, and local hardware stores to see and feel the products and to select what you want. You can then decide either to buy there or order from the suppliers and save the markup. Realize though, that your time is worth something. It may be worth paying retail for the convenience.

There are also many mail order catalogs available for home improvements, especially for renovating older homes. Many have products you can't find locally. However, there is usually a long shipping delay. Also, you have to be careful how you order. Shipping charges can add up over several orders. Plan carefully.

You can find used building materials at salvage yards and some flea markets. Many such places are listed in the Yellow Pages, too, under Building Materials, Used. This can be a wonderful source of architecturally rich materials. Many architects and remodelers spend countless hours at these yards. Some materials, such as brick, look better used. Other items, such as windows, are probably better new due to modern advances in insulating qualities, etc. But you can get some great bargains. Windows that might cost $200 new can be had for $10—if you can find the right size.

Don't always go with the cheapest materials. Check the quality. You want the lowest-cost reasonable material. Quality, or the lack thereof, shows. You will not get the full potential value out of your renovation if you skimp here. Remember, materials are not usually the major component of remodeling cost.

Building Codes and Permits

When you hire a contractor, he normally takes care of all permits, inspections, and other dealings with the city in order to complete the job and get paid. If you are doing the work yourself, you need to learn the codes, apply for the building permit yourself, and arrange for the inspections. Talk to the inspectors before you do the work. They can give you helpful hints as to what they will be looking for.

Permits can take anywhere from minutes to months to get. You don't want to hold up your project because of them, so plan the permits as far in advance as is necessary to ensure a margin of safety.

When the work is done you should get a certificate of completion and, if you are creating a new dwelling unit, a permit of occupancy.

Other Valuable Considerations

INSPECTING THE WORK

The simplest rule to follow is if it doesn't look right, it probably isn't. Aside from structural and services work, much of what you'll see, your buyers will see. If it looks odd to you, it will look odd to them and they'll get suspicious (rightly or wrongly) about the quality of work they can't see. Everything cosmetic has to look perfect.

A common practice of general contractors and architects is to do what is called a walk through. During the walk through, you point out to your contractor all the things that look wrong or are unacceptable. This is all spelled out in writing and the contractor is to fix it. If it can't be fixed, you should work out a compromise with the amount he's being paid (this is why you hold back money). It is recommended that you do two walk throughs, a preliminary and a final. Only when you are satisfied is the money released.

If you don't feel qualified to judge the contractor's work, hire an independent third party, such as an architect or professional home inspector, to do it for you. You don't need to be a structural engineer to know that walls should be vertical and that doors should close properly. Don't just go by looks. Try out each item. Your buyers will.

PRICE AND VALUE OF QUALITY WORKMANSHIP

Quality is a hard thing to quantify, but it does show and is more important as you go toward the higher-priced homes. It is amazing to see the garbage people will buy in hot markets. Anything will sell if it has four walls and a roof. But when times slow down, the owners that did poor jobs always seem perplexed as to why their property isn't selling. The rest of us aren't.

WHEN DOING YOUR OWN WORK PAYS

What kind of work can you do? The simplest is cleaning. This is time-consuming but easy. You could also hire a cleaning service. They don't cost too much. Demolition work and painting are reasonable, too. Some carpentry, sheetrock, mudding and taping, finish plumbing, and electrical may be within your capabilities. Landscaping can be very rewarding if you know what you're doing.

Key Players

In addition to the subcontractors, there are a few other workers and professionals whose services will be invaluable to you, whether you hire a general contractor or act as your own.

In a renovation project, as with most things in life, penny-wise can be dollar-foolish. Not using one of your key players in order to save a few dollars could become quite costly. There's an old saying that a good professional is never too expensive. A cut-rate one turns out to be very expensive when something goes wrong. You shouldn't have any unpleasant surprises if you use your key players properly.

These people are not usually considered subcontractors, but in the context of being a professional renovator, that is precisely what they are. They are providing a service to you. You are the manager and orchestrator of their work. Like coordinating subs on a building site, coordinating your renovation with the real estate agent, architect, and others is your job.

As with any subcontractor, you want to have good references and know they can perform. But there are also a few other items to check with these professionals. Many provide more services than you need. The following is an overview of the key people, some of the services they perform, and the ones you will want.

PROFESSIONAL BUILDING INSPECTOR

This person evaluates your project with you to determine if it's even a feasible renovation. He helps determine condition of the systems and of the structure and can give you rough cost estimates for repairs. Many problems that look severe turn out to be minor. The reverse is true also. A professional building inspector will be able to spot the difference.

An inspection by a professional also carries weight in selling negotiations. If you are buying a home to renovate and your inspection turns up many unforeseen problems, you can use the report to renegotiate on the price. An inspection you do by yourself won't carry as much weight with the seller.

No matter how many books you've read on the subject, get a professional who's insured and has a guarantee. Even some contractors hire professional inspectors just to make sure they haven't missed anything.

ARCHITECT OR DESIGNER

Especially if you are inexperienced or undertaking a major investment, a good architect can be a great asset. This person can save you many costly mistakes by giving you a road map of the renovation. Without a plan, money just seems to flow out the window. A well-conceived design is the best investment you can make. Major housing developers are realizing this and are now using design elements for impact and to be able to raise the prices of their new homes.

Whoever you hire, make sure she has experience with remodeling. New construction is a very different game and, in a lot of ways, much easier than renovating. An architect familiar with remodeling can give you a better idea of costs and knows some of the unexpected things that often pop up.

The architect can provide you with

Design services. This is the phase where the architect will create several concepts and potential plans. She can give a rough estimate of costs and work with you to create the design you want, with the impact you want at a cost that makes financial sense. Get a second opinion on costs and value. Many architects are not well trained in cost estimating and it is wise at this time to bring in your real estate agent or a contractor to help you determine future market value and actual cost. You are the master planner. You are designing this project for the particular housing market in your area. This means it is necessary to have the market knowledge and the design sense together to see what can be done with your structure to create a desirable and affordable project. I recommend a walk through with yourself, your architect/designer, and your real estate agent. When suggestions are made by one, the other can determine whether they will work or not.

Working drawings and specifications. Once the design is finalized, an actual set of drawings and specifications will be drawn up to submit to the building department and the contractor.

Supervision. Many times an architect will supervise the construction work for a nominal fee. This can be insurance that a quality job will be done.

An alternative to using an architect is a design/build contractor. These people know costs better than most architects and will be with the project from conception through final product. However, many firms lack the imagination and quality of design a trained architect can provide, so be careful in the design/build firm you choose. When selling, you want to get the buyers excited about your home. If it costs a little extra to create this, it will most likely come back to you.

Even though you will probably be using a design professional if your renovation is of any large degree, there is no substitute for doing your homework. You will get more for your money if you can ask intelligent questions and have some knowledge of the market and what you want. Read all the books on renovation you can and watch television programs on home renovation. Doing this will open your mind to possibilities and allow for a better give and take with your architect or designer.

REAL ESTATE AGENT

This person can help you get a handle on values in your neighborhood and on what people are looking for. Every day, agents are out viewing other properties, seeing what prices are being asked, and finding out what properties have sold for. They will also know what properties have sat on the market for a long time and may have a good idea as to why.

A good agent will also market your property effectively when the renovation is finished and can find you future properties with renovation potential. Agents have a network of other agents with buyers and can put the word out for the type of property you're seeking. And you don't pay them unless they perform.

But for renovations, a key function of the real estate agent is to take information, such as is in this book, and help you hone it for your particular market. A good agent knows what prices people will pay in certain neighborhoods and for certain types of homes. With this knowledge, you can decide what renovations are a necessity, what ones are optional, and what ones don't make any sense in your particular market.

ATTORNEY OR REAL ESTATE ATTORNEY

Many people have a fear of attorneys or at least a morbid dislike for them. However, the law is a way of life and these are specialists. Many of your renovation projects, especially ones involving zoning and variances, may hinge on legal issues. A good attorney is necessary here. She can also catch items at the closing. Although the attorney is not technically a part of the renovation, the fact is we are dealing with real property and all the laws that affect it when we enter this game.

It is also good to have an attorney when dealing with construction projects and contractors. She may be there to draw up contracts or to answer questions should disputes arise. Hopefully, you'll never have to use her for a legal action but it's nice to know she's there should the possibility arise. If nothing else, just having an attorney tends to keep the other party from making threats or ignoring legal obligations.

THE HANDYMAN

Many tasks are small and don't require the cost or skill of professional tradesmen. This is where the handyman comes in. The cost is usually low ($10–20 per hour) and handymen can do a multitude of tasks—you don't need to hire a separate person for each trade. Their work quality can be as good as that of a professional. They are always unlicensed. Just check out references before using someone you don't know.

Finally, put everything in writing and be detailed. If your contract just says to paint the house but doesn't specify the quality paint or whether it's one or two coats or the amount of prep, you could get a job far inferior to what you anticipated.

CHAPTER THREE

Estimating Remodeling Costs

ESTIMATING IS MORE OF an art than a science. Few skills are more important to the success of your remodeling than being able to estimate your costs accurately. Fewer still are less well understood.

Before you can begin to estimate accurately, you have to know what you want. Start by imagining what would improve your home the most, what would make it the most salable. Would you like your kitchen to be like a kitchen down the street? Write this down as a renovation possibility. Would new tile in your bathroom help sell your house? Write down that idea, too. Only after you have written down all possible renovation ideas can you start to calculate costs and see where savings can be made.

Now that you have an idea of what you want, and you've made notes on paper, it is time to make sketches. Don't worry that you are not an expert draftsman. Even rough, though accurate, sketches are helpful here. It is not necessary at this stage to have finished construction documents (and it may never be necessary). You just want an accurate idea of sizes to calculate material and labor costs. If you know that the tile you want sells for $6 a square foot and you know that the labor cost is $2.50

per square foot, but you don't know how many square feet you have in the bathroom, you're no closer to getting an accurate cost than if you didn't even bother pricing items.

If your project is starting to look too big and expensive, don't worry. You can always scale it down. It is possible to do more with less. Spaces and functions can be combined to create wonderful rooms. Costs can be cut by doing the labor yourself, allowing the money to be spent on the finest materials. You can cut costs by learning the dimensions in which certain materials come. For example, linoleum comes in 6- or 12-foot widths. If you're designing a 13-foot wide kitchen, you will be adding significantly to your costs. This applies equally to wood lengths, wall coverings, and any other material that comes in a standard module.

Not respecting a material's module size adds so much to the cost because of the labor. Whether it's your time or your money that is covering the cost, the extra time involved in measuring, cutting, and hiding seams can be as great for a little extra piece as for the rest of the project. For example, cutting tile adds greatly to the length of time needed for installation. Quite often, cutting and installing the tiles around the perimeter of a room takes more time than doing the whole rest of the room's floor, even though it might be four times greater in area.

As you pay attention to the building process in your planning and are aware of labor-adding items such as cutting and fitting, the skills of estimating and the skills of design will soon incorporate themselves into one another so that you create a beautiful, functional design at minimal cost.

As you design your renovation plan, be aware that many older homes are not designed to accommodate certain modern appliances or other items. If your attic floor is inadequate to handle the weight of the new jacuzzi tub you want in the master bath, it may not be worth installing—even if jacuzzis are all the rage in your neighborhood—because it would mean rebuilding your entire floor.

When planning rooms, in addition to thinking about cost, think about lighting, ventilation, circulation, functionality, and, of course, aesthetics. A building that is solely designed around cost considerations shows it.

Estimating Methods

There are three basic methods used in estimating—rule of thumb, square footage cost, and unit by unit cost. Rule of thumb estimates or ballpark figures are useful only in the earliest stages of a project proposal. This method seems to be the most common and is probably the least useful, but it does allow you on a moment's notice to decide if a project warrants further investigation. The square footage methods work pretty well as a next level of approximation of cost. Many contractors carry rough square footage estimates for different types of construction in their heads and will tell you whether it's possible to build your bathroom for $50 a square foot or not. (Of course, the quality you desire will affect these estimates.) The third method is the true professional and most accurate method of cost estimating, although it takes more time than either of the first two. There are many books on this method of estimating, whereby a project is divided into separate tasks and then a cost per unit of task is assigned.

STICK AND UNIT METHODS

These methods are the most complete and accurate methods, which most contractors use when making estimates. Both these forms can be found in books such as R. S. Means' *Repair and Remodeling Cost Data* or *Dodge Remodeling and Retrofit Data*. These guides are used extensively by the trade but are just as useful to the homeowner planning a remodeling project.

The way to calculate stick method costs is to go through the whole process of the renovation from the start to finish. This includes demolition, carting the debris away, framing, plumbing, finishing, etc. All of the activities are mentally done in their proper order. You count every piece of material that will be needed, add them up, and get your total material costs. You then calculate how long it will take to perform each section of the renovation to get your labor costs. Figure 3-1 shows an estimator's shopping list.

Another detailed method of calculating, and one used commonly by builders, is the unit cost. In unit cost, you calculate your cost per material unit, such as cost of siding per square foot, multiplied by the amount of wall square footage of your home (less doors and windows), or the cost per linear foot of concrete foundation multiplied by the perimeter of your home. In this regard, it is very similar to the stick method. But labor costs are not figured by the job but rather by the unit. Figure 3-2 shows an example of unit estimating.

Using the unit method will give you an estimate that compares favorably with actual figures reported to the estimating guides by thousands of contractors. The problem is adjusting for costs in your particular area versus the national average. Just remember, these calculations are only an "estimate."

All estimating breaks down into three major components—materials costs, labor costs, and contingencies.

Estimating materials is simple and straightforward, although it can be time-consuming. Estimating labor costs, on the other hand, is an art. The estimating guides will give you a rough idea how long it takes a professional crew to do a certain task. How long you will take depends on your level of skill and confidence. Some items you will be able to perform nearly as fast as a pro. Some will take two or three times as long. Make sure to account for all hidden labor costs in your estimate. These include unloading the lumber truck, covering materials after a day's work, and cleanup.

Description of item	Unit	Unit cost	Quantity	Total cost
1/2" AD plywood	Sheet	$21.00	1	$ 21.00
Cabinet Varnish	Gallon	$12.00	2	24.00
2 × 4 studs	Linear foot	$0.30	400	120.00
Door Hardware	Door	$18.00	6	108.00

Figure 3-1 *Estimator's shopping list*

Description of item	Unit	Unit cost	Quantity	Total material cost	Labor hours	Labor cost/hour	Total labor cost	Total cost for task
Install oak plywood paneling	Square foot	$1.95	450	$877.50	9	$16.00	$144.00	$594.00
Paint bedroom walls and ceiling	Square foot	$0.04	2700	$108.00	25	$8.00	$200.00	$308.00

Figure 3-2 *Example of unit estimating*

Contingencies such as weather delays (especially if you are renting equipment), chasing the neighborhood kids away, getting the dog out of your freshly poured concrete, and time driving to the hardware store for that one missing part all need to be calculated in. Perhaps an extra 20 or 25 percent should be tacked onto your labor costs to figure in these items. Things always take much more time than expected. There will also be unknowns in the walls. Perhaps you discover rotted wood, and now you have to fix it. Or perhaps there is wiring in a wall you were going to remove. That takes extra time, and extra money. Many contractors won't even touch remodeling because of the unknown contingencies.

When estimating, you must be very thorough. Forgetting all the little items will cost you in the end. They seem to have a way of adding up to a great big item. Nails, hardware, the cost of cleanup (in time), the cost of hauling away debris can add up until the little things that you forgot to add into your estimate become a sizable chunk of your remodeling costs.

Don't forget about costs such as loan fees, carrying costs, insurance, and other costs not directly related to the physical structure. How about the costs of eating out while your kitchen is being remodeled, or the psychological costs of inconvenience? Many times it is these costs that make or break a project. When figuring costs,

Item	Estimated cost	Actual cost	Over or under
Bath:			
Install bathroom floor tiles	$400.00	$432.00	$32.00
Install sheetrock	$100.00	$125.00	$25.00
Skylight installation	$535.00	$476.00	($59.00)
Install new vanity	$295.00	$295.00	$0.00
Totals	$1,330.00	$1,328.00	($2.00)

Figure 3-3 *Worksheet*

calculate in everything. It's the only way to assess if the project is worth doing. Figure 3-3 is a worksheet to keep you on budget.

You want to break items down into the smallest reasonable components to calculate your costs.

SQUARE FOOT METHOD

Developers and remodelers never do a detailed estimate on their first look at a project. This would take too much time and money. They rely on rules of thumb to make quick judgments, the most accurate of which is square foot estimating.

Tables have been compiled based on builders' experience as to how much a particular type of renovation should cost on the average per square foot. Imagine a vertical slice through the living room of your home. Imagine this slice being one foot square at its base and cutting through the floor joists, subfloor, carpet, any wallboard and studs, any wiring or plumbing in the wall, the ceiling joists and light fixtures, and you have an idea of what is involved in coming up with the square foot calculations. Using your experience or consulting a table, all you need to know is what type of renovation you wish to do (bathroom, kitchen, bedroom) and the square footage of the room. Look at the table and multiply. R. S. Means puts out a book called *Means Square Foot Costs*, which breaks down construction costs in this way. (Although primarily geared for new construction, it is handy for remodeling, too.) Many local builders have compiled their own lists based on experience.

ORDER OF RENOVATION

Renovating, and all construction, has a logical order. Certain items must be finished before others may be started. An obvious example is that the foundation and framing must be done before the roof can be put on. But there are smaller and less obvious tasks involving the same concept. For example, you don't want to cover any of your walls until all pipes have been tested with water in them. This seems obvious, but it is hard to count the number of times people have had to tear open freshly covered walls to fix a leak.

Plan for all inspections. You don't want to sit around for five days because the electrical inspector is backlogged and you need to sheetrock the room, covering the wiring. Phased construction is the answer. Have several projects going on at once that can cover each other's lag time. This way, while waiting a day or two for the bath tile to set, you can work on installing the new front door.

BALLPARK ESTIMATING

The roughest form of estimating and the one most likely to get you into trouble is using ballpark estimates. Ballpark figures provide the quickest way to see if a project is worth pursuing. If it seems to be economically viable using ballpark figures, one might put in the time to see actual costs. If it doesn't even work under ballpark, the project is dumped with little if any time invested.

Kitchen renovation	$3500–8000
New roof	$1500–3000
Paint, interior	$100–200/room 6 Rooms
Paint, exterior	$2000–4000
Bathroom renovation	$1500–3500
New electrical service	$500–1000
Totally new electric	$1200–2000
New plumbing	$1500–2500
New carpeting	$1700
Landscaping	$500–3000
Total	$14,500–29,900
Contingencies (15%)	$2175–4485
Total estimate	$16,675–34,385

The table on the previous page shows how you might do a quick ballpark estimate on a two-bedroom home that needs some upgrading.

In the rough estimate for bidding purposes, you can use ballpark figures to estimate what you should offer for a house. Get more realistic figures before you actually buy.

Estimated value of house at resale	$ 325,000
Estimated cost of renovation	$ 30,000
Carrying costs	$ 12,000
Sales costs (real estate commissions, closing costs)	$ 20,000
Profit required to do deal	$ 30,000
Maximum bid you can make	$ 233,000

By working backward this way, you can learn what your maximum allowable purchase price is. This will let you pass by many average deals until the right house to renovate comes along.

As a final tip, remember to estimate your costs high. If you start with your estimates too tight, and a problem or unexpected occurrence arises, you may run out of money or go over budget. Always use a contingency amount for unexpected problems.

LEARNING ESTIMATING SKILLS

Experience is the best teacher—either yours or someone else's. If you haven't done any renovation work before, you can learn from books and from talking to other people who have renovated. Many book stores contain some information on home renovation, and in larger cities there are even architectural and construction specialty bookshops.

Owner-builder centers have recently started appearing across the country. Many of these teach renovation classes in addition to being a great source of information and collective experience. University extensions have real estate and construction courses. Materials suppliers sometimes hold classes to talk about new products.

Tips for Maximizing Productivity

This chapter will conclude with a few recommended tips to help keep costs down.

Plan accurately. It costs a lot less to fix an error on paper than it does to correct it after you've started construction. Accurate plans are also essential for getting realistic estimates of construction costs.

Decide which items you want to handle yourself and which should be left to a professional. Then plan a schedule and flowchart to maximize productive time and minimize down time.

Order materials correctly and issue specific delivery times and places. It costs more to run back and forth to get little pieces of forgotten hardware or plumbing from the hardware store than to have ordered the correct amount or a little bit extra in the first place. Your time is valuable, and other people's time costs you money. Also be careful how material piles are arranged. You don't want to have to dig through a ton of lumber to find the 1 x 2 at the bottom.

Keep the site clean and store materials neatly. A cluttered floor is a hazard around power tools and machinery. Injuries have occurred and people have been hospitalized because of carelessness. Keeping tools and materials organized doesn't waste time, it saves it. Knowing where to find everything is invaluable. Many a beginning remodeler has had to stop a job because he needed just one more valve, all the plumbing stores were closed, and he couldn't find the one he "knew was around here somewhere."

Reduce fatigue. Don't try to work long days. Fatigue leads to low productivity and possible injury. Schedule your work for humans, not supermen.

If you have large glass windows or a sliding glass door, before starting construction, take some masking tape and put an "X" over the glass. You will prevent some serious accidents, not to mention having to replace the glass.

Use the appropriate worker for the appropriate task. Much of construction work requires unskilled labor. To pay a carpenter $12 an hour to haul lumber around is a waste of money. Hire a grunt laborer at $5 per hour to do that type of work. If you have two jobs going on at the same time, the grunt can shuttle between them.

Schedule work flow on paper. There are two types of tasks that must be performed in a renovation project: sequential tasks and parallel tasks. Sequential tasks must be done one before the other, such as pouring a foundation before you frame the floor. Parallel tasks are tasks that can be done independently of one another, such as laying a new kitchen floor and hanging wallpaper in the bathroom. By putting down all the necessary tasks on paper, you can clearly see which are sequential and plan your time schedules accordingly.

Plan for contingencies. Nothing ever goes as planned. You will find unexpected decay in the walls, or the night before you're to receive your concrete delivery, the concrete truckers go on strike. Interest rates may rise, or you may fall ill. Don't make your schedule so tight that you do not allow for change.

CHAPTER FOUR

The Process

NOW IT'S TIME TO begin. Refer back to the chapter on getting started to remind yourself of the feelings that you want to generate in a buyer.

There is a whole hierarchy of renovation, from cleaning, to major foundation repair, to adding another dwelling unit. Many rooms will need only a light touchup, others may need a full overhaul. You must decide which level you will be undertaking.

Minor remodeling might include

Cleaning

New paint

New carpeting/linoleum

New doorknobs, window hardware

Minor repairs

Installing mirrors

Changing light fixtures

Moderate remodeling might include

Modernizing the kitchen

Modernizing the bath

Refinishing floors

Removing interior partitions

Major remodeling might include

Adding a new room as value dictates

Remodeling the attic

Adding a second story

Adding a second dwelling unit

You need to decide how much you are willing to do to your home. What is your budget in time and money? The extent and quality of your remodeling needs to be geared to the location and value of your home and its relation to the other houses in the neighborhood. But no matter what the cost or quality of your home, all homes can benefit from applying the basic principles discussed earlier in the book.

All homes can use a sense of drama and elements of surprise. It's what keeps an environment interesting. As you look through the chapters on renovating particular parts of your home, keep several thoughts in mind.

First, rooms do not exist totally alone and of themselves; they are part of the total that is your house. If your bathroom looks like a Roman dream but the rest of the house is one step away from being condemned, the bath will not help sell the house.

Second, the chapters start with some small elements and work up to a major renovation. All these suggestions may not be appropriate for your home, but they will increase value in general. If you have no fireplace and we talk about improving the fireplace to give a sense of warmth to the living room, it doesn't mean that your home won't sell unless you rush out and buy and install a fireplace.

Third, every home has a mixture of good elements, neutral elements, and shortcomings. Your home may not require an extensive renovation. A market-oriented remodeling will emphasize the positive and try to neutralize the negative. As you go through your home, look for the problem areas but also look for the pluses. These will be key selling points and may determine the direction of your renovation.

You must seek out the problems because whether you do or not, buyers will. This isn't Alcoholics Anonymous, but acknowledging that problems exist is the first step to coming up with creative solutions. It is the people who think that selling a house means sticking a "for sale" sign out in the front yard that get into trouble when the buyers bring their army of inspectors through.

Fourth, be creative. You will come up with many of your own ideas about what is appropriate for your home. The suggestions in this book are merely proven items consistently sought by buyers.

Fifth, it is crucial for you to know who your potential buyers will be. Are they first-time buyers, or current homeowners who wish to move up to a larger home, or move down to retire. Although not easy to generalize, certain elements are especially desired by each of these different groups.

Finally, enjoy. You have a chance to beautify your home and make a lot of money in the process. Remember, your house is going to become a visual treat, a stunning example of residential design. It is possible to transform your home profitably.

Mistakes to Avoid

There are many mistakes that beginning renovators seem to make consistently. This list should save you countless hours, headaches, and dollars.

Probably the worst mistake beginning renovators make is to use inferior materials in order to save money. People can usually tell when a product is inferior and they won't pay top dollar for your home if it's composed of junk. There are reasonably priced quality materials available; they may take some searching to find, but it will pay off in the long run.

The second major mistake is the use of dull, tired, or out-of-date materials and features. This includes putting used appliances in the home (with outdated colors), buying dull, dark carpeting because it was a leftover on sale (why do you think they're trying to get rid of it), or painting with colors that scream "outdated" to the potential buyer (such as mustard yellow living rooms or pink kitchens).

You need to learn what buyers want. Don't guess; look around. Go to as many open houses as you can. Check out new home developments, especially ones professionally decorated. Go back a few weeks later and see if the house has sold or not. All this information will give you an idea of what is hot and what is not.

You can learn a lot by looking at real estate flyers. Notice which features are being emphasized. Look at magazines to see what the professionals value. Talk to tradespeople, real estate agents, kitchen and bath appliance retailers, and fixtures salespeople. This research will give you clues as to what is popular.

A third mistake is to do only partial remodeling of a major system such as plumbing. Many older homes have galvanized iron pipe, which has a life span of approximately 25 years. Over the years the pipe builds up deposits until there's very little room for the water to get through. Replacing a portion of the plumbing system will not improve the water pressure because the water still has to pass through the restricted sections. Electrical systems work the same way. Many people will upgrade the service electrical capacity coming into the house but will leave all the old two-pronged electrical outlets ungrounded.

Paying too much for work is another common mistake. Always get at least two estimates. Three is the classic number recommended. You might find that the first quote was way too high. It is not uncommon for one estimate to be double another estimate for the same work.

Also be wary of paying too little. Look carefully at bids that seem too low. It usually means either inferior work or that the contractor has missed a vital piece of information in preparing his estimate. If you get a very low bid, be sure to check references. Review the contractor's previous work and find out if it went over budget. If the references check out, great, you've found a true bargain. Remember, however, you usually get what you pay for.

Another mistake is underestimating the cost and the psychological toll of a renovation. Renovations always seem to take twice as long as planned and cost considerably more than budgeted. The process can be a heavy burden, especially if you are living in the middle of it. You can't just leave—it's your home. So, if you decide to do a major renovation, be prepared. Have a planned retreat to escape to when the going gets rough.

The next on the list is lack of a good plan. This is perhaps the most important common downfall of beginning renovators. It isn't enough just to think about one room at a time. The overall picture must first be in your mind before you can work on individual elements.

Measure every room to get an idea of the layout of your home and to see how it works and how you can alter it. You may find a treasure in extra hall space that can be incorporated into a room or used to carve out some more closets.

Without a plan, you'll find yourself tempted to add a little here, and a little there, until you find that those little things have added up and now you've gone way over budget.

The final, and perhaps most important item, is lack of imagination and believing it can't be done. Many contractors or other experts will give you their opinions on some proposed renovation you have. But if they can't give you an answer that is satisfactory, keep asking. You may find that there really is a way, and that it's not that expensive.

Recently, we attempted an attic conversion. But the floor joists were only 2 x 4's. Everyone said the only way to do the floor was to nail 2 x 8's or larger members to the existing floor to make it strong enough. The problem was the attic didn't have much head clearance and those extra four or six inches of flooring would have made the project unfeasible. The books said it couldn't be done, contractors said it couldn't be done. Finally, we found an architect who had a brilliant suggestion of bolting steel beams to the floor joists to give them the required strength—making the attic conversion possible and affordable. So think big, and try to come up with creative solutions to any problem.

CHAPTER FIVE

Getting Buyers into Your House

YOU MAY HAVE THE most charming house on the block. You might have a kitchen to die for, a sumptuous bath, and the largest master suite on the block. But unless you can get potential buyers into your home, they're not going to buy. "Curb appeal" is the key. Curb appeal means making your home so inviting from the street that buyers want it before they've even walked through the front door. This chapter will tell you exactly what you need to do.

It does not have to take much money to improve the look of your home dramatically. To figure out what can be done to spruce up your home's appearance, check out neighbors' homes for ideas and then look at yours again. Take some photos of the house and study them; perhaps trace over them and try adding on little elements or landscaping. Or consult with a designer for an hour for some good professional suggestions.

As you look at your home objectively, take note of the displeasing features from the street. If you can't find anything, ask your friends or a stranger, or a local real estate agent.

Drive through the better neighborhoods in your area and notice what makes the homes seem stately or warm, cozy, and inviting. Is it the landscaping, the arch over the front door, or the fence in front? What appeals to you? Decide what character is best for your home. Are there similar homes to yours in the neighborhood that are already renovated or that have recently sold for high prices. Check them out. You might be able to get a few ideas from other homes in your area.

Just remember, as you do your investigations you will probably see houses with so much in front they resemble fortresses, and others with so little that they appear no better than industrial parks. Ignore these and look for appealing properties. Your purpose is to create an entry and a facade that are so inviting the buyers can't wait to get inside.

Psychologists have shown that it's better to set a good impression from the outset than to have to correct a negative impression. Newton's famous law of physics seems to apply here—an object in motion tends to remain in motion. That can be altered for home buyers: An idea or impression in motion tends to remain in motion. If you get a "no" in the beginning, it takes a lot to change it. Salesmen have known this for years and always try to get a yes answer from the start.

Getting the Buyer Excited

It is said you never get a second chance to make a first impression. Sure, people shouldn't judge on appearances alone, whether they're judging people or houses. But they do and you need to be ready.

The impression of your home starts before the buyer even gets to the house. The neighborhood plays a big role. The conditions of the neighbors' houses, the abandoned cars along the curb, the cracked sidewalks or potholes, the broken fences or weeds in the yard all affect the buyer and the price she's willing to pay.

It's hard enough to get the house in shape, let alone the whole neighborhood. Yet the appearance of your neighborhood is crucial. Most people would like to improve their street, they just don't want to put in the effort. If you feel your block seriously lowers the desirability of your home, it's time to organize. Many cities will provide trees, fix potholes in streets, and make many other substantial improvements if enough fuss is made about them.

If you are going to be putting in many hours on your home in order to make a profit, it won't take much more time to increase that profit significantly through upgrading the neighborhood in whatever way you can. You will also be improving people's lives.

SIDEWALKS AND ROAD

Your buyer's first impression starts at the road. Are there potholes? Get the city out immediately. Is a junked car sitting out front? Have it towed, even if you have to pay for it. No one wants to feel he's moving into a slum. The towing cost will be nothing compared to the cost of lost buyers and the weeks your home languishes on the market.

Look at your sidewalk. Is it buckling or cracked? In many towns, the local government will make repairs free of charge. If you must pay for it, the job is quite easy to do or can be contracted out for about $40 per two-foot concrete square. Is the concrete just stained by oil or paint? This can be scrubbed clean using many driveway cleaners (available at auto supply stores) or by using muriatic acid. Be careful if using the latter, as it is highly caustic.

DRIVEWAY

The same applies to the driveway as to the sidewalk. Is it uneven? If so, it could be a landslide problem. Is it cracked? Are weeds growing through the joints? As driveways tend to take up a large chunk of the front yard, your driveway needs to look its best to give an overall good impression.

If your property is on a hill and you have a visibly cracked driveway or retaining wall, most buyers will see this as a danger signal that your home is about to slide down the hill, and they will run the other way. If a problem looks serious, consider obtaining a structural engineer's report. This way, if the problem turns out to be mostly cosmetic, you can fix it. If it is truly serious, all parties should be aware of the extent of the problem. Many times defects look worse to the uninitiated than they actually are. A professional report will ease any irrational fears.

If you have an asphalt driveway, make sure there are no potholes. For an even better appearance, apply a driveway sealer ($30). It will give the driveway an even coloration and a new feeling.

If you have a dirt drive, laying two parallel rows of brick for the car to drive onto can upgrade the appearance significantly, especially if you then plant the remainder of the driveway. Rather than asphalting an entire 8 x 20 foot area, only 20 percent of which will ever actually be driven over, you save considerable money and create an attractive and utilitarian driveway. There are also special pavers designed to allow plants to grow through them. This improvement permits a green lawn look, even though there is a hard, drivable surface just below.

Additionally, the vehicle parked in the driveway will have a major impact. Is it a Mercedes or a candidate for the demolition derby? Even if two houses are exactly the same, the one with a new luxury car out front will subconsciously affect the buyer more positively than the one with the old VW bus. If you own an old jalopy, park it around the block and walk home. You might consider renting a nice car for a week or borrowing a friend's new car. Just make sure it doesn't look forced. A limo in front of a $30,000 house sends up red flags.

GATES AND FENCES

Gates and fences can give your home any feel you desire, from elegant and stately to warm and inviting. Studies have shown that a barrier of some sort in front of the house makes it appear more valuable to buyers.

Whether it be wood, stone, or iron, a fence can add dignity, warmth, privacy, or security to your home. Take a look around town and in books to get an idea of the many fence possibilities. A nice fence and gate can also improve the foot traffic through an otherwise bland or ugly house. That's because a buyer will only see the fence from the approach and won't have time to form a negative impression and just keep driving by.

Fences can be used to block an unpleasant view or to help insulate from street noise. Many people have made a dramatic increase in value just by blocking the view of a commercial area or blighted site. Concrete and brick fences are commonly used by developers to block freeway noise. Although sometimes unsightly, they are still better than feeling like the freeway is going right through the living room.

One way to repair a tired-looking fence without going to the cost of replacing it is with ivy or flowers. Ivy is a longer-term solution but flowers are instantaneous and can provide distraction from the fence.

Fences or walls can be used to control the views from the home or yard. A five-foot-high wall blocks much of the neighbor's home and activity yet leaves many of the surrounding trees within view.

Low walls create outdoor rooms (see chapter on outdoor spaces) but more importantly, they make the house look bigger by extending the facade to the lot line. Low shrubs and flowers can ease the transition from brick or stucco to lawn.

WALKWAY

Several treatments can be done to improve the appearance of the approach to the house. Give the front walk a little character. Edge it with plants, flowers, bricks, or treated lumber. If your walkway itself is in bad shape, consider replacing it.

If you're going to be showing your house a lot after sundown, lighting the walk becomes a crucial issue. Proper night lighting can add much to the impression of a home. The light can create a calm mood that entices the buyer, or can direct attention to areas you want to highlight.

Whatever night lighting you choose, it has to look good in the day, too. You might want to put in a lamppost along the walk to light the way. But beware of tacky-looking ones. Observe how lighting is handled in the wealthier neighborhoods.

Make the walk of handsome brick rather than concrete. Brick can be set in a herringbone or basket weave or other interesting pattern.

Other materials buyers like include flagstone and slate. Many a home has been transformed into a more expensive-looking house just by relatively simple and inexpensive material changes such as these.

The walkway need not be straight. If you're putting in a new walk, think about gently curving it for a more peaceful approach. Or you can make the walkway exceedingly grand and formal, with symmetrical benches, plantings, or built elements.

A new set of front steps may be necessary. If yours are worn and warped or contain dry rot, you have a chance to redesign them to appeal to buyers. You can have a nice rail installed or have planters built into the side.

UTILITY AND SERVICE STRUCTURES

Sometimes items like garbage cans or a recycling area can be an ugly distraction from an otherwise immaculate home. In a case like this, constructing a service area from redwood lattice is a good way to screen unsightly spots from general view.

SIGNAGE AND WELCOMING SIGNALS

Polished brass numbers, classy mailboxes, door knockers, potted plants, a fresh welcome doormat, and working doorbell all can add to the illusion of quality in your home. Little details go a long way.

Before beginning to correct individual elements, step back and look at your house as an entire picture. You may even want to cut out a cardboard frame and look through it to see your home as a picture. That way, you can see what elements just don't seem to belong or perhaps what needs covering up.

Look at the overall concept of your landscape. Do the decks work with the plantings? Is the color of the flowers working with the house color? Connect all the elements like in a painting and the whole will be greater than the sum of the parts.

Look at the mailbox. A nice home with a beat-up mailbox is not as appealing as one with a good one. Polished brass mailboxes look very good if all the other metal around the home is brass, too.

Does your home have a security system? In upscale homes, this will add selling value.

Landscaping

Mature landscaping can greatly enhance the value of any home. In a recent survey, home buyers judged mature trees as the single most desired outdoor amenity to a home. Part of the reason so many people put up with antiquated homes is the lovely setting the landscaping provides.

Unfortunately, if you don't already have large trees, the cost to plant them is prohibitive. But if you have such trees, you have a valuable asset.

As undesirable as having no trees is, overgrown old trees can detract from a home's appearance, too. If you have mature trees, you may want to consider trimming them. If your trees are looking sickly, call in a tree surgeon. He can do wonders and perhaps save an asset that adds hundreds or thousands of dollars to your home's value.

An area of landscaping over which you have more control is hedges and shrubs. Hedges can act as a natural fence and sound barrier. Hedges grow relatively quickly, too. If you are planning on selling a few years down the road, these plants can make a significant difference in the impact your home has from the street.

Your plantings can be used as a welcoming sign or as a wall. Lush landscaping around serpentine walks can glide visitors into your home. Or a wall of shrubs with a gate can keep them out. Look at the image your home is projecting and see if it's the one you want to project.

All your plantings can be viewed as architectural elements, guiding a person's eye, and the actual person, from the street to your front door. If you want them to look toward one area and ignore another, plant color and contrasting plants in the area you'd want them to see and many bland plants that blend together in the area you'd rather they not see. Color and contrast excite the eye and brain, and our tendency is to look toward them.

When planning your yard, plant in asymmetrical groupings. This will allow the eye to glide over imperfections. If something is supposed to be perfectly symmetrical and a plant dies, it can make the yard look strange or untended.

Another way to cause the eye to flow over your plantings is to plant smaller bushes in front of larger ones. This gives a three-dimensional effect and makes the landscape look less instant and forced. The same principle will be applied to the home. Front porches, trellises, low walls, and other items help ease the eye's transition and soften the appearance.

In general, use accent plantings of various colors to contrast with duller but fuller plants. Many plants are flowering and their colors can make the yard bloom.

If you are planting near the house, make sure you leave enough room (about three feet from your home) to provide ventilation and to allow the sun to penetrate to the walls. It shows carefully considered planting and prevents mildew from forming on your home—a red flag for home buyers and inspectors. Also, plantings around the home should not be deciduous. Bare shrubs look worse than no shrubs in the winter.

Foundation plantings can not only camouflage bare concrete, but will serve as a bridge between the home and yard, visually linking the two together to create a more harmonious effect. Your home will appear larger if you extend the plantings out past the corners of the foundation and around the sides.

One way to enhance the appearance of already-existing trees and bushes is to dig up the grass around the base of trees and cover the area with a rich, dark mulch. White river rocks also look good around shrubs. Be sure to prepare the ground properly or you'll find yourself weeding every other week.

To prepare the ground properly, clear it, then cover it with a thick black plastic available at most garden stores. Anchor this down with metal coat hangers stuck through the plastic into the ground like large hooks or with a brick or rock border. Punch some holes in the plastic near plants so they may get water, and cover with the cosmetic pebbles or mulch.

Trimmed plants form a smoother surface for the eye. If yours have limbs flying in all directions, give them a manicure. Also replace any dead plants with live ones. A dead bush or a hole in the ground where it used to be seems to call more attention to itself than the rest of your landscaping combined.

Fertilize your plants, especially the month before sale. It will make them greener and healthier.

Think about your plants in relation to timing the sale of your home. If you have all deciduous plants and you are planning on listing the home in the winter, it may appear cold and barren. On the other hand, if you know the large maple in front of your home looks best in September and October when the leaves are turning, your sale may be easier if you can time it for the fall.

Put some flowers along the walk or driveway, potted plants by the door or in a small planter box. Hang planter boxes under the windows and fill with flowers. Color adds a great deal to the overall impression of your home and can attract potential buyers.

Make sure the lawn is mowed and edged. Make sure hedges are trimmed and plant beds neat. For a softer look, curve trimmed edges around flower beds and plantings.

Make sure the lawn is in top condition. If you have a front yard that looks like the Sahara desert and you want to sell next week, then you'll have to go sod. Sod is very expensive and is only to be used on either very small lawns or in rush situations. The lush effect it creates, though, should bring people into your home. If the only problem with your home is the lawn, spend the money on sod and hire a professional lawn service to maintain it. If you can't get the buyers into your home, you can't sell them.

Although the front is the most important part of the house, make sure all improvements extend around the sides. You never know from what angle a prospective buyer is going to approach.

Many homes have tiny side yards, some as small as five or ten feet. If you have one of these and everything you plant consistently dies, consider building it into an outdoor room. This can be a court with trellises and vines or perhaps a bricked patio (see chapter on outdoor spaces).

Keep in mind when buying all plants that they are seasonal. You may want to have plants that bloom in the spring, others in the summer, and others in the fall. You never know exactly when your house will sell. Otherwise you may end up doing what many renovators have done when a house sits on the market. You'll find yourself digging up all your flowers every two months or so and having to replant new ones.

As a final note to planting, don't overdo the flowers. You want the home to appeal to buyers. But many dual-career couples will view your yard as a maintenance nightmare if it looks too labor intensive.

The House Itself

Your home should at least equal the exterior appeal of the average homes in your neighborhood. Usually, all a house needs is a good cleaning. On the other hand, many homes are in such bad shape on the exterior that they really need the addition of some elements. It might be new trim, or a trellis over the front porch, or something to make it distinctive and give it warmth and charm.

The front of the home sets the tone for a buyer's attitude toward your home. It is so important that if you have only a little time or money to devote to the exterior of your home, put it here. A buyer will carry a first impression of your home with him throughout the building. Make it a good one.

It is common practice for home builders in California to put the best windows, the most detailing, and the best materials on the front of the home and leave the other three sides almost barren. Yet these homes sell as fast as they're built. Concentrate your money on the front entrance to your home. Buyers like it because not only does it impress them when they first see it but they figure it will impress their friends, too.

Other recent building trends point out the importance of the street facade even more in selling impact. The "wide-shallow lot" concept turns the home so that as much as possible faces the street. Many times the home is angled to the street to make it appear even larger and more impressive. Another trend is to build duplexes that appear to be one large home. This gives the impression of a wealthy homeowner from the street, although it's obvious once you've entered the home that you are in a small duplex.

How your home influences a buyer starts with the building material. Siding is the dominant visual element.

WOOD BUILDINGS

Paint

There are few improvements one can make to the exterior of a home that will increase its value more than repainting. The power of new paint is so great that countless quality homes have languished on the market for lack of a new paint job while many structurally unsound homes have sold because of a fresh coat of paint.

If your home has cracking, blistering, or peeling paint, a new coat of paint is in order. You can do this yourself or hire a professional. It's one of the easiest tasks for the do-it-yourselfer.

Prepare the surface well. Imperfections and a poor prep job show through the finished coats.

Remember, paint color is a vital selling consideration. Blending in with the neighborhood is usually recommended. If your neighbors' homes are in earth tones (yellows, browns, reds), then do not paint yours blue. If the neighbors' homes are cooler (blue, gray), yours will stick out if it is not painted in similar tones. You may not want to do this, but be conscious of how the color of your home relates to others.

Paint can be used to affect the apparent size of the home. Small one-story homes (bungalows) will appear larger if painted one color. If a house has a lot of trim or accessories, this should be painted a tone lighter or darker, rather than a contrasting color. In fact, tones can be used to pop out or hide bays, to create detailing and shadowing where little or none exists, and to help correct an otherwise bland exterior. Light and neutral colors are always a safe bet and will not offend anyone. They are the most popular and the most likely to stay in style.

It is not necessary to repaint the whole house if your budget does not allow. The front approach is the key side if all the paint is in pretty good shape. Many times, though, the southern exposure is more worn than the others due to its exposure to the elements. Check this side to see if it needs repainting, too. If it's in good shape, the rest is most likely okay, too.

Spray painting can make a large job go more quickly and cheaply. If your home has large flat surfaces and needs to be painted, you should investigate this option.

Your house may only need a good cleaning. Many homes, especially stucco homes with a cottage cheese surface, collect much dirt. Hose it down. That alone will work wonders.

Trim

Sometimes a little ornamentation is all that is needed to transform a home. In San Francisco, many Victorians were stripped of detail in the 1940s and 1950s. These homes now command significantly lower prices even though the interiors may be exactly the same as the homes with all their trimmings. Conversely, many people have made a lot of money just by upgrading the facade. Figure 5-1 shows some samples of trim.

Upgrading the trim does not have to entail redoing the whole building. A few carefully placed details can alter the impression of quality on a home.

Trim can be made of wood, plaster, vinyl, or a host of other materials. Unless you are intending a natural wood look, any of them will work fine. If you want to match existing trim on your home, you may find it is no longer sold as a stock item. In order to do your upgrade, you can either have the trim custom-made at a cabinet shop (expensive) or cast a plaster mold of the remaining trim (cheap). The latter method will only work if you are painting the trim.

Think about shutters, awnings, and window boxes.

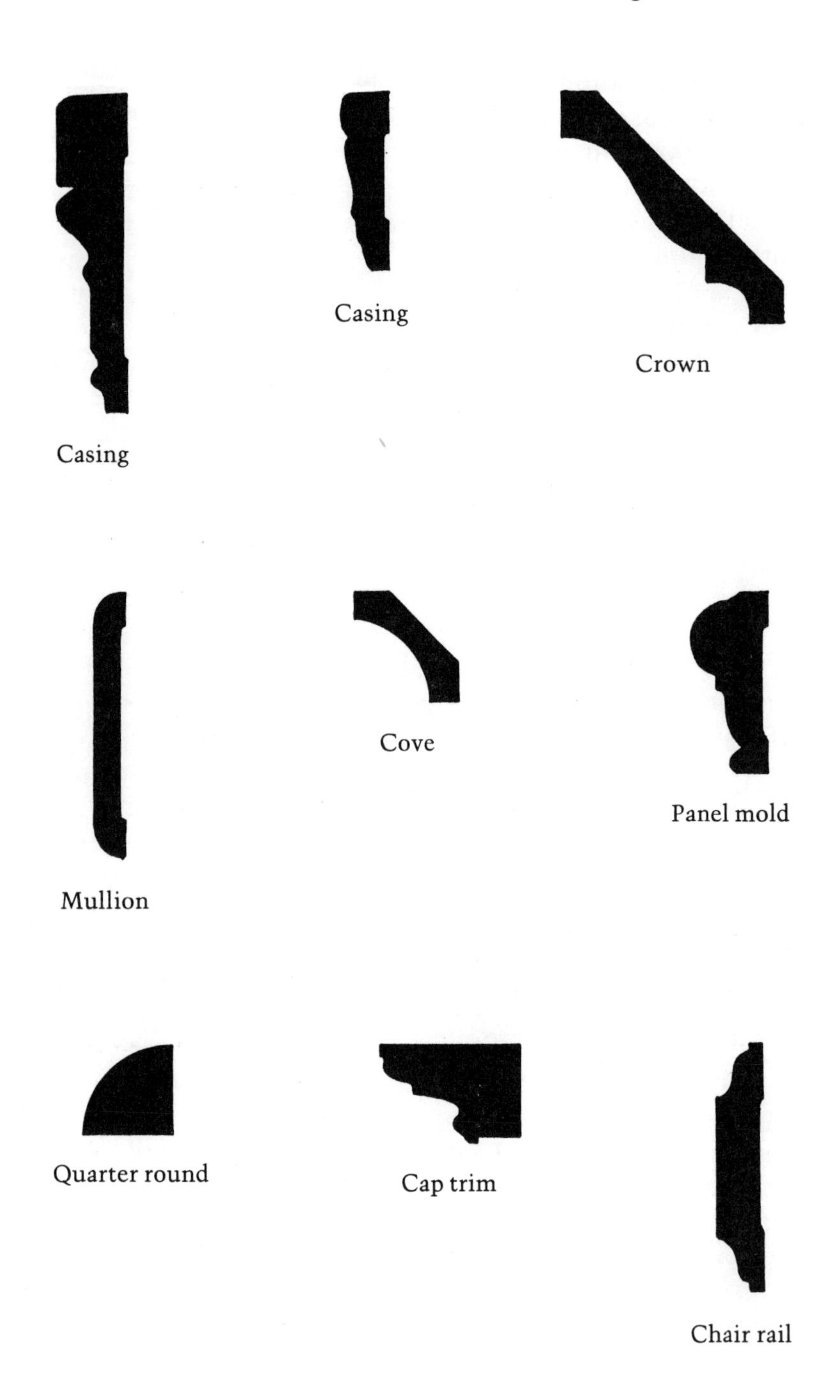

Figure 5-1 *Samples of trim*

Could your house use these to help make it seem homier? Most homes look better with the addition of a flower box.

Take a step back and look at your home as a picture. In fact, photograph it. Then try coloring in some changes. That's the easiest way to see the possibilities in your home.

Windows

How are your windows? Are they ugly aluminum sliders or are they warm wooden double hung? What condition are they in? If your home is one of the many that were bastardized by misguided renovations in the past, you may just have to live with that. Replacing all the windows in a home can be costly ($200 material, $200 installation per window) and you rarely get back more than 60 percent of your cost at resale time. If you received a discount on the purchase of the house because of the windows, this may be a time to upgrade. It will help the home sell faster. In any case, even though replacing all windows is usually a losing proposition, replacing key windows, such as kitchen or front facade windows, can more than pay for itself.

When replacing windows, check the style. Traditional double-hung wood windows look out of place in a modernist home, just as aluminum sliders look out of place on a Victorian.

Have consistent window treatments on the windows facing the street or entry facade. If they are all different, they will make the home appear smaller, as the buyer's eye is interrupted by all the changes.

WALLS ON ALL TYPES OF HOMES

The exterior walls should be weathertight. Almost all sidings will last longer if kept dry. This is why a house with an overhang is preferred by buyers and home inspectors. If your home doesn't have one, chances are your siding has deteriorated faster than it needed to. Different sidings show deferred maintenance in different ways.

Brick

Brick is the most popular exterior siding material in the country. This does not mean, though, that you should rush out and redo your home in brick. In some areas, such as northern California, brick is rare and would actually lower the value of the home because it would be an oddity.

Brick is an expensive material to install but a relatively low-cost one to maintain. That's one of the reasons for its popularity. However, it doesn't last forever. Look at the condition of yours. If the mortar between the bricks is crumbling, it probably needs to be replaced. This is called repointing. It is a time-consuming task and can get expensive.

If the brick is stained or has old paint on it, repainting or sandblasting the paint off are your options. Only use the sandblasting if the brick is mostly natural already. If it's painted and the paint is in reasonably good shape, just repaint.

Check the condition of the windows and the trim. These are usually made of wood and may need a repainting. Also check the appearance of the windows. The installation of shutters will help warm the outside of a cold brick building.

Stucco

Look for cracks around windows, doors, and chimneys. If they are small, hairline cracks, they can be easily repaired. Fill all minor cracks with a stucco repair compound and paint. If you have wide cracks, they could be structural. Long running cracks may indicate that the foundation is settling. If you suspect a structural cause, have the cracks inspected by a licensed engineer or contractor before repairing. Otherwise you could have an expensive legal action on your hands.

If the large cracks are non-structural, chip out the loose stucco and repair. It may take two or three layers of stucco to bring the wall back up to the original surface. If the damaged area is more than four feet square, the whole wall may need to be restuccoed. Allow several days for the stucco to dry before painting it.

Replace any broken roof tiles viewed from the street. Check for signs of moisture penetration before replacing the tiles. Make repairs if needed.

Aluminum and Vinyl Sidings

Aluminum and vinyl siding are both maintenance free and inexpensive. However, few buyers desire them. If your home is sided with vinyl or aluminum, check its condition. Patch all dents or cracks. Repaint if necessary. Replace any damaged sections if they are too far gone.

Vinyl siding has some advantages over aluminum. The color tends to go all the way through the material, so scratches do not show. Also, it is a better insulator than aluminum.

Traditionally, aluminum siding was applied directly on top of the existing siding. You may have a beautiful clapboard house underneath the aluminum. Be aware, though, that it is not cheap to bring back the original luster. In higher-priced neighborhoods, upgrading the siding may bring significant returns.

Changing Sidings

Sometimes, although not usually, it makes economic sense to alter the siding on your building and replace it with one that is in vogue. Many homes have been bastardized with asbestos shingle siding or other alteration. On average, you can get back 40 to 70 percent of your re-siding cost immediately on resale. In wealthier neighborhoods, you can recoup the value of changing the siding and then some if you can change an ugly duckling into a beautiful swan. Many homes have been reshingled from asbestos to cedar and the home's value has skyrocketed.

If you decide to install new siding, check to see what is appropriate for your home and also what sidings are on the higher-priced homes. Some ideas and cost examples are below:

Cedar shingles or shakes ($2.00–2.40 square foot installed). You can install them individually or you can buy shingles pre-cut in decorative designs and mounted on panels, usually eight feet in length—a real timesaver.

Cedar siding is the most widely used wood siding. It is an excellent insulator and is naturally resistant to rot and decay. It comes in smooth or rough surfaces and generally runs from $2.00–2.60 per square foot installed.

Redwood siding is also available. This costs a little more, generally about $3.00 per square foot.

Cheap sidings include plywood sawed and grooved to look like separate wooden boards. It comes in 4 x 8 or 4 x 9 sheets and reduces the cost of labor tremendously.

Hardboard siding is similar to plywood siding but without the defects of natural wood.

Redwood siding comes in boards at $2.95–3.30 a square foot.

Aluminum siding and PVC (vinyl) siding are much cheaper at $1.80–2.30, and they require no maintenance, but they can make a home look cheap.

THE ROOF

Roofs should be unobtrusive, but if your roof is prominent from the street, the street side needs to look its best. If some shingles are worn and peeling, have them replaced. Many times the new shingles are a different shade than the old ones due to age and weathering. If this is the case, you have but one choice—make them match.

If your roof is asphalt shingles, the shingles can be spray painted an appealing color to go with the rest of the house.

If your roof is cedar shingles, you could still paint, but usually people want the natural look (that gives your home the greatest value). You can stain the new shingles to match the weathered ones.

The Front Door and Entry

The front door and entry area are very important in making a good first impression. Just updating this area can color a buyer's perception throughout.

The front area should be well defined and welcoming. You can choose to focus attention on the front door through the use of symmetrical elements such as side lights, or you can focus it away and onto the entry as a whole, depending on your home's strengths.

Since this area is seen close up and is so important, detail is crucial here. Make sure the paint is in impeccable condition. If not, repainting it should only take a day. Brass numbers, door knockers, and plants all add to the value statement your entry makes. Good lighting and a cheery welcome mat help, too.

If your door is plain, consider replacing it with a raised panel door, or one with stained glass. There are many beautiful doors on the market for under $200. A handyman should be able to install it in three or four hours. If you don't want to buy a new door, it's possible to dress up your old one with molding. A plain door can become a classy painted lady with a few pounds of the hammer and some careful applications of paint. Everything must look good in the entryway. Even the weatherstripping should be in good condition.

If you have room, and your home is in an upscale community, consider installing side-by-side double doors where your front door currently is. More than 60 percent of luxury home buyers want double-door entries to their home.

Make sure the doorbell works! If not, you may have lost the buyer already. You don't want them to think anything is broken in the house. If you start them off like this, they'll be looking for other problems.

Also, if you have a screen or storm door, unless it's very attractive, please remove it if possible. Although practical, its aesthetics may influence the buyer.

You might try putting in a new exterior light fixture. This is especially important if your home will frequently be shown in the evenings. Or, you can install glass sidelights on both sides of the door to let light into the home. Because of cost considerations, do this only if you're doing a major renovation on the entry area.

Potted plants and flowers are also a welcoming touch by the front door and add warmth to the home.

If you're renovating your front door area, now is a good time to consider the other side of the wall. Is your foyer large enough? There are many ways you can make it special without killing your wallet. For under $4000 (less if you do it yourself) you can pop out your entryway six feet and essentially transform both the exterior and interior of your home. You will probably not get this money back directly, but it may lead to a quicker home sale.

CREATING A FRONT PORCH OR ENTRY

Front porches and other entry transitions used to be standard items on homes built before World War II. But when the war was over, housing demand was so strong that many standard items became extras, and the porch was one of the first to go.

Walking up to many homes is like walking up to a wall. There's no transition between the outdoors and the interior. Creating an attractive transition can greatly upgrade a buyer's initial impression of your home and the price he's willing to pay.

A front porch need not cost much. A simple one can be constructed for under $1000. Covered decks run a bit more.

If the garage is your home's dominant visual element, consider making the path to your front door more prominent and attractive. Buyers want to walk into a house, not a garage.

You can also create a sense of entry before you get to the actual house, softening the transition from yard to home. By building a low wall near the house, you provide an illusion of passing through an imaginary gate and entering the inner sanctum. Another advantage of a low wall is it can stretch out the house and make it appear visually larger than it actually is.

The Neighbors and Neighborhood

It should be emphasized that people are not just buying your house, they're buying the neighborhood and a certain quality of life. If your neighbor has a junker up on blocks, stereo blasting, and garbage on the front lawn, it's going to discourage buyers no matter how nice your house is.

If you can get your neighbor to clean up, or if you can get him to let you, do it. It will more than pay for the cost, inconvenience, or embarrassment. As a last resort, you could always build a fence. It will look nice, add privacy, and shield you from the eyesore.

Hiring Professionals

You don't need a contractor to do landscaping, unless you're planning some major earth moving. Trees, shrubs, and grass can all be planted and cared for by the homeowner. You may want to get professional advice as to what plants work best for your area. This advice can sometimes be given by a nursery, but hiring a gardener or landscape architect for an hour is probably a better use of your time.

If your plants are in trouble, hire a tree surgeon or gardener to come out and look at them. Many problems are correctable if caught early enough. Landscaping is invaluable to the resale value of your home and costly to replace, so investing a few dollars here is money well spent.

Exterior painting can be a dangerous job if your home is two stories or more high. Scaffolding and high ladders require one to be agile and have no fear of heights. However, there is no single element of the painting process that cannot be handled by a homeowner. It's just that the total task can get quite large. Doing the work on weekends could end up taking several months including the prep work.

Building a front porch or new stairs is another task easily handled by the homeowner or handyman with carpentry skills. Replacing worn stairs and building planter boxes are perhaps the least difficult of carpentry tasks on a home.

Replacing the front door is an afternoon task for the homeowner with the right tools. However, because the look of this area is so crucial to a potential buyer's impression of your home, it is recommended that you use a professional carpenter. Adding sidelights or replacing the door with a double door should also be handled also by a professional carpenter.

If you are planning a major remodeling of your front entry, perhaps extending the foyer or enclosing the front porch, once again, use your discretion. None of these tasks is too complex and the do-it-yourselfer should be able to handle them all.

If your bricks need repointing, this is a task professionals can do a lot quicker than you. Stucco repair, if minor, can be handled by the homeowner, but if a significant section needs to be redone, it is best left to a professional.

Fences are another easy homeowner project. Gates are a little more complex, with ornate ones requiring someone who's skilled in woodworking. Putting in a brick or concrete walkway is another easy homeowner project.

Siding replacement can also be done by a homeowner. But it is a time-consuming task and might better be left to someone who can do it full time.

Conclusion

The house and yard need to be neat and clean and inviting. All debris, hoses, rusting lawn furniture, and unattended toys need to be removed.

One of the key factors in curb appeal is directing the buyer's approach so that he gets the impression of your home that is most positive and shows all its good qualities. Keep this in mind as you plan your streetscape and landscape, and as you renovate your facade.

CHAPTER SIX

The Foyer and Entry

THE ENTRY HALL IS the first glimpse people get of the interior of your home. It should be welcoming and inviting. Recent trends in new construction are to create grand entries with vaulted ceilings and sweeping vistas. These are going over well with buyers. In all likelihood, your home will not physically allow for such a modification, but there are still many things you can do to create the best entry possible.

The entry to your home should make people feel welcome. If it's dark and cluttered and doesn't have any personality, it will create a negative impression.

Getting Started

Look at the overall impression your entry creates. What kind of statement is it making about your home and the people who live there? Bring some friends over who have never been to your home and let them tell you what they feel your home says to them upon entering. Go with first impressions, as that is what will be registering with your potential buyers.

The entry is the keyhole to the rest of your home. People will peer through with extra alertness and curiosity as they first open the door. This tends to set their mental framework once they're inside. So you really want them to like your home from the start. If they liked the exterior, this may just push them into your court. If they didn't like it, it's a chance to win them back.

FLOORS

The entry is a small but highly visible area. People have just been wiping their feet on the welcome mat, and now their focus is your entry floor. It's a place where you can use even the best of materials and not go over budget. You can use marble, tile, hardwood, or even carpeting, although the latter is not recommended because it wears so easily. This area gets the most wear in homes and much of your competition will probably have tired-looking entries. Make yours stand out.

Look at your current floors. If you have wood floors, they may require refinishing ($1 per square foot by a professional) or at least a waxing and buffing. Chances are the floor has had much abuse and is deteriorated. See the section on refinishing wood floors later in the book for details.

If your entry needs definition, installing an ebony border in the hardwood floor will set visual boundaries. There are many pre-made border designs that can be easily installed.

If you have carpet, make sure it is shampooed and that there are no excessively worn areas. Because it is hard to replace a piece of carpet with a matching new piece, if you must remove the worn piece, use this opportunity as a chance to contrast your entry with a different material. Perhaps you would like a wood or tile entry. One especially nice entry combines the two—a tile inlay surrounded by a hardwood border.

If you have a tile entry, does it make the statement you want? Some varieties of tile will date a home. Does it look like a fleeting memory of a bad nightmare in Mexico? Check. It's probably fine, but you want to leave no stone unturned. Examine your entry floor with the eyes of one seeing your home for the first time.

You can retile an entry for about $10 per square foot in materials. Even the best marble can be bought for under $20 a square foot. When you calculate the total cost, because of the small size of the entry, it should come out to be quite reasonable.

You can install a new hardwood floor for from $4 a square foot for parquet up to $10 a square foot for wide plank flooring or fancy inlays. It will cost substantially less if you do it yourself.

There are many techniques you can use to add visual excitement to your entry floor. If it is made of wood, you can cut out an area in the center and recess a diamond-shaped area of marble into it. Or insert some beautiful cobalt blue ceramic tiles. This contrasts nicely with the wood and gives a custom look to your entry.

Another technique is to paint parts of the floor, for accent. This does not refer to the floor and deck paint used to cover up floors that are hopelessly beyond repair. (You would never use this in the home—if your floors are in this condition, it's time for a new flooring.) It means paint techniques such as marbleizing, stippling, or sponging, which would normally be used on walls.

Don't paint the whole floor, but use the paint to create a pattern that accents the wood and adds to the total picture. You can paint a small pattern in the center of the entry, surrounding it with freshly sanded wood, or perhaps border the wood with a thin line of paint to accent it. Both the natural and painted woods will be covered with three or more coats of polyurethane.

Wood floors can also be bleached to give a lighter and more modern look, or they can be stained to highlight grain patterns and alter the color of the wood. A little trick you can do is to use several different color stains to create borders that appear to be made of another wood. Score the wood lightly before applying the second stain to prevent it from running off into the first.

Some homes, especially post–World War II tract homes, do not have formal entries at all. A change in flooring materials is one of the cheapest and most common devices used by homebuilders to designate entry.

WALLS

Paint the entry a light color to make it look large and bright and welcoming. You can also mirror a wall to increase the apparent size of the room, bring in more light, or reflect an interesting view from another room or from outdoors.

Entry walls and those going up the stairs should be decorated the same color throughout unless there is a reason for a change, such as an abrupt change of materials dictating a different paint color.

If your entry is small and dark and you can't alter it, don't get frustrated. You can use that as an asset. Make the entry feel warm and cozy. Natural woods and soft lighting will appeal to people's emotions. The key is to create a sense of drama and destination as the buyer emerges from the low dark entry into a living room with vaulted ceiling and awash with light.

This technique can be used for good effect throughout the home. Passing from a low, narrow, or dark space can be offset by arriving at a room of contrasting sensations.

Mirrors, in addition to increasing the apparent size of the entry and the amount of light available, serve another useful purpose. Placing a mirror in the front hall provides your guests a place to pause and see how they look. Play up to the vanity in all of us. A mirror can also double the effect of any special items you've put in the room, like a vase full of flowers or a special heirloom.

Creating a wainscoting out of molding will add immeasurably to the perceived value of the entry. There are many different patterns you can create, as shown in Figure 6-1.

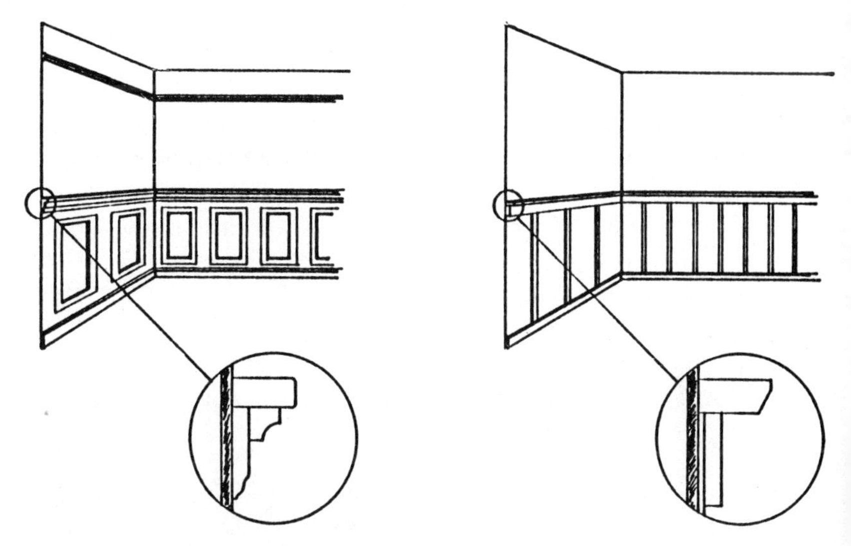

Figure 6-1 *Types of wainscoting*

Another way to open up a narrow or tight entry is to change the walls from drywall to glass. This can have the effect of making your living room an elegant showcase. Adding French doors will add to the effect.

LIGHTING

A bright entry is undoubtedly an asset. If you're replacing your front door and you have a dark entry, consider putting in a door with some glass in it. Or, if you're doing a larger remodeling of the area, install sidelights on either side of the front door.

Another way to increase the natural light is to place a skylight directly over the entry. By filling the room with natural light from above, it will almost feel like you're still outside and will ease the transition from outdoors to indoors. If you have a very dark entry, this trick, although relatively expensive ($200–600), will more than pay for itself if it transforms your entry from a turnoff to a turnon. Just make sure the rest of your home lives up to the entry. Operable skylights can also be installed if ventilation is a problem ($350–900).

You can achieve effects with artificial lighting to highlight elements. Backlighting, small table lamps, or a chandelier can all add character to your home. A matched set of wall sconces can add a touch of elegance to your entry.

You can use lighting to create an initial dramatic mood in your home. Think about the possible colorings the light can have. Or perhaps it can focus on particular architectural elements in the room.

There are several different types of lighting sources, which all produce different effects in the home.

> Incandescent lighting is the standard lighting used in most homes. Incandescent light tends to cast sharp shadows and create bright highlights. This effect can be muted by frosted glass or by using a light shade.
>
> Fluorescent lighting is a low energy user and highly efficient compared to incandescent. But fluorescent light tends to create a dull, cold effect that is generally unflattering. It connotes offices to most people and should rarely be used in the home. There are full-spectrum fluorescent tubes out now but few attractive fixtures to hold them.
>
> Tungsten-halogen is a recently introduced form of incandescent lighting. It creates a very high concentration of light for a given wattage. It produces a nice color rendering and is very stylish today. However, it also produces a lot of heat and needs some sort of protection around the bulb.
>
> Neon is a wonderful decorative light. It's not usually used in homes but when it is, it can produce a great effect. It can be bent to any shape, to further highlight its impact.

The type of lighting you choose, in addition to the shape and style of the fixtures, will have a great impact on the visual impression of your home.

SPATIAL ORIENTATION

The transition from the exterior of your home to the interior is always noticed. The questions you should ask yourself once inside are: What does the arriving person see? Where will he automatically go? What room will attract him?

Is there a corridor or stairs at the entrance or does the buyer burst right into the living room? What are the views? If you have to go down a long dark hall to get anywhere, it will create a bad impression. A short transition can be good.

If you find yourself looking directly into a room, evaluate whether or not it is a positive or negative item. Perhaps you want to screen it better.

New home entries today are being built in two basic ways—starting low and proceeding into a grand two-story space (such as the living room) or built as a grand space themselves and then entering into the other rooms.

Many new entryways are also built at 45-degree angles to the home in order to create a longer view within the home and thus make it appear larger. If you can incorporate this visual trick into your home, it will give a favorable impression to buyers.

Builders are also currently producing tall entries and accenting them with skylights and clearstory windows that pull the eye upward. Occasionally, instead of spending the money on a skylight, you can add a tall window set way up high to break up a large, blank wall and draw the eye up.

There is much to be said for a grand front entry. It turns buyers on, especially in the luxury market. Yet, unless you are planning to remain in your home for awhile, you will probably not recover the expense of creating such a foyer. The entry is a non-room. It is simply a show space. Because people do not spend much time there, your money will be better spent in an area like the kitchen or master bedroom, places where owners spend much of their time.

The only time creating such an entry will pay for itself in remodeling is when adding an addition. If the old entry can be turned into some other useful space and then a new entry built to current buyer preferences, the conversion of the old area will recover some of the cost.

OTHER ELEMENTS

Some added elements will help define an area as an entry that is both elegant and usable. For example, a small ledge or table for items such as keys or the mail is always desirable. If you face a wall as you enter, it is an ideal place to build a mantel or place a piece of furniture to act as a table.

A large potted palm or other plants will help add warmth and elegance to the entry. Other items such as a fresh vase of flowers will start your home off on a cheery note.

Odor is very important. Remember, your buyers have just come in from the fresh outdoors. Your home must not smell stale. Potpourris or other fragrances are one solution. Another is to thoroughly air out your home before showings. Fresh-cut flowers will add beauty as well as scent to the entry.

If you have a tall entry, a ceiling fan can keep the air flowing and provide an elegant visual touch.

The Illusion of an Entry Hall

In the rush to build housing after World War II, many shortcuts were taken to reduce costs. One of the areas that suffered was the entryway. Many builders in their rush for profits decided the entry was an unnecessary luxury. If your home is one of the unfortunate ones, don't lose hope. There are several things you can do short of building an entry that will add appeal to your home by creating the illusion of an entry hall even if you don't have one.

Remember, there was a purpose for an entry, it is not just a room title. Certain activities were to happen there. It was the place to greet guests, hang coats, and drop off packages and keys.

Steal a little space from your living area to make room for these activities. Build a half wall or create a division of space with a column. These are relatively inexpensive and can add character to the room. Change the flooring in this area. Have a place to put things, perhaps a table or an open bookcase.

Another way to call attention to this area as a separate space is through lighting. Make certain the entry has its own lighting, whether it be a hanging ceiling fixture, wall sconces, or an attractive table lamp. Lighting can define spaces.

If you have room, create a hall closet. People don't want to spend several hundred thousand dollars on a house only to have to throw their coats on a bed in the guest room for lack of closet space.

Hiring Contractors

Many jobs in the entry can be done by the homeowner should he elect to do so. However, the quality of the floor is crucial in the entry, and if you do not have the necessary facility to do any major work, a contractor or skilled tradesman should be hired.

Tile is easily installed by the handyman. Many tile shops will loan out tile cutting tools when you purchase the tile there. Because of a lack of grout lines, extra care needs to be taken when installing marble. Marble requires special tools to cut but in general is installed by the same method as ceramic tile.

Hardwood floors can be sanded and refinished by the homeowner. There are many ways to put excitement into your entry floor. If you are careful, you can inlay some tiles or marble into the wood floor.

Installation of a new hardwood floor is best left to experienced carpenters, although there are now kits of prefinished flooring that the average homeowner can install. These kits allow for easier installation of the floor. Instead of using individual boards, the flooring comes in sections.

Changing light fixtures is easily done by the do-it-yourselfer. You should be aware of and respect the dangers of electricity. You could be killed if the power has not been shut off properly.

Running new wires in the walls is not hard either, but may require a lot of patch work to the walls, which costs time. Many jurisdictions will require you to use an electrician to run new wires through the walls. Check with your local building department first.

Installing skylights is best left to a professional carpenter or a skilled handyman. There are several reasons for caution. Steep roofs or hard-to-get-to areas in attics make a poor work station for the use of power tools. Also, once you've cut a hole in the roof, it is recommended you seal it quickly to prevent potential damage. A homeowner installing a skylight on the weekend may find that by Monday morning, the job is still not done. Carrying a heavy and fragile skylight up to the roof can also get tricky.

Example

MINOR ENTRY RENOVATION

Many home entries are bland and nondescript. In the example shown in Figure 6-2a, there was nothing particularly wrong with the entry, you just would never notice it. The goal was to make a good first impression with potential buyers.

This was the original layout of the entry. We analyzed the room to see what could be done. We could play with

Light

Materials (floor pattern, etc.)

Walls (paint, wallpaper, mirror)

Furniture and decorating

The first thing to evaluate was where our attention was being drawn.

In the old layout, our eyes were not being drawn anywhere in particular. What the room needed was a focal point and some focus. The old carpet was torn up and a marble tile floor was put in its place in the pattern shown in the next figure. Notice how the pattern helps build a formality that draws the eye forward, thus strengthening the focus and symmetry of the room. A simple trim was added to the walls at a chair rail height (about three feet off the ground) to give the room some more character. We then placed a table alongside the wall for keys, mail, and incidentals. A mirror was hung on a wall near the table for both vanity and to help reflect light from the adjoining living room. Plants and art were added to fill out the room. Figure 6-2b (bottom) shows the entry after renovation.

MAJOR FOYER RENOVATION

Figure 6-3 shows the before and after of a major renovation. It involves some structural work, but the cost is not great compared to the improved feel of the home and the much higher price that could be asked for it.

In this example, we have a single-story ranch-style home with a nice sized entry. However, you will notice some problems with it. For one, the buyer looks directly into a blank wall.

In doing a minor renovation, you could upgrade the wall. Add some wainscot molding, perhaps a pair of symmetrical wall sconces and a dramatic print, painting, or tapestry as a focal point. Place a table along the rear wall

Figure 6-2a *Entry prior to renovation*

Figure 6-2b *Renovated entry*

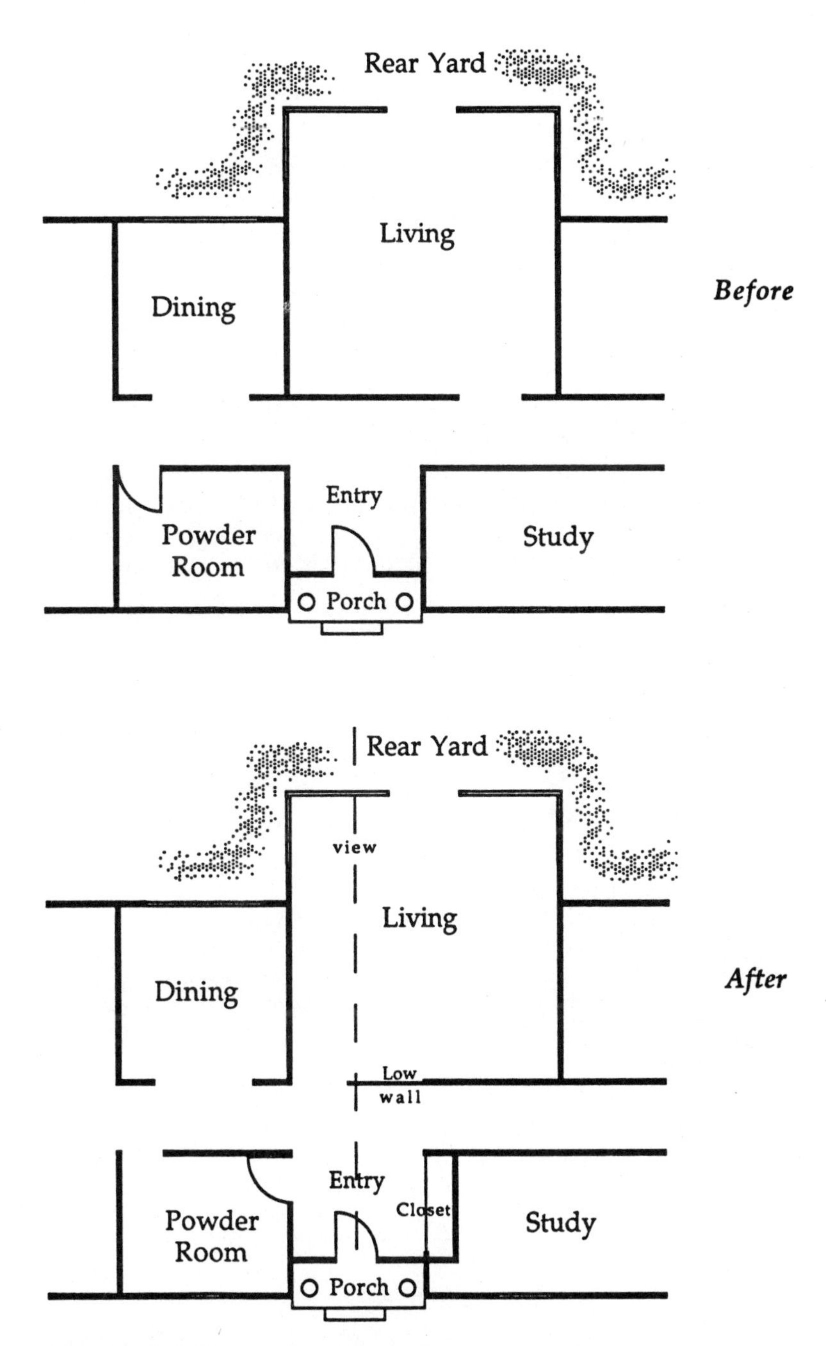

Figure 6-3 Example of a major renovation

for keys or packages and a potted plant or two near the door. Refinish the floor and place a mirror along a side wall for guests.

If you can spend a little more, perhaps change the flooring material to a nice marble laid in a classic pattern.

But in this case, it seems the most value would be created through a major renovation. The wall between the entry and the living room should be demolished. This creates a dramatic view out through the sliding glass doors to the rear yard. To help frame this view and to keep the rooms separate, construct a low wall. Use some short columns from the half wall to the ceiling for effect, and to structurally take the place of the wall that used to be there. Further add some sidelights to the front door to help balance the light and change the door to the powder room to make it more convenient. A hall closet is a highly desired item so one should be added. Steal the space from the neighboring study. Finally, decorate to fill out the room.

The total cost for a renovation like this is

Demolish existing walls	$ 160
Reset door of powder room	$ 300
Repair wall where door was	$ 50
Replace front door	$ 230
Cut wall and install new sidelights at front door	$ 400
Build closet from study. Install closet doors.	$ 400
Construct half walls and columns at living room	$ 500
Change entry flooring: install marble tile	$1000
Install new light fixture in entry	$ 200
Total renovation cost	$3240

The return, because of the new vistas, was many times the cost when it came to sales time.

CHAPTER SEVEN

The Living Room

Character

OF ALL THE ROOMS of the house, the living room is most like a stage set. Remember when your mother put plastic on the living room furniture so that it would "look good for company." Well, luckily, those days have gone but the living room is still the room to make an impression. Like the kitchen and master bedroom, the living room is a turnon room. And because it is the first one most buyers see, the impression it makes is most important.

The living room must be inviting yet convey the image the buyer is seeking. Treat your living room as a stage setting for the theater of your life. In general, buyers want the living room to look formal yet inviting. It is a place for entertaining as well as lounging around. Be careful about going to extremes. It should not look cold and sterile, but having the kids jumping up and down on the couches is not good form either. Remember, it is a *living* room, after all.

The elements of the living room need to be chosen with care. This room, more than any other, reflects the lifestyle to which its owner ascribes. The living room is usually the first of the main rooms that a buyer sees. The way it's furnished, the colors and textures of the walls and floor, the feeling of light or volume should all be coordinated to reflect a certain lifestyle.

Surfaces

WALLS

The most common wall surface for living rooms is plaster or sheetrock, although brick and other materials are acceptable to buyers as an accent wall. Walls in the living room serve primarily as neutral backdrops for hanging pictures and other wall accessories. The key is to have the walls looking in top condition. No matter how nice the home, cracks and holes in the wall turn off buyers.

PAINT

The easiest way to spruce up the room is with a new coat of paint. Paint has a nice habit of covering up minor blemishes and surface defects. To carry it even farther, walls can be sponged lightly or marbleized to add character to an otherwise bland wall. This works especially well in formal rooms like the living room or dining room. There are literally hundreds of textures you can sponge onto the walls. What would otherwise be bland walls become something special and make the room a room people will remember and want to buy.

Light-colored paints make a small room seem larger. Also, if you have a low ceiling, lighter colors raise it. The opposite is also true; if your ceiling seems too high, dark paint will make it seem lower.

MIRRORS

Mirrors add both light and the illusion of space to a room, for minimal cost. Look for a defined place to put the mirror or else do the whole wall. One area that usually looks good with mirroring is above the fireplace mantle. This helps create a focal point for the room in addition to increasing the available light.

WALLPAPER

Another way to dress up the walls of your living room is with wallpaper. Wallpaper can add a lot of class and character to the room or it can ruin it depending on the style of paper chosen. Be very careful. Look at home magazines for ideas. Unless you've got a designer's eye, try to match a pattern you liked in the magazine rather than just looking at samples in the wallpaper store. Very often a 4-inch piece that looked wonderful at the store looks horrendous when suddenly there's 400 square feet of it in your living room. Neutral colors and patterns are safer, but copying a successful application is the safest bet yet.

MOLDING

Molding is an inexpensive way to upgrade the appearance of the living room. A simple horizontal strip four feet above the floor can add class to a simple room. Fancier moldings, such as wainscotings, can also be done. All add character and charm to a room and make it seem much costlier than it is.

In today's most wanted homes, moldings ring the ceilings and floors in the public rooms such as the living room. Wide crown moldings at the ceiling add architectural interest and give the room a more substantial feeling.

The use of molding cannot be emphasized enough. It is just about the most economical way to transform a room. A wooden chair rail or wainscoting can be added to the walls at little expense, totally transforming your living room from its former boxy self into a room with character.

MISCELLANEOUS

Details such as new outlet cover plates help make the room appear newer. Brass plates add even more of an upgrade. The famous architect Mies van der Rohe, when talking about what makes good buildings, said that it's all in the details. This should be a credo of home renovators.

Niches and nooks add much to a living room. Some built-ins such as bookshelves can make the room feel more substantial. Trim the bookshelves with molding for added classical effect.

Aside from adding charm to a room, bookshelves and cabinets provide much-needed storage. A window seat with bookshelves on the sides and storage beneath the seat can be installed along a wall for moderate cost, creating some of those homey feelings we all crave.

Ceilings

The living room is one of the few rooms where the ceiling gets noticed. Wood beam ceilings add a touch of class for little cost. You might also consider a ceiling fan. While not quite as fashionable as they used to be, ceiling fans are functional and are perceived as a desired feature.

If you have a unique ceiling such as a cathedral ceiling or a beautiful rosette, you need to call attention to that area so it gets noticed. Too often buyers are flitting through your home so fast to see it all that they never even look up. Dramatic lighting is a good way to draw the eye upward. Skylights are, too. Another way may be to hang plants or install a ceiling fan.

If you have a two-story ceiling, can it connect to another room or hall? Balconies make desirable sitting areas and the connections add more life to the room. Figure 7-1 shows some types of vaulted ceilings.

If your living room is on the first floor and you can't create a vaulted ceiling, the ceiling still may have interest. Wooden beams and other details look great in a tradi-

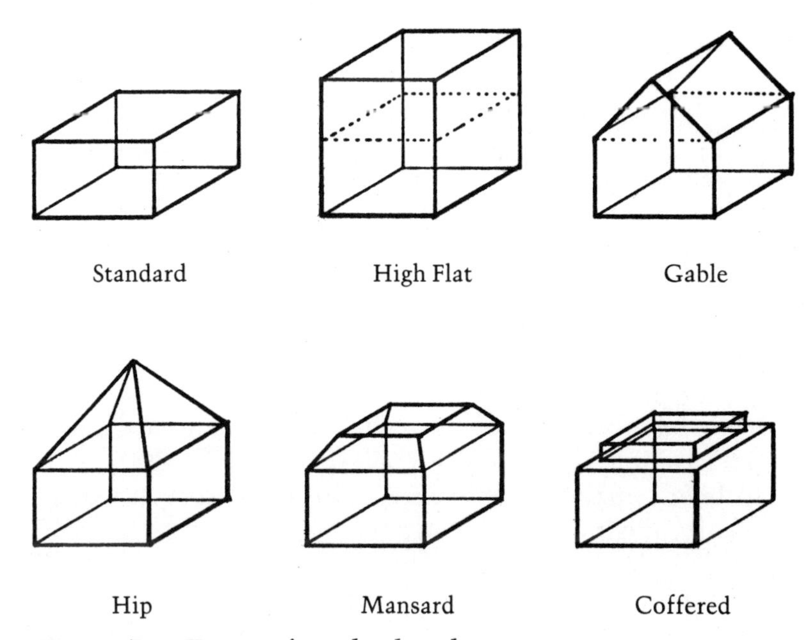

Figure 7-1 *Types of vaulted ceilings*

tional, Edwardian, or colonial home. Or perhaps the ceiling height allows for a coffered ceiling.

Floors

The floor is a key factor in your living room's impression. Wood floors are highly valued, as is a good quality carpet. If you have hardwood floors, refinishing can be done for a couple of hundred dollars and will add a luster to your room. If you have an old carpet, get it steam cleaned. If it's beyond repair, put in a new one.

If your carpet needs replacing, and you just have plain floorboards underneath, consider installing new carpeting with a hardwood border. This creates a wonderful effect, is cheap to install, and looks like a custom designer job.

If you are going to remain in the home for awhile and you have children, consider getting a more textured or mottled carpet. This will help hide any stains or abuse the carpet may suffer.

Furnishings will play a key role in shaping the living room. There's probably more furniture in this room than any other room. If you have wood floors, area rugs under different furniture groupings will help warm the way the room is perceived.

Doors and Windows

If you have a doorway leading into your living room, consider the installation of French doors ($200–300). This will perk up the sense of entry. This is a luxury, not a necessity, and its value to you depends on the impact it will provide. Many experts claim it works better in a small apartment or condo than in a large rambling home.

Whatever you do, upgrade the doorknobs with new brass, porcelain, or cut-glass knobs. Also upgrade any obvious window hardware.

If you have any plain doors, consider dressing them up with picture moldings. Or replace them with paneled doors if cost allows. Hollow-core doors feel cheap. If you have a door that people will be opening a lot as they go through your home, it should be the first to be replaced with a solid-core interior door ($100). Your home should feel solid, not cheap.

Wood windows are preferred. Aluminum sliders look cheap and detract from the grand appearance of your living room. If you have cheap windows, replacing them may cost $300 or more per window. Instead, you can invest in window coverings to camouflage the bastardization. If you are going to replace the windows, get energy efficient ones.

Lighting

Perhaps because the living room is a key room in the house, the use of lighting is at a premium in living rooms.

Since this is usually the home's showcase of expensive objects, lighting is used to highlight elements in living rooms perhaps more than in any other room. In any event, dramatic light is more at home here than anywhere else in the home.

NATURAL LIGHTING

Plenty of natural light is the rule for living rooms. We all want a living room bathed in warm natural sunlight—a place to sit and read a book on a weekend or chat with a friend. However, not all living rooms were designed with the sun in mind. There are dark, north-facing living rooms. There is little one can do to change a room's orientation, but the use of mirrors and light colors can help mitigate whatever defects exist.

GENERAL LIGHTING

The usual source of artificial light is a ceiling fixture or a wall lamp. The fixture should be either bland and unnoticeable or very special. Make sure there is enough light to illuminate the room well. Recessed lighting is very popular in living rooms.

ACCENT LIGHTING

Here's where you can let lighting sell the house. You can set the mood in your living room with various lights that don't cost very much. Floodlights can be placed behind furnishings or plants on the floor. These can be white or colored and provide a dramatic effect.

Track lights can be aimed to accent your furnishings or to emphasize some art. Wall sconces are also a popular item. They add an air of elegance to the room. Notice how often they appear in the living rooms of homes in designer magazines.

Fireplace

Studies have shown time and time again that fireplaces are a highly desired item in most homes. Other studies have shown, though, that unless you have something to work with already, installing a fireplace doesn't usually return 100 percent of its cost. So we will be talking about improving upon what you already have.

If your fireplace is ugly or just plain, there are a number of cosmetic touches that can be inexpensively performed. One place to start is the mantle. If your fireplace doesn't have one, consider a purchase. They can usually be found in salvage yards or can be ordered from the back of magazines such as *Home* or *Fine Homebuilding*.

You can also cover the facing of your fireplace with new tile, brick, or even old lithographic plates. Anything that might make it attractive and a focal point is good.

As mentioned earlier, a mirror over the fireplace is a good way to accentuate its focus. If you're selling a furnished home, quality fireplace accessories and some logs in the fireplace are also important. Even in an empty home, a vase of flowers on the mantle will catch the eyes of all who wander by. A fireplace is a key asset. Use it.

If you've got a huge space you want to make feel cozier, a fireplace in the center can break up the mass.

Bookshelves can be added to either side of the fireplace at a relatively modest cost and will perk up the room considerably. Built-in bookshelves top the list of items homebuyers prefer on their walls.

Ideas for Major Remodeling

If you are creating a new living room as part of your home's remodeling, here are some things to keep in mind.

Create volume. People want high ceilings and lots of light. It's an impressive feeling to walk through a low entry and have a grand living room open out around you. Unusual effects, such as coffered ceilings, are also desired yet cheap to build with simple framing and drywall.

Make use of the volume with balconies or views to the second floor. Vertical connections in homes have moved out of the design studios and into the mainstream. A balcony off of a second-floor room or hall overlooking the living room is a feature that has rated high among home buyers.

Large rooms are in, barns are not. Americans want open flowing spaces so they may entertain, but the rooms also need to function when there are just one or two at home. In an open plan, break up the space by creating subspaces with stairs and half walls. Think of how the room would work with 5 people or 35.

Improving What You Have

If you have a view, you can enlarge the living room windows to make this the focus of the room. Many a spectacular view has sold an otherwise ordinary house. If you can build a deck or patio off of the living room, even better. This is not a cost you can recover directly, but it will upgrade the general feeling about the entire house.

If your home has all standard eight-foot ceilings and your living room has nothing above it, you may be able to upgrade its appearance by going through to the roof. This will give you a higher, volume ceiling that can be filled with skylights to create the type of room over 85 percent of buyers crave. This is not cheap ($2000–5000) and should only be done if your living room is exceedingly dull and the market warrants it.

Opening up the ceiling gives you a chance to reevaluate your lighting plan. It is a great time to install recessed fixtures, which are a high-preference item for buyers in terms of lighting.

The living room needs to be of sufficient size for people to meet and gather. This is proportional to the number of rooms in the home. If you find yourself thinking about adding bedrooms, make sure the living room is of an appropriate size (or can be made so) or you will discourage many buyers.

Some people have knocked down the barrier between the living room and dining room to create a single great room. This is a good strategy for increasing the roomy feel in a small home.

You can add a fireplace if it seems to work with the room ($1300–3500 depending on how much you do yourself). Studies have shown that fireplaces return anywhere from 50 to 150 percent of value. If planned well, a fireplace can't be a loser. Fireplaces often become the focal point of a room. An otherwise dull or uninteresting living room can be given selling appeal just by adding this feature.

Because of the cost and difficulty in installing a masonry fireplace in an existing home, the trend is to use zero-clearance prefabricated fireplaces and then use a marble facing. Craftsmanship of the surrounding area becomes important, as this is where buyers' eyes will focus.

Hiring Contractors

Most work in renovating the living room involves carpentry, especially finish carpentry. If you are handy with wood and if you have a good eye for detail, there is no reason you should not be able to do the work.

However, depending on how ornate you wish to get, you will require many special tools such as a table saw, jig saw, and special sanding equipment that most homeowners just don't own. Remember, the quality of the job is crucial because that is what people see.

Painting and wallpaper are a matter more geared for the homeowner. Be sure to prep the walls properly. If you need some advice, there are many good how-to books from the Sunset or Ortho series that explain how to do everything.

Carpet should be installed by a professional. Installation doesn't cost much and goes very quickly.

Cabinet work goes along with finish carpentry. If you've got the skill, great. It will save you a lot of money. If you don't, you need to talk with someone who does about how to keep the costs low on any cabinetry you do install.

The handyman should be capable of opening up the living room ceiling to the rafters, insulating, installing new sheetrock, and finishing off the job. However, it is a large undertaking and you might want to hire a carpenter or contractor. Any wiring for new lights can be done by the homeowner, if city ordinances allow and caution is used.

This type of renovation can be dangerous. Any time you are working high above the floor and removing pieces of ceiling, you need to be cautious. You need to check with an architect or engineer to learn how the house can remain structurally sound once the ceiling joists are removed.

If you desire a fireplace, you should be able to handle most of the installation yourself. The most complicated part you will encounter involves cutting ceiling and roof openings. It is recommended that you leave the installation of the flue to a contractor. Also, because quality and craftsmanship are so important on the facing and hearth, it is recommended that you hire a professional mason or tile setter.

Examples

ENLARGING THE FEELING OF A LIVING ROOM

Since the 1940s and until the last few years, eight-foot ceilings were the norm for new homes. Many a home now suffers from a lack of architectural excitement and interest, with all the rooms being the same height. Although this may not seem like a problem after you've lived in the home for many years, you must remember that an active homebuyer is comparing your home to others, including ones with vaulted, spacious ceilings and other amenities that give the living room a grand feeling. When it comes to the decision of which house to buy, yours may be passed by.

As seen in Figure 7-2, a low dark living room can be transformed into a spacious light-filled wonder. This remodeling can be accomplished for a minimum investment and can make a nondescript home sell quickly.

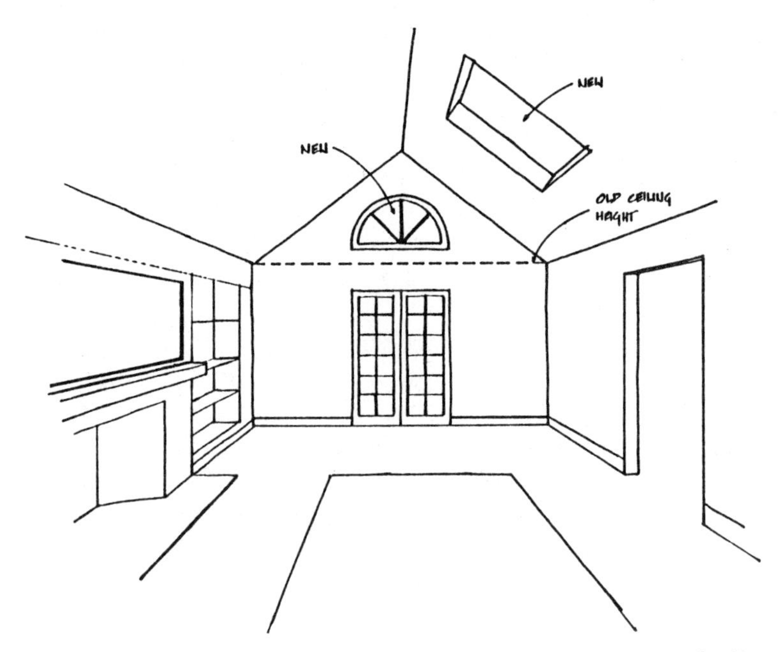

Figure 7-2 *Renovating a dark living room to increase light*

ADDING MOLDING AND CHARACTER TO A BOXY ROOM

In the first drawing of Figure 7-3, we have a standard room. In order to get maximum value out of the room at minimal cost, we decided to do the following:

***Figure 7-3** Renovating to open up a living room*

Add trim and moldings. We installed a beam ceiling and made the fireplace mantle more classical.

Open up the room. We tore down the wall between the living room and dining room in order to give the home more spaciousness and light. In order to separate the rooms visually and yet keep the openness, columns were installed. If the removed wall had been a bearing wall, this would have been a necessity.

The floors were then refinished. This created a wonderful living space that was enjoyed for a few years before the home was eventually sold for a profit.

CHAPTER EIGHT

The Dining Room

THE DINING ROOM IS a room that impresses, but it no longer sells the house. A formal dining room is more for show, with few families actually eating there every night. In many older homes, the dining room once was one of the most lavish rooms in the house, but no more. Today's home uses the kitchen to sell.

As homes become smaller, the dining room is taking on many of the tasks other rooms used to handle. Your dining room may also be your study, or your library. Whatever the function, dining is still the main focus and the room should be oriented in that fashion.

Walls

The walls of the room must bespeak elegance, whether quietly or not so subtly. A wainscoting is a common way of upgrading appearances for low cost. An even less costly way is to use wallpaper with a chair molding dividing the two portions of the wall. As in other rooms, repair all cracks, then paint to give it a fresh feel.

The dining room is one of the few rooms where a person can get away with using darker colors on the wall. Dark, rich tones work to add a sense of formality to the room. Bright colors work well, too. Much of what you choose depends on the mood you wish to convey.

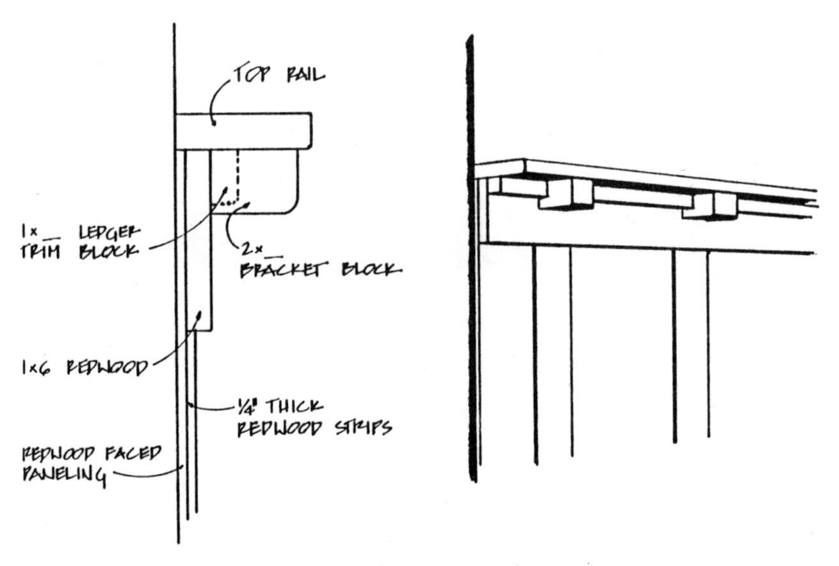

Figure 8-1 *Example of craftsman-style wainscoting*

There are many tricks you can do with molding to add class to a room. One is to create a wainscoting. This can be of many different styles. Figure 8-1 shows a craftsman-style wainscot. This consists of wide vertical boards placed along the wall with narrower boards on top between each one, all capped with a horizontal ledger and rail.

Moldings are not limited to wainscot designs. Near the ceiling, an interesting and dramatic effect may be created. By placing two strips of molding near each other but not touching, you create a dark recess that seems to separate the wall from the ceiling.

If your home already has some nice moldings, take care of them. They are a true asset. If the wainscoting has been painted, you can repaint it or strip it and refinish. Keep in mind that stripping wood is hard work and you may find some reasons why it was painted over in the first place, such as boards that were replaced with a nonmatching wood, or holes that had been drilled and patched with a substance not matching the wood.

Stripping wood is a tedious job. Only undertake it if: (1) You know you have fine hardwood underneath and you will see the job through to the end, or (2) there's already a varnish or shellac but it has darkened unattractively with age and you want to upgrade the finish, or (3) you've got nothing better to do.

Floor and Ceiling

The floor should be neat and clean. Most different floorings work in the dining room. Linoleum should be avoided, as that implies a breakfast nook rather than a formal eating area.

Hardwood is a very appropriate material in the dining room. An area rug, such as an oriental carpet, looks good under the dining table and adds a touch of formality appropriate to the room.

Carpeting works visually, too, although it tends to be soiled with dropped food and spilled drinks. Make sure the carpet has been thoroughly cleaned and vacuumed before showing your home. If it's ruined beyond repair, replace it. An area rug usually works better than wall-to-wall carpet. It is easier to get cleaned and can be removed and replaced more easily if it's beyond all hope of repair. Ceramic tile works around the dining area, too. It is easy to clean—a fact some buyers will notice.

As with all rooms, check the ceiling for water stains. These can point to potential leaks. If the leak has been fixed, use a stain killer and repaint the ceiling. Few things scare buyers more than water leaks. Check for other defects. If the surface is very irregular, darker paint will help mask some of the imperfections, but it will make the ceiling appear lower. A light color is recommended for the ceiling unless a specific effect is desired. A rosette pattern on the ceiling makes a nice touch for a formal classic dining room.

China Cabinets and Other Built-ins

One item most buyers desire is the built-in china cabinet in the dining room. Built-in cabinetry can be expensive to have installed, but it might make the difference between a bland room and one that's noticed. If there is an already-existing cabinet, try to refinish it either by painting or stripping and staining.

Storage space is desired in the dining room. Even if it's not a fine china cabinet, shelves and other cabinetry are in demand.

If you have a fireplace in the dining room, make sure it is clean and functional. See the section on upgrading fireplaces for some ideas.

Lighting

Most lighting in the dining room focuses on the dining table. As such, it tends to be a directional downlighting fixture or perhaps a chandelier. Both these fixtures are very appropriate. Sconces on the wall provide nice fill-in lighting but the main focus is usually on the fixture over the table.

Have a dimmer switch installed to create a nice mood light for dining. Dining room light should be subtle and romantic. If you are showing your home in the evening, add candlelight to complete the picture. A mirror over the fireplace or on the wall will reflect the flickering.

Connection to the Kitchen

The pass-through is as old as the Wright Brothers, but it's a concept that still goes over well. Today's version isn't a little hole you push the food through; it's a large opening that can be shut when needed. When open, it allows light to pass into the dining area from the kitchen. When closed, it can be a formal cabinet so no one suspects the connection. An alternative closure would be one of translucent glass, so light still passes through from the kitchen, but not the smells or distractions.

In smaller homes, it is common for the dining room to connect with the kitchen even more. Perhaps a bar or a half wall is all that separates the two rooms. The dining room needs to be separated from the kitchen to give the home a more upscale feel. There are many ways to accomplish this.

Change the flooring. Switching flooring materials helps to define rooms. If you switch from the kitchen linoleum to a hardwood under the dining area, the distinction will be noticed.

Change the wall finish. Wallpapering the dining area helps separate it, as does adding a special light fixture over the dining table.

Build a platform, or have your kitchen on a platform. If your kitchen is not undergoing major remodeling, a good separation is to place the dining area on a small platform. This architecturally separates the two rooms. Conversely, you may decide to put your kitchen on a platform, especially if it's a small area, to physically remove it from the main dining and living spaces and to provide an area for pipes and electrical lines to be run.

Access to the Outdoors

If your dining room has a nice view of the yard, opening it up onto a patio can be a way of making it truly special. This type of upgrade will run about $1250 but can transform a tiny or nondescript dining room into a wonderful place to eat.

Visually opening up to the outdoors will increase the perceived square footage of the room and, if you live in a mild climate, provides a chance for wonderful outdoor dining.

Contractors

A good finish carpenter is an asset in working on the dining room. There's probably more woodwork here than practically anywhere else. Of all the rooms of the house, this one speaks of elegance and formality. Wallpapering and painting can be easily done by the homeowner on a weekend. See Chapter 7 for other suggestions on hiring contractors for your dining room, since many of the tasks are the same as for living rooms.

Tearing down walls is an easy task for the homeowner. Cutting a pass-through is also something the average person can do with a little skill and care. Before ripping into a wall, check to see whether it is bearing or not. There are several ways you can tell this. One is to check if the wall is running parallel to the roof ridge or not. If it is not, it is more likely just a partition wall. See if there is another wall built on top. If not, it's even more likely just a partition wall. Most building departments require a permit to tear down any wall that may be structural.

Example

SIMPLE TRANSFORMATION

We transformed the room in Figure 8-2 through the simple use of building up a wainscoting onto an ordinary, blank set of walls.

A sense of formality was created in the symmetrical treatment of the room. Notice the mirror in the center to add light and increase the apparent size of the room.

A bad view was blocked using louvered shutters, which also lent a graceful air to the room. A chandelier was put in, and a dining table set up.

Figure 8-2 *Renovating a dining room*

CARVING OUT A DINING AREA WHERE NONE EXISTS

In this example, we were renovating a condominium. As is true in many condos, there just wasn't the room for a separate dining room. Yet creating the appearance of a separate dining area would significantly increase the unit's appeal and selling price. Notice the difference in the floor plans in Figure 8-3.

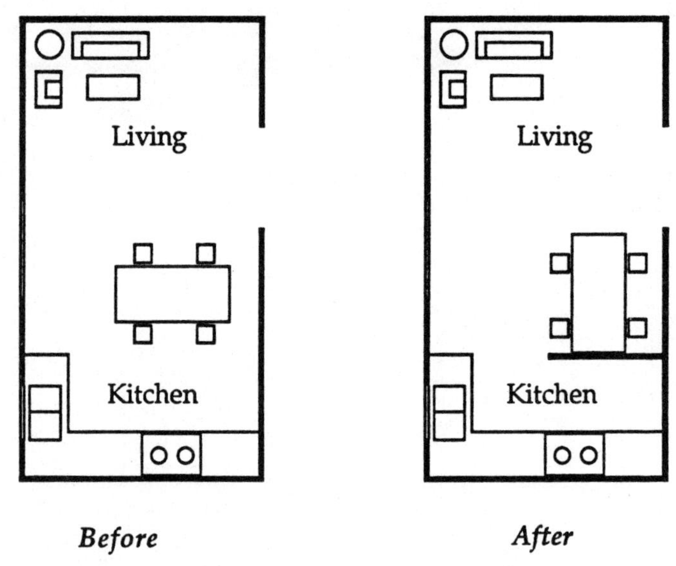

Figure 8-3 Renovating to create a dining area

CHAPTER NINE

Kitchens

Importance of Kitchens

IF THERE IS ANY one room that sells a house, most experts would agree it's the kitchen. The state of a kitchen sets the tone for a buyer's reaction to the whole house. While old wood in the living room may be charming and the odd window in the hall might be interesting, the funky old kitchen will send many buyers running to the competition.

If the kitchen shines, buyers will overlook many shortcomings of the home, such as undersized bedrooms or a less than perfect family room. A kitchen alone won't sell the house, but it will go a long way.

But there's more to a good kitchen than looks. A good kitchen must also be functional. Food must be stored, prepared, and cooked. Meals must be served and guests entertained. Of all the rooms in the house, the kitchen is truly the workstation.

The current vogue is for gourmet kitchens with every professional gadget around. Most of these kitchens are too expensive to be practical to the average home buyer. Although your kitchen may not be able to adopt every idea and device shown in the designer magazines, many can be integrated into even the most economical renovation.

Kitchen renovations can cost anywhere from a couple of hundred dollars to over $50,000. Anyone can give you advice about how to spend lots of money improving your kitchen (and many will—especially the kitchen remodeling contractors). In this chapter, we'll talk about low- to medium-cost renovations, as that's where you can make the greatest return.

Bear in mind that a kitchen is not just a place for cooking any more. It's a place to congregate (people always end up there during parties), to chat on the phone, to pay bills, to study, or to write. Many of these auxiliary activities can be integrated into the architecture of your kitchen at a relatively low cost. Most buyers, although not looking for some of these possibilities, will be delighted when they come upon a kitchen that offers a small worktable or a corner for writing. It just may be the item that swings them over.

Different types of kitchens appeal to different types of buyers. More than most other rooms, you want to target your kitchen to a specific audience. Will your prospects be first-time homeowners or move-up buyers? First-time buyers want a kitchen that is efficient and looks new and that they know will not cost them any extra money to upgrade (money they do not have). Move-up buyers require a kitchen that has more of the look of the designer magazines. They want their kitchen to be luxurious and warm. There are similarities, too. Both groups want a clean efficient kitchen with the latest appliances.

The kitchen has more built-in devices than any other area of the house. It is a hodgepodge of surfaces and textures—cabinets and counters, walls and flooring, appliances and light fixtures. The key is to make it all blend harmoniously. Stay away from contrasting colors and textures. The eye should flow, not be jarred from corner to corner. Do not be afraid of an all-white kitchen. Dish towels, plates, and other items will add all the color necessary.

Besides being the workstation of the home, the kitchen is a very emotional room. Many people have sentimental memories of baking cookies, family gatherings, and grandma. Don't let efficiency go too far. A kitchen that looks as sterile as a laboratory may make *Progressive Architecture* but it has little appeal for the average American home buyer.

Types of Kitchens

There are many styles of kitchens, from country French to modern. Each one has to be treated slightly differently in its decor and in the choice of accessories. However, the major distinctions between kitchens are made based on the work triangle. The work triangle is the shape that connects the stove, sink, and refrigerator.

There are four basic layouts of kitchens, each with its own "triangle," as shown in Figure 9-1. The U-shaped kitchen contains the most compact triangle. It works best with the sink in the center of the U and with the re-

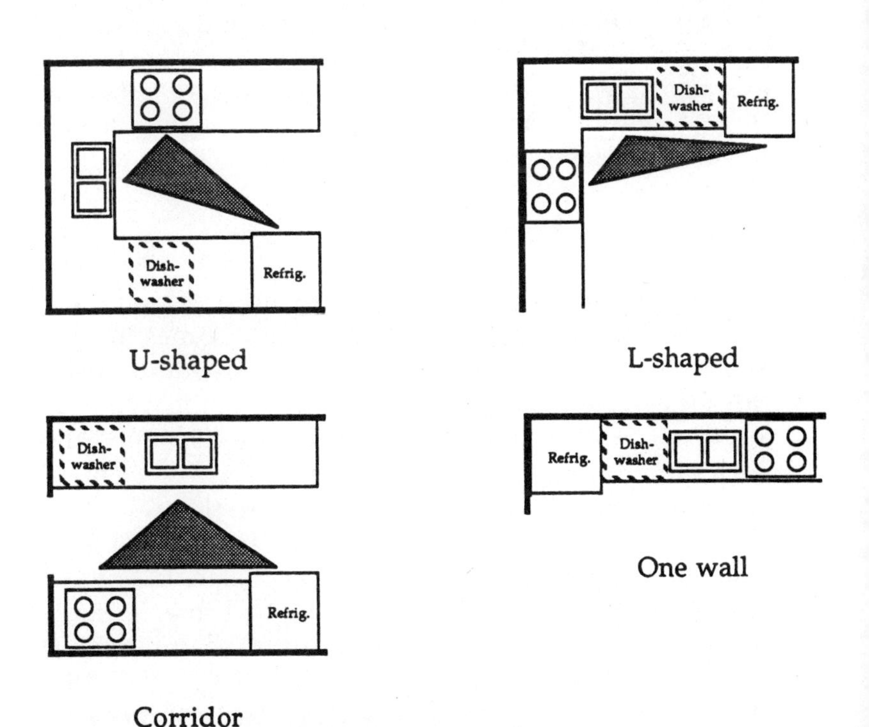

Figure 9-1 *Basic kitchen layouts*

frigerator at the end of a counter to allow an unbroken work area.

The L-shaped kitchen puts the three points of the triangle on two perpendicular walls. Once again, having the refrigerator on the end leads to the most efficient layout. An L-shaped kitchen works very well with an island.

The corridor kitchen puts two points of the triangle on one wall and the third on a parallel wall. It can be a difficult kitchen to work in because of traffic patterns going through the middle. When looking at this type of kitchen, be aware of what rooms are beyond and how often the kitchen will become a true corridor. The best layouts have the sink and stove located on the same counter, resulting in fewer interruptions of the cook.

The one-wall kitchen, also known as the open-plan kitchen is only for the smallest of spaces. It is undesirable from the buyer's viewpoint. It tends to work best in rentals and in-law quarters.

All of these layouts can be altered by the introduction of an island, creating four more layouts. According to recent home buyer studies, an island kitchen is the preferred kitchen layout.

Getting Started

Compare your kitchen to others in your neighborhood. How does it stack up? Now look at new homes in your area in a similar price range. Notice the layouts and features they offer. See if any of these can be incorporated into your kitchen. Check the higher-priced homes and notice their kitchens. What makes them feel like a higher-priced kitchen? What do you like about them? Is there anything that turns you off? Look at your kitchen with your new knowledge and rate the kitchen with the eyes of a home buyer. You may even want to bring in some friends or a local real estate agent to help. Just be objective.

Don't be discouraged. There are many things that can be done to alter your kitchen dramatically. Have fun, this is what designers get to do all the time. Your kitchen probably also has some wonderful features. Perhaps it has good light or a good view. Maybe it's spacious. Maybe it's cozy.

You might be surprised to discover that your kitchen does not have to be totally remodeled to be attractive. Even if it looks ugly, it may not cost too much to upgrade significantly. There are many small items that, when combined, will give a charming effect. There are times when a total remodeling is called for, and we will be exploring that option later.

Degrees of Renovation

A minor renovation might include

- New paint and/or wallpaper
- A butcher-block inset into the counter
- New cabinet hardware and hinges
- New paint or finishing on cabinet faces
- Up-to-date appliances to replace outdated ones

A moderate renovation might include

- Retiling or replacing the countertop
- Creating built-ins for minor appliances
- Replacing cabinet fronts
- Buying all new appliances
- Replacing flooring material
- Replacing a solid rear door with one with glass

A major renovation might include

- Redesigning the kitchen layout
- Adding a skylight
- Adding or enlarging windows
- Buying all new cabinets

Costs and Benefits of the Upgraded Kitchen

Few buyers can view a room with the eye of possibility. Many seem to think that what they see is all there ever will be. By upgrading the kitchen you will be selling them a lifestyle they want but couldn't imagine for themselves and you'll earn a premium doing it.

It is the rare kitchen that cannot pay for itself in a renovation. Unless your kitchen is in very good shape, the upgrades will give you your investment back or at least help to sell your home more quickly. In a recent survey of remodeling contractors on the costs of upgrading a kitchen, a $7000 kitchen remodeling that included refacing all cabinets, replacing counters, installing new lighting, and other moderate items returned between $3500 and $15,000 to the value of the house. Note that this was paying full general contractor prices and was probably not going by the value-added design concept. Even then, most people recouped their costs. You could do many times better.

Strategy

As with all items of the house, we must first get an idea of our competition. Then we can see what we can do with the kitchen we have.

The first step is to determine the degree of renovation you think you will need. Before deciding on a total overhaul, take a good look at your kitchen. Does the floor plan work well? How's the lighting? Is there a good view out the window? Consider all the items we'll talk about in this chapter. Many times a facelift and a little major work is all that is necessary.

There are many elements that go into a kitchen renovation, and just naming them could take the page. Some of the key items to consider, in order of importance, are

- Appliances
- Cabinets/storage space
- Counter space
- Flooring
- Lighting
- Accents, small appliances, and specialty items

Remember, this is the key room in the house. Don't be afraid to invest a little extra money here. But think seriously about how you can get the best results without breaking your bank account.

APPLIANCES

Appliances are one of the major features, and expenses, of a kitchen, whether it be old or renovated. They're also one of the easiest to replace. Like clothing, cars, and trendy restaurants, appliance styles and colors go in and out of fashion. Few things date a kitchen as quickly as the appliances.

Colors date an appliance more than anything, so if your appliances are avocado green, harvest gold, or copper brown, you might want to consider replacing them or at least having them repainted. (Don't attempt to repaint them yourself, since it usually looks like an amateur job.) Having an appliance professionally refinished will cost $60–150.

Many manufacturers today are trying to sell completely coordinated stoves, refrigerators, and dishwashers as a set. Don't buy into this without thinking through your needs.

Appliances can look good together without being from a perfectly matched set. It may not be necessary to replace all the appliances.

The other key to appliances is to keep them clean and looking new. Greasy stoves turn the buyer off. Keep all appliances polished, waxed, and looking like they just came out of the showroom.

When buying new appliances, get all the warranty information. You can use this as a selling point as you pass the warranty protection on to the next buyer. Also, people look at brand names. Buy a known one, and if it's top of the line, make sure you point it out.

STOVES

A stove can be unobtrusive within the framework of the kitchen or it can be the focal point. Stoves can vary from a standard 30" white ($279) to a professional 6-burner Wolf range ($5000). Who your buyers are and what competing homes in the neighborhood offer should give you an idea of what is best for your kitchen.

If you're doing major remodeling, you might want to consider a separate cooktop and oven. Cooktops in the island are an upscale feature, yet are not that costly to install ($200–500 for the cooktop, and installation may be free or under $100). If you haven't been to a kitchen showroom lately you might be surprised. Kitchen appliances come in a full range of styles.

Even if doing only minor remodeling, you might want to consider putting money into one top-quality appliance that you can use as both a focal point and a sales tool. Look at home magazines to get some ideas. Many of these publications feature kitchens every month.

The more upscale a home is, the more buyers look at the features the appliances offer. Self-cleaning ovens, timers, digital readouts, and programmable cooking are just some of the features offered. Use your best judgment. Most of these extras are just ways for the manufacturer to make more money. An appliance that looks upscale will sell better than one that doesn't, even if the latter has more features.

When choosing appliance colors, white is the safest, as it never goes out of style. If, however, you're planning on selling right away, then a kitchen done with "today's colors" could sell quickly. Black is currently the popular color and signifies "new" to buyers. The catch is that fashionably colored appliances will tend to cost more.

REFRIGERATORS

Make sure your refrigerator is clean inside and out. There's no excuse for a sloppy refrigerator. It's an easy item to clean, and it will affect your buyer's perception of the whole kitchen.

If you're replacing your refrigerator, stay away from all the fancy upgrades unless your neighborhood warrants it. It's just an extra cost, not to mention having to run a separate plumbing line for that automatic ice maker. A clean, standard size, new refrigerator is all most buyers ask for. Make sure it's an automatic defrosting model.

Make sure the new refrigerator's door opens in the proper direction. Manufacturers make both left- and right-handed refrigerators.

In the luxury market, zero-clearance refrigerators are the rage. These are refrigerators that are flush with the cabinets. In any other market, these are too costly and just don't return the expense.

MICROWAVE OVENS

These are now standard items in new kitchens. If renovating your cabinets, construct a built-in for the microwave. In fact, mounting the microwave under some cabinets will free up counter space, making your kitchen counters appear bigger.

SINKS

It's hard to find a basic sink these days. The sink catalogs are starting to rival Webster's dictionary in their thickness. One-, two-, and even three-basin sinks are popular now. They come in a full variety of styles and shapes. At least a two-bowl is recommended, especially if it is fitted with accessories such as a cutting board. A garbage disposal is also a must these days.

Stainless steel is the most popular kitchen sink, but the new two- and three-piece enamel over cast iron are a sign of an up-to-date kitchen. If you are replacing the sink anyway, go with one of these models, especially in a more expensive home. But do not tear out the kitchen sink just to upgrade if it's an older stainless steel in good condition and of a reasonable size.

Space is probably the determining factor for the size of your sink. Get the largest one you can that will fit in your cabinet and counter space. For a really luxurious effect, add a second sink in the island for washing vegetables.

DISHWASHERS

Dishwashers are also now a standard item and will help sell your home. However, moving electrical and plumbing lines can be costly so take this into consideration. The best location for a dishwasher is near the sink. It makes for convenient loading and unloading of dishes. If buying a new dishwasher, get one that's quiet when running. Many people will test them.

Dishwashers are a less critical item for sales than some of the others. If you must skimp a little on your appliances because of budget, do it here rather than on the stove or refrigerator.

GARBAGE DISPOSAL

Another item that helps to sell (or hurts through its absence) is the garbage disposal. All that is necessary here is one that works. People aren't very impressed if you brag about your new 5-horsepower disposal that can eat table legs or anything else it's fed. A small 3/4-horsepower unit should be fine. A garbage disposal can cost $50–75 for the unit, and up to $200 to install depending on location of power source.

Trash compactors are not necessary. Don't spend the money to put one in.

New Fixtures and Surfaces

Tile is the preferred material for kitchen countertops. It is usually used in a 4″ x 4″ tile or 6″ x 6″ tile. Don't try to create complex patterns; the kitchen already has too many different elements that must blend harmoniously. A single base color with a contrasting accent on the backsplash looks nice. Simplicity is the key here. Tile is not cheap, but if you do the work yourself, it doesn't have to be too expensive either. The cost can range from $30 to $50 installed or $12 to $24 without installation. These prices are per linear foot, assuming the common countertop depth of two feet. Variations depend on the type of tile and the backing you use. It's a good idea to use a tile sealer to seal the grout and prevent food particles and bacteria from getting stuck there.

It is standard for countertops to have at least a backsplash to prevent water from hitting the walls. A very nice touch is to tile the backsplash all the way up the wall to the underside of the wall cabinets. This is not very much tile, perhaps 18 inches to 2 feet in height, but it can add a lot to the kitchen in sex appeal. Depending on the style of your kitchen, you might want to put in a few hand-painted tiles or a contrasting color every so often to heighten the effect.

Laminate is also very popular. It is sometimes called by the brand name Formica. It can be cut to many shapes, including curved corners (a recent trend). Although considered a fine material in its own right, there are several ways to dress it up and make a more expensive-looking counter without the high cost of tile. One way is to combine new inexpensive laminate counters with a more expensive tile backsplash. Another way is to use an edge trim in a contrasting color or wood on the laminate counter. The results can be quite incredible in resale return.

Laminate counters can be bought as cheaply as $6 per linear foot for the preformed units with a built-in backsplash and lip, up to $20 or more per foot for custom cuts and inlays. Laminate is very easy to install if the counter is straight, with no corners. The key is to hide the seam at corners. If you have good carpentry skills, you should be able to handle this installation easily.

Butcher block is also popular. It makes for great accents in a tile counter or a laminate counter. It's also good for covering an island. Many people associate good feelings with butcher block and it's quite handy for the gourmet cook. But do not do all your counters in this material. It's costly and labor intensive to keep looking good. Many buyers know this. One of the sales points of a kitchen is that it should feel maintenance free.

Warning: Stay away from laminate designed to look like butcher block. It doesn't fool you and it doesn't fool your buyers. It's the sign of cheap and shoddy remodeling.

Corian is a beautiful material and looks especially lovely with inlaid wood on the edge. However, it's also very expensive and must be installed by a professional, quite expensive in itself. This is only for the upper-end markets.

Granite or marble make for a good accent for the complete kitchen. It makes sense to do a small counter in one of these materials in a very upscale house. These materials, though beautiful, are not very practical as counters. Dishes break easily, knives dull quickly, and your wallet empties at a very fast pace.

Remember, sleek, clean surfaces are the key. The counters will help smooth the transitions the eye must make when jumping from appliances to cabinets to windows to floor.

Faucets

In recent years, the variety of faucets with their myriad of features has increased tremendously. Any given manufacturer today produces literally hundreds of different faucets. The question is how does one choose the appropriate one.

The first key is quality. The faucet must feel solid and real. A nice-looking faucet that is nothing but chrome-painted plastic will look good until the buyer goes to try it. If it feels cheap then, she'll start wondering about the quality in the rest of the home. Quality does not have to mean expensive. Building supply houses and home improvement centers regularly have sales on different faucets, and some lines are standard and thus much cheaper than the upscale models.

The chrome single-handle faucet seems to be the most popular in the kitchen. Buyers also find the black spray nozzle with hose a desired feature. Practicality and beauty are the keys. Buyers are thinking function and work in the kitchen. You can get fancier in the bath.

Recently, bright plastic faucets have become popular. They are offered in white, red, black, and occasionally other colors. These work well with ceramic sinks and denote a more upscale lifestyle, but are not as safe a bet as the standard chrome.

Kitchen faucets range in price from $29 to $329. Most fall into the $50–$125 range.

Flooring

The floor is a substantial part of the visual impact of the kitchen and thus requires our attention. Look at your existing flooring. Look at its condition. How easy is it to clean? Does it appear dated? Now look carefully at the floor. Notice any uneven or sloping areas. This could indicate a subfloor or underlayment problem. If this is the case, the flooring will have to be replaced.

The three main requirements of a kitchen floor are durability, resistance to moisture, and ease of cleaning. Vinyl flooring, tile, and hardwood all fit these requirements.

The most popular flooring is vinyl, also referred to as linoleum. Vinyl floors are generally easy to maintain, resilient, and comfortable to stand on. There is an almost unlimited selection of patterns and colors. Choose a light, neutral pattern. Flooring more than pays for itself. A medium-quality material ($10–30 per yard material, $45–55 per yard installed) will give the best return. Avoid the cheap stuff—it looks it. Avoid dark patterns, bright colors, or simulated ceramic tile or brick patterns. They turn off most people.

Vinyl tile floors can also be made quite attractive if a little imagination is used. This is by far the cheapest floor to install and requires no professional labor. Be careful, though, that it does not look cheap. Some patterns built from these tiles look quite good, such as the traditional checkered black and white pattern.

The color and pattern in pure vinyl tiles goes all the way through. There are also rotogravure products where the pattern is just printed on a thin sheet that is attached to the backing material. The quality of the finish and whether the vinyl is pure or just a thin veneer will affect the price. (Pure vinyl tiles range from $3 to $8 a square foot. Composition tiles cost from $.50 to $4 a square foot.)

Many times, vinyl flooring can be laid right over the existing floor, provided it is a smooth surface. This saves time and money.

Although vinyl is the most popular, tile is still the most preferred material of home buyers. Because of its cost compared to vinyl, it tends to appear mostly in costlier homes. Large tiles work best. Quarry tile can be bought cheaply, and provides a very nice custom look.

A durable, non-skid surface is the best flooring for a kitchen. Six-inch or larger tiles should be used in the flooring. With an almost unlimited variety of colors and textures, tile allows you to use your creativity to the fullest to upgrade the look of your kitchen. You can tile in a border of contrasting color to give the floor a custom look or you can use more traditional patterns. Look at designer magazines. Notice the kitchen floor. Many times you will see an imaginative and beautiful pattern. You can create that, too, at an cconomical price.

Tiles range in price from $2 to $12 per square foot, with some decorative tiles costing as much as $14 or $15 per tile.

Wood also makes a beautiful kitchen floor. Use at least three coats of polyurethane to make it water resistant. It's still unique enough that many buyers fall for a kitchen just because of this. It does require a little more maintenance than tile or vinyl.

When choosing materials, remember, economies of scale work both ways. Although the cost per square foot may be more for a small kitchen, the overall cost will be less than for a large one. If you are upgrading a very small kitchen, you can use the best materials without the cost getting out of control. The impression of quality will go a long way toward selling the home, even with the inadequate size.

Wooden parquet flooring, available at most home improvement centers, looks exceptional in smaller kitchens ($3.50 to $8 per square foot). If you are sanding and refinishing it, use a professional, as it's hard to sand parquet.

Evaluating What You Have

KITCHEN SIZE

Does the kitchen's size relate well to the rest of the home? Do you have a four-bedroom house with a kitchen that seats three? If this is the case, no matter how nice the kitchen, it will be perceived as inadequate. Conversely, if you have a mammoth kitchen in a studio apartment, perhaps you would do better to carve out a dining area or other useful room.

OLD APPLIANCES

Take a good look at your old appliances. If they are relatively modern looking and perhaps the only thing wrong with them is the color, you can have them refinished. The only other appliances worth saving are some truly antique stoves and refrigerators—the type people pay premiums for in antique shops, not your old round-top International Harvester brand refrigerator. Most old appliances are worthless and are impossible to sell. In fact, many places will charge you to haul the old appliances away. Remember, people want a carefree kitchen with carefree appliances. To most buyers this means brand new. If your appliances look worn or from some bygone era, budget in their replacement now.

CABINETS AND CABINET SPACE

If the cabinet space in your kitchen is adequate and well arranged but the cabinets don't shine, updating may be all you need. New cabinet doors and drawer fronts can totally transform a kitchen, or, for even less money, perhaps painting or refinishing cabinets is all you need. A combination of updated cabinet fronts and a new countertop will give the appearance of a new kitchen although it only costs a fraction of one. You'll get the full retail value at sale.

Cabinets can be transformed through paint magic. Faux granite and other textures can take the plainest, cheapest-looking cabinets and make them appear as works of art.

The three most important concerns buyers have about cabinets are how they look, how much storage they provide, and how well they're constructed. All three should be concerns of yours as you plan your renovation.

The cheapest way to update cabinets is just to replace the hardware. Go for nothing but the best. Solid brass (about $4 each) or porcelain knobs ($3) and appropriate hinges can be a surprisingly effective way of giving your kitchen an upgrade. This item rarely costs over $100 total. A few new knobs and newly painted cabinets have totally transformed many a dark kitchen into a beautiful new one.

As mentioned earlier, one step above just replacing knobs is to repaint or refinish the cabinet fronts. This can be easily done. For painting, spraying is recommended as it doesn't create brush marks. Be sure to mask off all nearby areas that you don't want to paint. For natural wood refinishing, there are products that remove old stain and varnish, allowing you the chance to refinish cabinets and make them appear like new. If the doors are just a little scratched, there are products available in hardware stores to hide the scratches.

If painting, stay with the whites, off-whites, and almonds. Colors tend to look either strange or amateurish. Take off all hardware or mask it well. If you want a more professional-looking job, you can have the doors refinished by a cabinet shop.

It's possible to upgrade the kitchen while keeping the old cabinets by making it "country." Paint your existing cabinets with a fresh coat of a light-colored paint and just wallpaper the walls around the cabinets with traditional patterns. It will give a homey effect.

The next step up in cost is totally replacing the cabinet and drawer fronts while leaving the cabinets intact. This has become a hot trend lately, as it allows one to install the modern raised-panel doors in cherry or oak or to create a Eurostyle kitchen with laminate. It costs about one-third to one-half as much as installing new cabinets. You can find firms to do this in the Yellow Pages. There's a high markup on this item so try to negotiate a lower price ($2300–4500 per kitchen).

Finally, if none of this will work because your kitchen is laid out horribly or the cabinets are severely inadequate, consider putting in new cabinets. You can do this yourself or have them professionally installed. New cabinets will transform your kitchen and may not cost that much for smaller kitchens. We talk more about layout later in the chapter.

If installing new cabinets, be aware that more is usually better. Also there are now many wonderful inserts and types of cabinets that provide the sizzle buyers need. Many local cabinet shops can manufacture cabinets to your specifications for a cost very competitive with the "off the rack" variety sold in many home improvement centers.

Cabinets cost a lot and if you have a substantial expanse to cover, the total can really add up. A cheap alternative to cabinets is open shelving. It can look quite beautiful and dramatic and can save you hundreds of dollars. Also, plastic-coated wire grids can act as places to hang items. They're cheap but also help the kitchen stand out.

Glass inserts in cabinet doors help add to the classy feel. These cost a bit more, but you only need to do two or four to get the effect. Another way to get more bang for the buck is to mirror the back of the open shelving. The mirror adds to the spaciousness and sparkle of the room.

One inexpensive yet nice-looking effect is to use open shelving on the corners of cabinet layouts. This makes a nice display and also costs significantly less than a standard cabinet. Any shelving will be cheaper than cabinets and can usually be worked gracefully into a kitchen design.

You can replace the fronts of your cabinets with glass cabinet doors, creating a nice display effect for little money.

STORAGE

Storage is crucial to a kitchen. Most storage needs are covered by the use of cabinets. Make sure you have enough. Pantries and broom closets also provide places to hide things. If you don't have the space, buyers will notice. You can make what you have appear larger by discarding anything you do not need. This will make the cabinets look less cramped and may not signal a red flag to the buyer.

Many older homes have walk-in pantries. Cabinet companies have in the last few years introduced adjustable full-view pantries— cabincts that have an incredible capacity for storage yet take up very little area. You can replace a 25-square-foot pantry with a 3-foot-wide pantry cabinet, thus freeing a large amount of extra square footage in your kitchen for other purposes.

Lighting

NATURAL LIGHT

Natural light in the kitchen is essential to give it that homey feel. If yours is dark, do whatever you can to bring in natural light. If you can't do that, make the artificial light bright. We'll talk about these items in this section.

Try to make your natural lighting work for you as much as possible. A single window may illuminate the kitchen unevenly, creating such a contrast between light and dark that it causes glare. Try to balance the light with another window or a skylight or artificial light.

Proper lighting will greatly enhance the selling appeal of your kitchen. A well-lit kitchen can appear cleaner, larger, and warmer. New fixtures and appliances combined with pleasant lighting can make the whole kitchen appear new.

To get natural light into the kitchen, you can

Install a new window. Look for views, etc.

Install a skylight or two.

Install a greenhouse window. These are relatively inexpensive but add a lot of light and a feeling of spaciousness to the kitchen. Fill them with plants for a homey effect. These work especially well over the sink.

Add mirrors to bring in more light.

Put in a back door with glass panes.

Make a connection to a room that has natural light. Many times the dining room is light in old houses but the kitchen is dark. Times have changed and we can now make more of a connection between these rooms. Knock down the wall and build a counter divider. You can even have shutters or some other device to completely screen off the kitchen at times.

You can also use natural light to help define spaces. By placing a skylight over the dining area or breakfast nook, you can help separate it from the work area.

ARTIFICIAL LIGHT

In today's home, family life centers on the kitchen. Your lighting must take into account more than just food preparation.

As you contemplate your kitchen redesign, there are three types of lighting you should consider: general lighting to illuminate the room, task lighting to illuminate specific work areas, and accent lighting to show off a special personal item or to create a mood.

General illumination can be either a luminescent ceiling, a series of recessed high hats, or just a nice fixture in the middle of the ceiling. Aside from the luminescent ceiling, fluorescent lighting is discouraged. It reminds people of school or work. People see it as a sign of a cheap kitchen.

The key to the artificial lighting is the accents. These may be track lights, carefully arranged spots, or an unusual fixture. These can provide a mood that says to your buyer "buy me now." Perhaps arrange a series of spots along a wall of framed photographs or art work, creating a gallery effect. A nice hanging fixture over the eating area is always a plus.

A fixture that hangs below a ceiling generates more light than a similar-sized recessed fixture. If you want recessed fixtures, the layout of the kitchen, the ceiling height, and the type of fixture and bulb will determine how many lights you need. A crucial rule of thumb is that the light from one source should always overlap the light from the next. You don't want to create any shadows.

Task lighting is used over workstations and under cabinets. It is both functional and says to your buyer this is a quality kitchen. Light sticks under the cabinets cost about $25 each plus the cost of getting the power there.

Task lights can illuminate work areas directly, but be careful to avoid the "operating room effect" where the kitchen is too well illuminated. Control is of the essence. Remember, a kitchen is a gathering place in addition to a workstation. You want to be able to create moods. Provide as many switches as possible and put dimmers on those switches. That provides for the maximum possible lighting combinations, allowing a full range of activities.

Eating Areas in the Kitchen

Unless you have a very small kitchen, an eating area should be incorporated. We rarely spend our casual meals eating in the dining room. Even if it's just a bar, people prefer to have an informal place in the kitchen to eat.

The breakfast nook can be used as an asset in remodeling your kitchen. If the kitchen is small, create a sun space addition to house the nook area. This will add more natural light to the kitchen and significantly increase its appeal.

The island can double as an eating area. If updating the surface, reconstruct it to allow for a 12–18-inch overhang. This is enough space to allow people to sit around the island on stools for casual coffee get-togethers.

Design and Layout

The kitchen is probably the most complicated of all the rooms to plan. You must consider both functional and social needs, structural and mechanical systems, and budget. However, as the most important room in the home, it deserves your attention.

If you've decided your kitchen is hopeless, if the quality of the neighborhood has significantly increased since you first moved into the house, if you really need the kitchen to help sell the house, it may be time to consider doing a major renovation. In planning a major overhaul of your kitchen, the first step is to analyze how the room is used or could be used. Is it for entertaining or just for throwing items in the microwave? Is the kitchen an integral part of the house or tucked away in some corner? What would you like it to become or what would your type of buyer like it to be?

Draw the floor plan of your existing kitchen on a sheet of graph paper. Show all existing windows, doors, cabinets, and appliances. Make special note if any of these are in bearing partitions. Remember, though, this is only to give you an idea about what is there and what you have to work with. The trick is to see past that to all the possibilities.

When planning the kitchen, break it up into its use components. What is going to happen here? You need an area for preparation of food, a cooking area, a cleanup area, and an area for food storage. In addition, you might want to have a workstation or desk area for bills and business or an area geared more toward entertaining. These areas can overlap but they must be present.

Plan your work triangle and locate the major appliances. Make sure the stove, refrigerator, and sink are out of the traffic flow. Allow sufficient counter space around each appliance and for each function.

Try to store small appliances in appliance garages or place them in a special area. The kitchen should look uncluttered. Too many of these appliances in view will use up all the available counter space and will make the kitchen appear poorly planned.

Provide adequate clearances in aisles and near work areas. Even a large kitchen will appear cramped if buyers have to squeeze around the table to get to a view of the cooking area.

Place tall appliances or cabinets at the ends of a run of counter to avoid interrupting the work flow and to make the kitchen aesthetically pleasing.

During the design phase, consider

Traffic pattern. Avoid making people walk through the food preparation area. Allow for people to congregate in certain areas.

Appliances. Locate appliances to avoid requiring a total overhaul of the infrastructure—the plumbing and electrical—to keep costs low.

Counters and cabinets. Keep counters flowing with the eye. Avoid a jumble of different surfaces. The more cabinets, the better. Work cabinets and counters together to allow breaks between different activity areas.

Elevations. Always see how the kitchen will look from eye level, not just from an overhead plan view. A kitchen can look great in plan but not work in elevation due to window heights, bad juxtapositions of counters and cabinets, or other reasons. You want to know how your kitchen will look from all angles before you invest a significant sum in it. You might even build a scale model.

Work triangle. This is the basic layout of your work space. Consider how it relates to the dining area and the exterior. Keep traffic patterns out of this area.

Views. Check for views or potential views. Then decide if you would rather enjoy the view while dining or while washing dishes. Check all the possibilities. Is there a fabulous view behind that solid wall?

Breakfast nook. A must for today's home. If there's not enough room for a full nook perhaps a counter can be widened to become an eating area with stools.

Islands. The island isn't extra chopping space any more. It can be an extra eating area, storage, a cooking area, or just about anything. Think about the potential of this extra counter space.

Focal point. Grab the buyer's attention. The kitchen is now the most dramatic room in the house. Look around. Perhaps you could use a work island jutting out at an interesting angle or varying counter heights. But don't use drama to cover up lack of quality. That needs to be there, too.

Planning a Smart Kitchen

In the kitchen, the geometry of the work triangle is the basic key to planning. The work triangle is the shape that connects the stove, sink, and refrigerator. Studies have shown that in the most efficient kitchens, the three legs of the triangle will add up to at least 12 feet but will not exceed 23 feet. Don't worry if, in order to capture a special view or include a unique feature, your kitchen must fall outside these guidelines.

The sink and dishwasher will work most efficiently if close together. They share a common drain and both work together in cleanup. Try to keep the dishwasher on the outside of the work triangle.

With refrigerators, keep in mind two items: The door should swing away from the work triangle and there should be at least fifteen inches of counter space on the side next to the door handle.

You may wonder at the staggering cost of all you are conceiving. Be forewarned that the cost of remodeling a kitchen will be higher than renovation of any other single room in the house.

The kitchen is a complex combination of electrical system, plumbing, appliances, working surfaces, and storage space. Kitchen remodeling will range from $5,000 to $50,000 and up, depending on your plans. However, if you are careful, you will always recover these costs or even make substantially more on a kitchen renovation.

Other Ideas

There are many features buyers desire in a kitchen. Some to keep in mind are

- A dining counter or eating area, at least in medium or large homes
- Dining area with easy access to but visual screening from the kitchen. A pass-through counter is a plus.
- Sink, range, and refrigerator conveniently located, with counter space near each one.
- An area for books, a phone, and a small desk is a big plus.
- At least one large sink is necessary. But a second sink in the island for washing vegetables is a hot item.
- A window, especially a greenhouse window, near the sink is always appreciated.
- Fire extinguisher and/or smoke detectors for safety.
- Wine racks/gourmet library.
- Islands, if you have the room.

Remember that buyers look for plenty of counter space and plenty of cabinet space.

Many ideas for kitchens can be derived from magazines and model homes in new housing developments. Costs can be controlled by paying attention to location of plumbing and electrical and by economical expansions of cabinet space.

Contractors

ARCHITECTS AND KITCHEN DESIGNERS

Because the kitchen is the costliest and most complicated room in the house (more wiring, plumbing, ventilation than any other room), it lends itself to consulting a professional more than other parts of the house. But this depends on the extent of the renovation you feel is necessary. Unless you are doing major remodeling, all the planning can be done by the average homeowner. All materials can be found at home supply stores or at kitchen, plumbing, or other specialty outlets; and the work can be subcontracted or attempted by the homeowner.

When doing kitchen remodeling, an experienced designer can be invaluable. If you do decide you need a designer, many kitchen contractors and showrooms will provide design services for a small fee. This fee will be applied to your purchase should you buy materials through them or have them do the actual installation. When choosing design services, don't just go by price. Your goal is to get the ultimate in resale value. Ask to see examples of their previous work or to see some recently completed jobs. If possible, call up past clients and ask them about the designer's creativity, ability to budget, and ability to provide value for the cost.

If there is going to be serious structural work involved in your kitchen renovation or if it's only part of a much larger project, you may need the services of an architect. His training can create a dramatic kitchen for you. If you just need someone to put your plans on paper, you can hire a draftsman more economically.

PLUMBERS

Because kitchen renovations are probably more common than those of any other room, a number of very good books have sprung up that outline how to install plumbing for all of the various appliances in the kitchen. However, if you have any doubts about your plumbing abilities, you might want to hire a professional to rough in the supply and drain lines. You could then easily do the finish plumbing—installing valves and hooking up the appliances. This could still result in a substantial savings.

One of the down sides to doing the plumbing yourself is time. The kitchen contains a myriad of devices that require plumbing. Remember, while you're remodeling, you don't have the use of your kitchen. Kitchen renovations have been known to take weeks to complete. Why stretch it into months?

ELECTRICAL WORK

As far as electrical work goes, the kitchen is the most complicated room in the house. Wiring for all appliances, lights, and ventilation carries a substantial load. Also, many kitchens have a 220-volt circuit. This is a room best left to experts. Electricians can get discounts on materials (of which there is much in the kitchen) and can be in and out of the job in a short time.

If all you're doing is adding a circuit, changing lights, or adding a few outlets, the average homeowner can do it with a good do-it-yourself book. Just be careful, and be sure it's legal. Some cities require that licensed electricians perform all electrical work.

COUNTERTOPS AND FLOORING

As mentioned earlier, a homeowner with carpentry experience should be able to install a new Formica countertop, especially if it's a straight run. Tiled countertops are not complicated either. A little patience and attention to detail can produce professional-looking results even the first time.

Because the floor is such an important part of the kitchen's overall impression, it must look excellent. With linoleum, this means invisible seams and no bubbles. With tile, this means straight and even grout lines. Too often homeowners do a less than professional job, especially laying linoleum. Seaming is probably the homeowner's weakest area. Be careful. If you're laying linoleum tiles, there is no need for a professional.

Ceramic flooring tile can be easily installed by the average homeowner, especially using tile spacers and other tricks of the trade. Ask your local tile supply store what items they have to ease your task. Marble and other tile can also be laid easily if you have the proper cutting tools.

OTHER WORK

If you're just putting some molding on the walls, wallpapering, or changing appliances, there is no need to hire a professional. There are so many books out on renovating kitchens, both with ideas and with how-to information, that the homeowner can easily do most of the tasks herself. Just be cautious. It must look professional or the savings is lost.

Kitchen and bath contractors are not my personal favorite because of the premium rates they charge. However, they usually do very high-quality work. Their sole income is from kitchens and baths, and they have much experience in remodeling. Ask first—many of them sub out all their work. You're paying a premium just for someone to get on the phone and get the real contractors out to your home. Beware of the hard sell types.

Many firms have excellent showrooms and are a good source for ideas. They even hire out designers. So you can get your kitchen designed at low cost. Their incentive is to credit that cost to you if you buy through them.

Examples

DETERMINING COSTS OF MINOR REMODELING

You observe your kitchen. There's nothing seriously wrong but it looks dull. In this example, we take a home built in the 1960s and update it cosmetically to meet the desires of today's home buyers. The cabinets are of the original installation and are a plain dark brown. The vinyl floor is showing its age and the counters are a speckled Formica.

Remember, the secret of a good minor renovation is to concentrate on the surfaces seen by the eye and never to spend more than half of what it would cost to do a major overhaul.

We had the cabinets refaced with raised oak panel cabinet fronts, replaced the Formica with a modern laminate in a plain ivory, with a cobalt blue tile backsplash for accent. The room was painted an off-white color and an island was constructed to enlarge the usable counter space. This was surfaced in butcher block. New linoleum was laid and a new light fixture was placed over the breakfast table.

KEEPING COSTS DOWN ON MAJOR REMODLING

The problem confronting many people is how to replace an obviously inadequate kitchen with an updated one, but still not spend too much. Kitchens costing $50,000 abound, but how about one for under $10,000?

There are many problems with the existing kitchen shown in Figure 9-2: lack of cabinet space, an awkward work triangle, an inefficient use of counter space, and a poor visual connection to the dining room. There is also the problem of a lack of a laundry room in the house.

By moving the door into the adjoining utility space, room was created to convert the closet into a laundry area. This made an effective use of plumbing lines while allowing for a more continual flow of counter space. This also created a U-shaped kitchen without traffic constantly cutting through the work area as it had previously.

Moving the refrigerator had a wonderful side effect of allowing us to open the wall to the dining area, thereby creating a less formal dining area and a more functional kitchen. With the increased counter space came in-

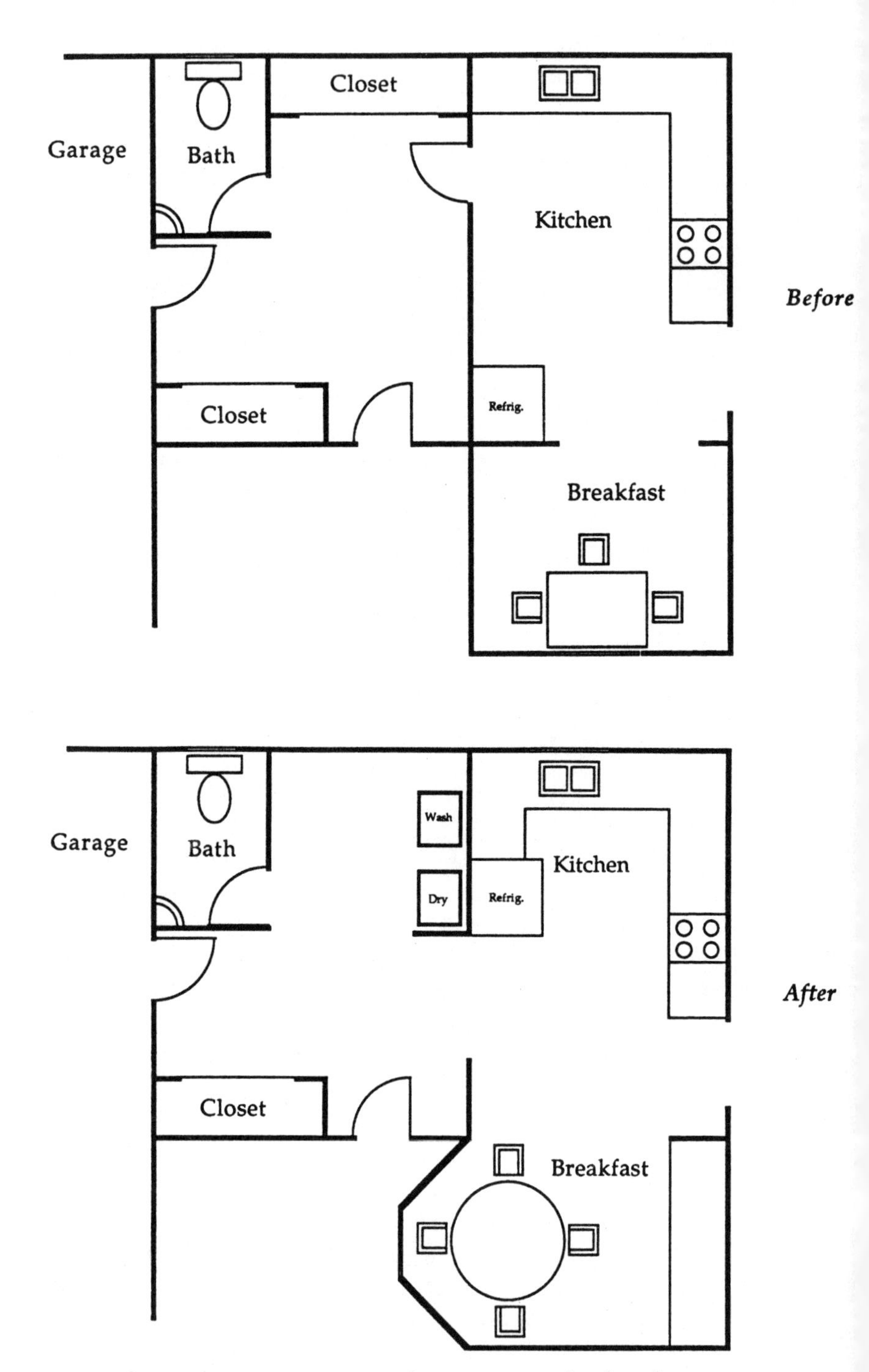

Figure 9-2 *Renovation revolving around a kitchen*

creased cabinets. These cabinets had modern amenities such as lazy susan corners and vertical storage.

The flooring was upgraded and the walls painted an off-white semi-gloss. The counter was a simple almond-colored laminate (to keep costs down) and a larger sink, with two bowls, was installed directly under the window. Costs are as follows:

	Materials	Labor
Install new kitchen cabinets (21 linear feet base, 14 feet wall)	$2665	$ 350
Install stock almond countertop	$ 130	$ 75
Buy new sink	$ 300	$ 45
Buy new stove	$ 450	$ 0
Reuse existing refrigerator	$ 0	$ 0
Buy new dishwasher (including plumbing)	$ 300	$ 45
Buy hood for range	$ 190	$ 85
Paint walls and ceilings (white)	$ 30	$ 75
Paint trim	$ 4	$ 75
Install vinyl floor (including underlayment)	$ 300	$ 400
Demolish wall	$ 0	$ 200
Build new walls	$ 150	$ 200
Install new faucet	$ 90	$ 30
Install bay window (breakfast nook)	$1800	$ 400
Install cabinetry and counter (breakfast nook)	$ 600	$ 50
Miscellaneous	$ 200	$ 400
Total	$7209	$2603

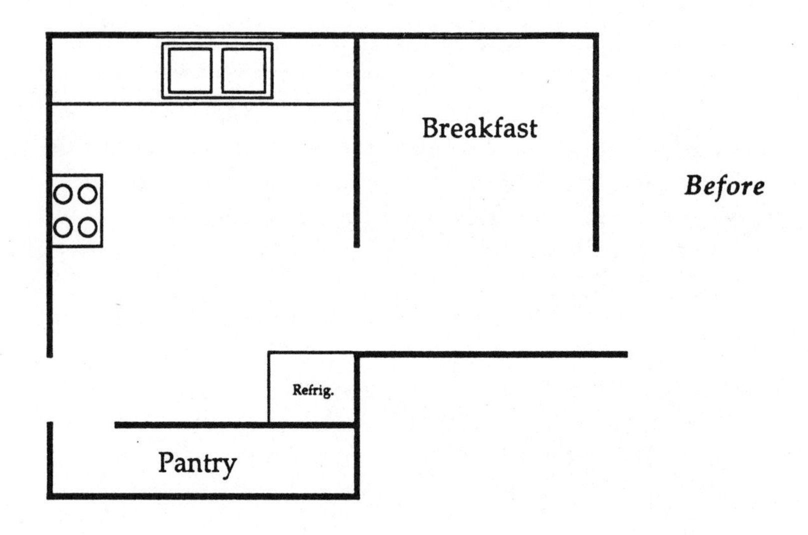

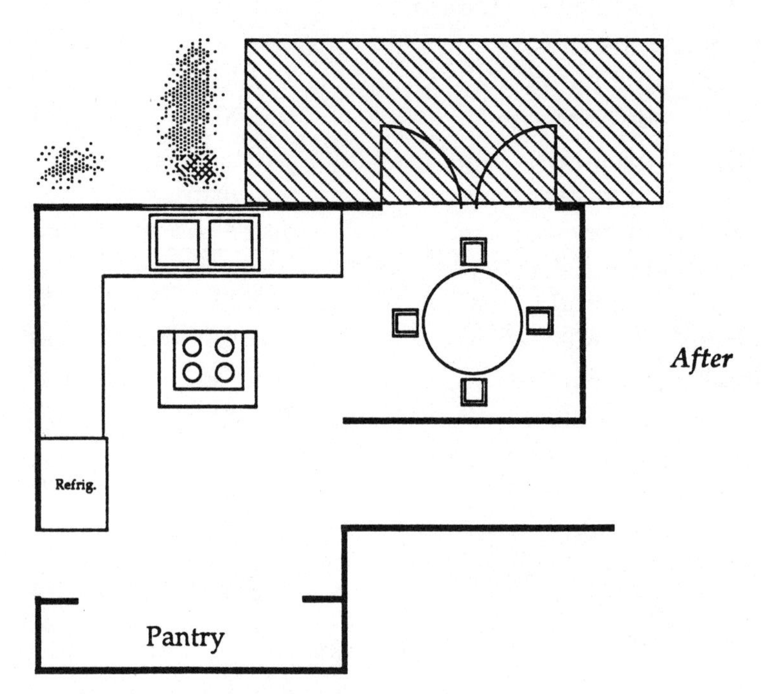

Figure 9-3 *Moderate kitchen renovation*

Labor was assumed at $15/hour unless the owner is expected to do the work (such as moving the refrigerator).

The kitchen is now a modern, salable kitchen and should add considerable value to the house.

A MODERATE RENOVATION

In this example, the kitchen was dark and, due to the inefficient layout, felt smaller than its actual square footage would indicate. Inadequate counter space and bad traffic patterns caused the cooking or preparation of food to be a hassle. The room also looked tired. It was still in its original 1920s configuration and the age was showing. Figure 9-3 shows the floor plan before and after.

An obstructing wall between the kitchen and breakfast area was removed to open up the feel of the room. This increased circulation space enough to allow a set of french doors to the backyard to be installed where a large window had been. A deck was built off the breakfast area to further enhance the home.

Of course the room was repainted, new flooring put down, and the light fixtures changed to a more modern look.

CHAPTER TEN

Bathrooms

Importance of Bathrooms

THE BATHROOM IS A very valuable room in the house, both in function and in resale value. It is a room where a little imagination and drama can go a long way in terms of dollars you put in your pocket. Probably only number two to a kitchen in terms of influencing buyers, a bathroom can make or break the sale of your house. Realtors and builders tell us that the bathroom is becoming one of the most important rooms in the American home. Gone are the three-bedroom, one-bath houses of the '40s and '50s. In a recent survey in *Builder* magazine, it was found that the average American home buyer in the '80s is looking for a home with 3.9 bedrooms and 3.1 baths! Abundant, spacious, luxurious baths are what the modern house is all about.

The possible styles and layouts of bathrooms are infinite. However, certain key elements distinguish the desirable bath from the ordinary or the all-too-common revolting one.

Buyers are often aware of the costs and hassle of upgrading a bathroom and are willing to pay top dollar not to have to deal with that. So a poor-looking bath can detract from a home's value as much as a great-looking one can add to it, irrespective of how much money a renovation would cost.

The number of baths, the degree of luxury, and the materials you use in your renovation are all keyed to the initial attributes of your house, the type of buyer you are targeting, and the neighborhood in which your house is located. How many baths are common for your neighborhood? What is the average ratio of bedrooms to bathrooms? Notice the bathrooms of a nearby neighborhood that you would consider a step up from yours. What do their baths look like? What is the feel? Note the layouts, the size, the materials, the lighting.

Now look at yours. Do you have fewer bathrooms than the neighborhood average? How about size, layout, lighting, and overall quality? These are all key factors in planning your renovation. Overimprovement for the neighborhood means most people looking at your house cannot afford it and most people who can afford it are looking somewhere else. However, with carefully planned spending, you can give your buyer more than he expects at a cost that will more than come back to you.

Types of Bathrooms

There are basically three types of bathrooms in a house.

- The master bath
- The standard (or children's) bath
- The half bath, quarter bath, powder room, and other variations of a partial bathroom

By and large, if you only have enough money to fix one of these, do only the master bath. This cannot be emphasized enough. This is where the people who are buying your house will be bathing. And who do you think they care about most? Why, themselves, of course. So remember, the buyer wants her bath to look good.

Next most important is probably the bath the guests will use. If you have a half bath near the entry, this should be brightened up as much as possible. Remember, when people come to check out your house, this may be one of the first rooms they see. This is also a very inexpensive renovation, even with the best materials, as the square footage of these rooms is usually quite tiny.

Getting Started

Did your house fit the typical neighborhood pattern in number and size of bathrooms? If so, you are in luck and all that may be necessary are cosmetic improvements. However, most people find that their home does not measure up in some way. This is good for you to know because home buyers are surely going to know. They are checking out homes every weekend.

If your house is not what is termed a fixer-upper, you may find it compares favorably with the neighborhood, or is at least not too much below. In this case, the bath may be the place you will use to differentiate your home from the others and allow it to sell quickly for top dollar. Chances are most of the homes in your neighborhood have ignored current trends in bathroom design. You may be able to appeal to the unwritten needs of today's buyer.

Renovating a bathroom can get expensive if you're not careful about what you choose to work on. Remember, you are going for maximum value for minimal cost. You are creating a feel, a mood. This may only require a minimal expenditure. You should check home and designer magazines for ideas but remember, many of these are showcase homes and they do not make economic sense in terms of resale value.

Degrees of Renovation

There are many degrees of remodeling that may be necessary for your particular house.

Minor remodeling might consist of

- A new coat of paint
- New towel racks and/or faucets
- Mirrors
- New wallpaper
- New light fixtures

Moderate renovation might include

- Items mentioned above in minor renovation
- Adding, resurfacing, or replacing cabinets
- Refinishing tub and/or other fixtures
- New flooring

Major renovation might include

- All items in minor and moderate renovation
- New fixtures
- New, enlarged, or altered windows
- New lighting
- Skylights
- Structural, plumbing, or electrical improvements
- Adding another bathroom

If you are looking for a special look, such as Victorian, scavenger yards are a good source as are the many companies that specialize in reproductions (see list at back of book).

Strategy

The strategy for remodeling will be similar to that of other rooms. The number of bathrooms in a home appears on real estate listings and on appraisal forms. So, unless it's out of line with the neighborhood, usually more bathrooms mean a higher sales price. Also, plumbing is a costly and hard to move item. Where you should locate bathrooms and what can be done within existing ones can be somewhat restricted.

After determining what it is you are competing against, it's time to evaluate what you can do to your property to maximize its value at a reasonable cost. Inspect your current bath with the eyes of a prospective buyer. What don't you like? What do you like? Inspect the fixtures, the faucets, the lighting, the flooring, the paint. Many elements of your bathroom will probably be worth saving. The key is to add only what is necessary.

If you have found that your house is deficient in the number of bathrooms it contains and that by adding one or two you could significantly increase the value of your home, that is an item you might want to consider despite the hassle and cost. However, in order to warrant this, you must get a minimum of 1 1/2 times your investment (unless you are planning on living in the house for awhile and you really want that extra bath). Your time and energy are worth a lot. Remember that.

It is almost a rule that homes with only one bath will always benefit by the addition of a second one. More than two might make sense if you have at least four bedrooms. See what is common for your neighborhood.

If you have found that the main problem is the size and/or condition of your baths and not the number, you may only need to do some minor or moderate work. This is good! Do as little as necessary.

When *Builder* magazine did a survey on what home buyers looked for in a bathroom, these are some of the top answers they got.

- Two sinks
- Separate shower enclosures
- Linen closet
- Mirrors
- Natural light
- Vanity storage
- Ceramic tile

You may want to evaluate the possibility of incorporating some of these into your remodeling.

Design and Layout

The key to creating a desirable bath is to compose a room with a sense of retreat. This can be done by being aware of three major elements in all your remodeling work: light, space, and cleanliness.

LIGHT

Get as much natural light in the bathroom as possible. This means if there is a window, keep it, enlarge it, or move it, but under no circumstances cover it. No window? Can you add a skylight? Put glass block in the wall? Put a stained or translucent glass window somewhere?

Artificial light is also crucial. A good modern overhead light is a start, but the real sales approach comes with the task lighting. Whether it be a set of Hollywood lights around the vanity mirror or the use of spots or a sconce on the wall, lighting can create a mood in the bath that says this place is special.

SPACE

If you cannot make it bigger, make it look bigger. Mirrors on the walls greatly enhance the apparent size of the bath. Also, properly framing a view out a window or opening the bath onto a patio can greatly enhance the apparent size of the room.

If there is potential to increase the size of the bath, it will probably pay to do so. See if you can steal some space from a nearby room. Storage space is also a necessity. Linen closets, cabinets, or even shelves over the toilet all add to the desirability of the bathroom.

It's easy to knock down walls to add space or to extend out or add a sun room style addition. However, remember, moving plumbing is not cheap. Plumbing for an average bath can run $1200 or more. So unless it will dramatically upgrade the room, consider just working on the cosmetics.

One idea, if your bath is dark and major renovation is necessary, is to completely open up the wall in front of you as you open the door and replace it with the equivalent of a sun space. That way, instead of looking at a dead-end wall, the buyer is looking directly to the scenery and sky. It makes quite a dramatic view for not too much more than the cost of a window and skylight.

CLEANLINESS

Americans like a sense of newness in the things they buy. That is why so many people are buying new cars while millions of perfectly good but old cars are being junked. The bathroom should look new, even if it's in a Victorian or other "old style." It's the unused, fresh feeling people want, not the exact age of the materials.

Specific Renovations

LIGHTING

Most people never give a thought to the effect lighting has on them, and yet a change in lighting alone can change the feel of a room. There are two types of lighting to be concerned about: artificial and natural.

Artificial Light

Lighting can be broken down into general illumination and task or accent lighting. General illumination should be bright. If you are located in a better neighborhood, pay attention to the style of fixtures used in magazines and in neighboring homes. The types of fixtures you choose can be very important in the look of the bath. In addition to being functional, artificial light can create drama and add class to a room.

Some recommended artificial lights are

- Hollywood lights around the vanity mirror. These denote class and glamor to many people and are quite inexpensive.
- Wall sconces, which can add elegance to a room for the cost of two fixtures ($50–300).
- Very special looking lights (for about $200), to make the main light fixture a focal point.

Make the room bright! It helps. People associate darkness with dinginess. Other hints include using spotlights for effect or installing heat lamps to add to the luxurious feel of the room. Even neon can be used to help turn an ordinary bath into a showplace.

Several recessed downlights in the ceiling will provide nice even lighting for the bathroom. Any mirrors, polished marble, or glazed tile will accentuate whatever light you provide.

The bathroom is overall a very task-oriented area. The lighting must reflect that intent, creating good even lighting at mirrors and other key areas. You can also alter the coloring of the light. Light bulbs that more accurately approach the spectrum of daylight are on the market. These might help the feel of your bathroom.

Natural Light

Even more important than artificial lighting, the key to a desirable bath is plenty of natural light. It can be windows, glass block walls, skylights, whatever. Just make sure you have it if possible.

If natural light does not already exist, putting it in is not cheap, but it must be done if at all possible. Installing a new window will run around $300–500. The value of your bath will be increased tremendously by attention to this one item.

Keys to effective natural lighting include

- Windows on two sides or a single window and a skylight to reduce glare and add to comfort.
- Maintenance of privacy.
- Views and vistas. Do not assume the existing windows capture all the views. You may find that adding a window in a dark room gives it the best view in the house.
- Garden plantings outside windows for a lush greenhouse effect even in tight city locations. This works especially well if your current view is of a brick or concrete wall.

If there are no windows and one cannot be put in, perhaps you can go up and add a skylight. It will help a lot, even if the ceiling is ten feet high or more.

If your only light will be a skylight, consider an operable one, commonly known as a roof window. This allows for better ventilation, and most major window manufacturers produce them. These cost around $400 for the window and about $200–300 to install.

If none of the above will work or if your bath will still be horrible, consider moving the bath and creating two back to back somewhere else in the house. This is an extreme case and only to be used where you can recover your investment.

VENTILATION

Good ventilation is crucial in the bathroom due to all the moisture present. If you have no exterior windows, a good mechanical ventilation system is a must. But please, get a quiet one. We've all had the experience of flicking a switch in a windowless bathroom and getting a ventilation fan that sounded like an outboard motor. It wasn't pleasant then, and it won't be appealing to your buyers either.

FIXTURES

Faucets should both look good and feel good to the touch. Faucets come in every style and shape imaginable. There are even ones with electronic thermometers built in. One thing to remember, though, is to keep the material and style similar between the different fixtures in the room, or at least the ones that are visible together.

You might also visit a bath showroom to try out their faucets or fixtures. These are the places with the luxurious displays, usually costing a fortune. Buy here when you feel like spending on yourself, not when you want to make a profit. For that, go to the plumbing supply house. However, look here all you like. The information and ideas you can get are priceless.

There is now a wider range of plumbing fixtures than at any time in history. Get the catalogs and look at the sample designs. You can find fixtures in many colors and styles to fit any taste. However, you should probably stick with white. White does not go out of style, it's usually the most commonly available, and it usually costs less because it's produced in larger quantities. The only exception to this might be in the master bath. But you must be very careful in color selection. You need to appeal to the person who will buy your house. If you are planning to live in your house a while before selling, be very cautious about the use of color, since colors go out of fashion faster than you might expect.

BATHTUBS

Check the bathtub. Unless you are doing major remodeling, it's not being moved. If it's chipped or scratched or just "looks old," it can be dressed up with a professional refinishing ($200–400). If this seems like a lot of money, it's nothing compared to the cost of removing an old tub, buying and installing a new one, and then repairing the wall area around the tub ($1000–2000).

If you are replacing the tub or you are building another bath, consider installing a whirlpool tub. Bathrooms are quickly becoming luxury spas and what better attraction than to be able to soak those tired muscles after a long hard day. These are becoming a favorite of builders in all markets, but they cost from $1500 up to $5000.

If you are replacing the tub, consider its placement. The bathtub has become the focal point of the bathroom and is rarely boxed into a corner these days. Stepping up the tub slightly or placing it on an angle will make the bath more interesting and more functional—you can use the extra space around the tub to place plants, a radio, or other accessories.

If you have an old Victorian clawfoot tub, this can become a focal point of the bath, almost like a sculpture. Please do not set it up as a shower too unless you must. They are wonderful as tubs (usually they are bigger than modern tubs) and should remain that. As showers, they tend to let lots of water run onto the walls and floor, inviting structural damage.

SHOWERS

If your shower is part of the tub, install clear glass shower doors. They are viewed much more favorably than a shower curtain, plus they do not tend to collect mildew the way curtains do. Clear ones are currently very fashionable. Most shower doors cost around $250 plus installation costs but they might add strength to an otherwise weak bath.

Of course, the faucets should be clean and of a high quality, with no leaks present. In luxury markets, two shower heads will make a favorable impression with buyers.

Tile is the material of choice. The fiberglass enclosures work best in apartments and low-end homes. You can tile a shower for $600 and increase its appeal drastically.

A shower apart from the tub is perceived as a luxury and works well in the upper-priced markets. If you are gearing your home toward a move-up buyer, this is a must. Outside of that spectrum the cost is probably not justified.

If your space allows for it, tile a shelf or seat near the tub. This can be a place for flowers or towels, or to sit on. It is a feature that adds to the bath without costing much.

TOILET

Not much to be done here. Make sure it's operable and that the flush handle is on securely. Buy a new toilet seat to help upgrade the whole look. If the fixture is very outdated or scratched, replace it. The cost of refinishing does not make sense here ($150–500 installed).

VANITY

Two sinks are becoming a very common feature in baths these days. Every survey of new home buyers lists two sinks near the top of the list of desired bathroom features. With the two-career couple, his and hers closets, vanities, and dressing areas are becoming popular.

The vanity should provide good storage space. Also, make sure the countertop is of high quality. Corian looks nice as does cultured marble. Spend the money for good-looking faucets. It will come back to you.

If you cannot put in two sinks because of plumbing costs but you have some room, consider keeping the one sink but extending the vanity countertop. People will appreciate all the extra room to lay out their personal articles.

Many builders use a vanity countertop that extends behind the toilet. This is a standard item but appreciated by home buyers. Another way to add interest to your vanity is to place it at a dramatic angle. There is a small danger of turning off buyers, but usually you get much more response for the same amount of money.

Sinks can be refinished just like tubs, but unless yours is unique, it's usually more economical to replace it. A new sink and vanity runs $200–400.

COUNTER AND CABINET SURFACES

If your bath is large enough, or if you are providing a separate dressing area, or if you just want a change from a traditional marble vanity, there are several other surface materials to choose from for your countertops.

Corian

This is the Rolls Royce of surfaces. Clean and white, it can be accented with wood or laminate inserts. The material is easy to clean and people perceive value when they see it. It is also very expensive: $80–100 per linear foot installed.

Marble

Most vanity surfaces are of cultured marble. You can also install marble tiles or sheets. These range in the $60–150-per-foot range installed, although the marble itself can be bought for only $8–20 if you would like to try it yourself. Most dealers will rent you a tile saw.

Plastic Laminate

Also called Formica after the brand name, it can be bought for as little as $5 per linear foot although it normally costs about $40 per foot installed. Available in an unlimited rainbow of colors, it can help tie in different elements of a bathroom. Versatile, it can be cut into practically any shape.

Tile

This is a great countertop material. By using a tile compatible with the tile in the rest of the bathroom, one can tie the bathroom together into a nice unit. However, counters, because of the small surface and angles, are relatively expensive and can cost up to three or more times the square foot cost of floor and wall tile installations ($35–60 per foot).

FLOORS

Examine the floor of your existing bathroom to see if it needs replacing. If it does, consider one of the following solutions.

Tile

Ceramic tile is the preferred material of today's buyer. Tiles come in all sizes, styles, and prices. One way to keep the cost down when installing tile is to put a pattern into the tile layout. This costs no more than laying all the same color and makes a large difference in overall effect. Patterns can range from something as simple as putting in an accent color tile every so often to as complex as creating an overall picture. Be careful not to get too personal in taste. Tile floors cost $10–20 per square foot, installed.

Linoleum

Vinyl flooring (usually called linoleum although it's technically not) is not considered a "class material" but a good, light, new linoleum floor can do wonders for the look of a bathroom at a price far lower than tile. This costs $10–25 per square yard plus $20 per square yard for installation.

Marble

If you are in an upper-end market, there is nothing like marble to make a bath look impressive. But its cost is similar to its expensive look. One place it might work in a more moderate household is in the half bath, as the square footage, and thus the cost, is quite small ($4–6 per square foot).

Wood

This is also popular and today is functional, too. The old taboo against mixing water and wood no longer applies with special woods and finishes. It works best to mix in wood with some tile accents, especially bordering the tub and shower. It makes quite an elegant combination.

WALLS

Sometimes all that is needed is a new coat of paint to add life to a tired bathroom. Paint probably gives you the best return for your investment. A couple of gallons and a little time can literally transform your bath. Stay with a white or light pastel. Unless you are a talented interior designer, you might want to stay relatively conservative. Most people are conservative in their tastes, so gear it toward the buyer, not the latest from *Progressive Architecture*. Also, colors go in and out of fashion like anything else, so be aware of what people are buying.

Paint in a bathroom needs to be resistant to moisture and mildew. Use a washable semi-gloss paint. Smooth surfaces work well in the bath, as they are easily cleanable. Leave the texturing for the other rooms.

Another relatively inexpensive item that can really improve a bath is wallpaper. If your walls are just bland sheetrock or plaster with a coat of paint, try adding a horizontal chair molding around the perimeter and then wallpapering above it. This works very well in smaller baths. Another option is to have an accent wall of wallpaper. Or, of course, you could do the whole room. When installing your wallpaper pattern, use an extra-strength adhesive that can resist the moisture present in a bathroom.

Bathrooms are one of the few rooms where wallpaper almost always works well. There are many good patterns available. It is recommended you find one you like in a home magazine or a friend's home and then order the same one. Many times the beautiful 4-inch swatch in the home decorating store turns into the 400-square-foot nightmare on your walls.

There are many other wall coverings such as natural wood or mirrors. As mentioned earlier, mirrors are a must in the bath in terms of adding light and increasing the sense of space.

Tile makes for a wonderful wall covering, but tiling whole walls can get expensive. One way to add excitement and to keep the cost down is to tile up to a chair rail height (about four feet) and then have a plain painted wall above. This gives the room a traditional feel that is appealing.

Tiling a pattern into the wall or floor adds an extra dimension that says "custom" even though it costs no more and is no harder to do than a single color of tile. You can create some wonderful designs with just two contrasting tile colors.

Wood can also be used for a bath wainscot. Polyurethaned heavily, it can warm a room with its natural patina, or the wood can be painted. This will add an old fashioned yet upscale feel to the home and appeal to buyers in markets with older homes.

Today, people like big bathrooms. That is not always physically possible. One of the easiest ways to give this illusion is with mirrors. Put a large mirror over the vanity. Or better yet, cover a whole wall. People love it. You can mirror a 6′ × 6′ section of wall for around $300 including installation.

If you have a big enough bath, a way to make the space more functional is to build a low wall near the toilet. This can act as planter shelf and hold books or magazines while shielding the toilet.

When deciding on wall materials, there are a few materials to avoid. Fiberglass tub enclosures may work for a year or two but they definitely lower the perceived value of the bathroom when contrasted to tile. From a maintenance point of view, they are also inferior. Usually the glue disintegrates within five years and allows moisture to penetrate the sheetrock, softening the wall and eventually leading to wood decay.

There is also another synthetic product on the market. It is a decorative hardboard coated with a waterproof surface. This material is available with a smooth finish or as a simulated tile finish. Either way the item is perceived as lower quality and may adversely affect the total perception of your home. This product works better in a rental setup or in low-end homes where economy is more of an issue.

ACCESSORIES

Check the towel bars. If they look cheap, replace them with some new ones. Brass or wood are best, depending on the motif. Just use what is appropriate. A lot of the elegant look in baths is just a set of plush towels hanging off some nice towel bars.

An easy way to create interest in a bath is to create a focal point, such as a pedestal sink or a clawfoot tub and work around that. Even something as small as hand-painted tiles interspersed among the others can add interest.

Putting a phone in the bathroom is another interesting idea. Place it near the vanity or toilet. It adds a sense of importance and luxury. People like that, it will impress their friends.

Another little touch is to replace the electrical outlets with GFCI outlets. These are special plugs with a circuit breaker built in. They can easily mark the difference between life and death if someone should touch electricity to water. Many buyers are becoming aware of safety items in the home. Having GFCI outlets shows care, concern, and quality, a feeling you hope people will carry with them as they wander throughout the rest of the house.

A little trick that buyers like is having your outlets or lights come through the middle of a mirrored wall. This costs little more ($25 per electrical opening) yet gives a nice effect that magnifies your light substantially.

If you have a small bathroom and there's nothing you can do about it, follow the old adage of making up in excitement what you lack in size. Unusual materials such as glass block will make the bathroom memorable.

A lot of the effect of a bathroom may not even be the major built elements of the room but the little touches—a vase with flowers, a prominent medicine chest, a wicker wastebasket or hamper, or some plush towels nicely displayed. People talk mostly about construction, but it's the little amenities that can really add life to a place both during use and at sales time.

PLUMBING

This is the single most expensive item in the bath and its layout should be carefully considered. You might want the suggestions of a plumber, contractor, or architect. Bathroom plumbing can run from about $500 to $1200, not counting fixtures. These costs can be more depending on layout and on accessibility to existing lines.

Many older homes have galvanized plumbing. Many of these pipes have had deposits settle in them over the years and have severely reduced water pressure. If this is the case in your home, you may have to replace them. Note that this is a cost. You will not get your money back for doing the work. However, you may have your sales price reduced out of all proportion to the cost of replacing pipe by some anxious first-time buyers. If you are looking at homes to renovate, calculate this cost in your purchase agreement.

ELECTRICAL

Make sure the electrical is up to code and the outlets are grounded. Mixing water and electricity is a deadly combination. Install GFCI outlets in the bath. These only cost about $14 each but will return their investment both in safety and in the perception a prospective buyer gets as to the quality of the house. (This is analogous to placing a fire extinguisher in the kitchen.)

Otherwise, as long as it's adequate and grounded, electrical follows the rule of out of sight, out of mind and should be left alone.

If you are redoing some wiring, consider putting outlets or a power strip near the vanity mirror for shavers, hairdryers, etc. This can be a selling point although it probably will not be missed if not there.

STRUCTURAL CONSIDERATIONS AND LAYOUT

If your structural inspection showed any flaws or damage, this is the time to fix them. It's quite common for old baths to have fungal or pest-related decay. Just make sure you remove all damaged wood before proceeding.

If you are thinking of expanding your bath or adding another, make sure you will not be upsetting bearing walls and that the structure can handle it. This includes the foundation.

Make sure the framing can handle any increased loads. Water weighs a lot. This is especially crucial if you are adding a bath in the attic. Some attics are not even designed to be walked in, let alone to support a full tub.

Remember, people's wants and needs have changed since that old home was built, and rooms may be too small or lack of insulation may make a room too drafty. Make sure the bathroom has good remodeling potential or you might find yourself sinking financially along with your house's foundation.

If you have a large bathroom, make part of it an exercise area.

If you have a very small bathroom and it feels too tight, replacing the bathtub with a shower will add lots of space that can be used for other buyer needs. Do this only if there is another bathtub in the house.

FLOOR PLANS

If the neighborhood warrants it, extra bathrooms can add considerable value to your home. You may be able to steal the space from an extra room or unused closet.

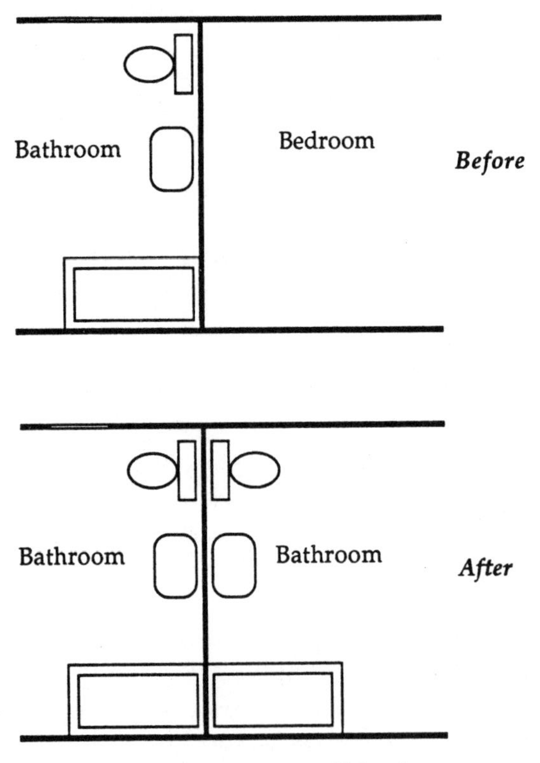

Figure 10-1 *Converting a small bedroom to a bathroom*

Many times, the space under the stairs is used to make a bath. Sure, it may not be the grandest, but its return might be several times the investment.

Adding a bathroom will always pay for itself if you are bringing the number of baths up from a deficiency to the norm for the neighborhood. If you don't have a master bathroom, this is the place to add it. Otherwise look for a place where the bath can be installed inexpensively. A standard rule of thumb is to provide one bathroom for every two bedrooms.

Because of the high cost of plumbing, the most economical way to add a bath is to locate it near existing plumbing, whether that be in another bathroom, the kitchen, or a laundry room.

Inspect your home for potential locations. When you think you have found some, draw a floor plan to scale on graph paper noting bearing walls and plumbing. Extend the drawing to include all rooms touching the one you plan to work on. Bathrooms usually have one plumbing wall, sometimes two. These walls are the ones the fixtures back up to. If you can tie into this your costs will stay relatively low.

Perhaps you can convert a small bedroom next to the existing bathroom into a second bath and some walk-in closet space, as shown in Figure 10-1. Then, you can rebuild the bedroom as part of an addition. This will save greatly on plumbing costs.

Another way to share common plumbing is to build above an existing bath, once again tying into the existing plumbing or, as noted earlier, work off the kitchen or a laundry room. Anywhere some pipes exist is a step cheaper in the cost of renovation.

You might be able to make a bathroom do double duty. Instead of just adding a bathroom, add one and a half as shown in Figure 10-2.

Notice how this allows for two separate bathrooms with only the tub being shared. Since the tub is not used as much as the other areas, there's rarely a conflict. The doors between areas can easily be locked.

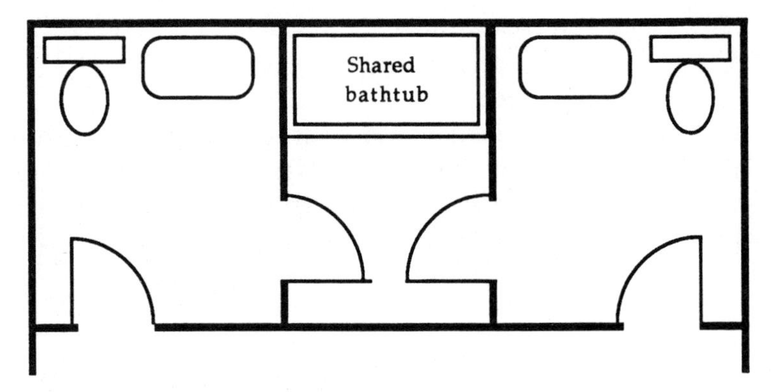

Figure 10-2 *Adding a bath and a half*

Perhaps you were planning on expanding into the attic. Consider the vertical alignment of the baths in your plan. Before proceeding, remember it's not just the number of baths but their location, beauty, and functionality. If you have to walk through the garage to get to your new bathroom, you are not going to get the kind of return you would get in building a bath off the master bedroom, even if it was cheaper to construct the first one.

If the problem is your bath is just too small, try to move only one fixture when you expand. This will keep the cost down. While you are at it, see if you can steal some closet space from an existing room to build a dressing area.

Check the traffic pattern. Sometimes you can change the entrance into the bath to give it a better feel.

You can add elegance to the bath through elevation. Building an arch over the bathtub or a vertical row of glass block in a partition wall gives your bath that extra custom look.

When planning bathrooms, keep in mind how they will be used. Many buyers like a separate area for a vanity just outside the main bathroom so that one person can use the vanity while another bathes.

Do you have an unusually large bath that can be made into two? Perhaps you were thinking of adding a laundry room. If you are, add a bathroom, too.

Sometimes there is a large bedroom or space that can be divided to create a bath, as shown in Figure 10-3. This is still cheaper than actually building an addition with a bath in it, although even that expensive extreme can return 100–200 percent of your investment immediately.

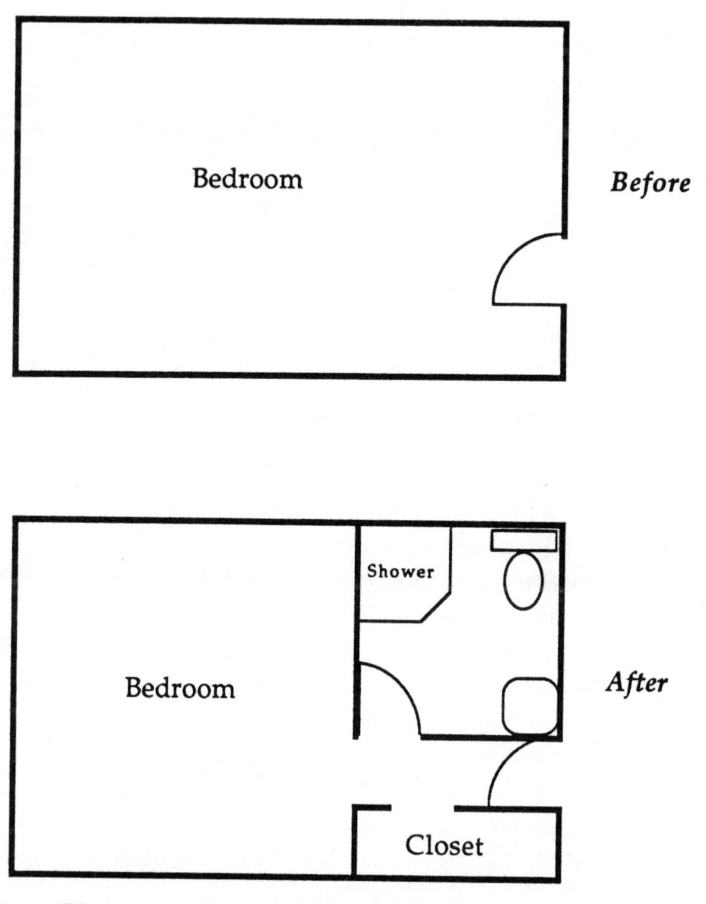

Figure 10-3 *Dividing a bedroom to create a bathroom*

In constructing these new baths, you might make them appear larger, lighter, and more luxurious by using the suggestions in this chapter. Also consider using some traditional architectural tricks such as level changes, glass block walls, half walls, and columns to separate spaces without making them feel confined.

Some other ways to dress up a bath might be to build a laundry area off of it behind some accordion doors or to build a dressing area off of it. Since this is not a fancy area, it's relatively inexpensive to build.

STORAGE

Storage space in a bathroom is highly valued by potential buyers. Of the top five items desired in a bathroom, two were general and/or vanity storage and a linen closet. This should be a clear signal of the importance of bathroom storage to buyers. (The other three items were: tile, two sinks instead of one, and a separate shower enclosure.)

Storage space is a must. A hall linen closet is okay, but cabinets and/or open shelves in the bathroom are desired. You can even have these match the kitchen cabinets for consistency as an added touch. Just be sure they also fit in with the bath motif. A luxurious touch is to make a dressing area off the bath. Steal the space from an adjoining closet or bedroom.

You can get extra storage from medicine cabinets. Or build shelves over the toilet. The bathroom is full of incidentals, from razors and toothbrushes to cleansers and medical products. Room must be found for all of these, and accessible room for those that are used often.

If you're putting in a new tub or shower, incorporate shelf space into the design. Rather than having the wall come right up to the edge of the tub, build a tile shelf one or two tiles wide or provide a tiled seat near the tub. This serves as a place to store shampoo, conditioner, and other items, or a nice place to put plants.

One final note. Bathrooms, like kitchens, can add extreme value to your home if done right. This may be the place to pay for an hour or two of an architect's or designer's time. The cost will more than come back to you in terms of lower construction costs and added design value.

Hiring Contractors

The question always arises as to what the homeowner can do herself. That mostly depends on your level of skill, your desire to do the work, and on what you can afford. But do not forget the big picture. The money you save on tradesmen, you may lose in terms of mortgage payments and aggravation. Note that, especially for work that shows, professionals have built up years of skill to make the work look better. You have probably not had that opportunity. Just make sure your contractor believes in the value of good workmanship. Your profit is directly proportional to the perceived quality of the job.

If you feel you have the skill or can tackle the job, then by all means do it. You will put much more care into your work than even the best contractor. You have much more at stake. Remember, though, even a project built with love and the best intentions can look bad if the skill is not there.

Aside from the kitchen, the bathroom is the most complicated room in the house due to the plumbing connections. It's also one of the most costly. If you're good at plumbing, you can save a lot of money here. If you're not, this is the place to hire someone who knows what he's doing.

Electrical in the bath is a relatively easy task if all you are doing is adding a few outlets or a new light. Even easier is just replacing fixtures and outlets. Most tasks are covered in do-it-yourself books such as the Sunset series. Just use caution, as electricity can kill you.

Plumbing in the bath is a major job and expense. Here, you should definitely use a professional. He can run DWV pipe or supply lines faster than you can, and the speed will more than make up for the cost. Most people have never been thrilled spending day after day crawling around under the house getting grimy installing plumbing, only to turn the water on and find a leak that must be patched. It does not do wonders for my mental health.

Changing bath fixtures is another matter. This is easily done by the homeowner or handyman and can save you $75 or more per fixture.

You should note that there is a high markup on bath fixtures and accessories. Perhaps you can get a plumber to use his discount—a savings of 25 percent or more on the cost of fixtures—even if he is only doing the rough plumbing. You might even give him something for his trouble.

Tile work can look wonderful or horrible depending on your ability to create an even surface. Although a relatively easy material to work with, if you have never done it before, it might be best to hire someone. Take the time to plan out an interesting pattern or color scheme in the tile. That will make the job look custom even if done to production standards without the highest quality materials.

Vinyl flooring can be tricky to install for the inexperienced. It does not take long to learn, but the first few installations can be rough. It is not recommended that you tackle such an important room on your first attempt. Remember, sloppy workmanship can detract from a house as much or more than all your effort and hard work can add to it.

Framing is relatively easy but, once again, especially if dealing with exterior walls, you may want to hire a professional. Most interior jobs can be done by a homeowner.

Just by acting as general contractor and coordinating the different trades, you might be able to save 10–20 percent on the cost of the project without getting your hands dirty.

The more upscale your market and the more luxurious your bathroom, the more you should hire out to con-

Adding a little curb appeal at low cost can greatly improve the overall image of a home. The top photo shows the house before any renovations. The photo below shows how the same house looks after the screen door was removed, a flower box was added, a large tree was removed, and a coat of fresh paint was applied. (Photos by Dan Lieberman)

Converting an unused attic is an excellent way to add rooms to a home, and to substantially increase its value. Notice the creative lighting possibilities and the addition of a fireplace. (Photos by Robert Malone)

This dramatic renovation demonstrates how a dated look (top) can be transformed into a modern, well-lit showplace (bottom). Notice that the dark beams have been removed, recessed lighting has been added, and there is new molding and fresh paint. (Photos by Jane Lidz)

Upgrading the look of these two rooms required no construction. The top photo shows the rooms before carpeting was removed, floors sanded and refinished, and new paint was applied. Also notice that the old green cabinet in the rear room was stripped down to natural redwood. The total cost of materials for this renovation was under $200. (Photos by Dan Lieberman)

The top photo shows a home before undergoing an inexpensive renovation. The front aluminum windows were replaced with wood, and the home was newly painted (bottom). There is a dramatic difference in perceived value. (Photos by Dan Lieberman)

The photos above and the photo at the top of the facing page show how adding a deck greatly increases outdoor living space and value. Combined with new paint and some remodeling, this deck offers a luxurious space for outdoor entertaining and relaxing. (Photos by Joanne Griese-Shefflin)

This is another view of the deck shown on the facing page. The home's desirability has been substantially improved by this addition.

This ultra-modern kitchen features a gallery along one wall. The spotlights above the artwork add a creative and distinctive look to what otherwise would have been wasted space. This is a kitchen a home buyer will remember. (Photo by Jane Lidz)

Materials, color, and texture can literally transform the feel of a room. The addition of new flooring, new light fixture, paint, artwork, and tasteful furnishings significantly increase the value of this room. (Photos by Joanne Griese-Shefflin)

The San Francisco Victorian home shown at right was average looking before its dramatic renovation (below). The addition of new trim, and paint in a unique color scheme provides an excellent example of what can be done to upgrade a home's appearance, thereby increasing its value. (Photo by Dan Lieberman)

The top photo shows a living room fireplace and wall that were severely damaged by fire. The floors were refinished, the walls painted, and the fireplace was faced with marble. This renovation was inexpensive and totally changed the appearance of this room, as well as greatly increasing the home's value. (Photos by Dan Lieberman)

The cramped half-bath (left) was made into a full bathroom by moving the sink to the opposite wall, and installing a shower where the sink had been. Patterns in the tile add interest to the room, and cost the same as one-color tile. (Photos by Dan Lieberman)

By replacing the dated, dark-paneled wall with a newly-surfaced wall and windows, this living room corner has been transformed into a light-filled, pleasant place to be. (Photos by Dan Lieberman)

tractors. Installing whirlpool tubs, doing marble cutting and setting, and working with other luxury items requires years of skill development to do well. Professionals do this all the time, day in and day out. If you've only done it once or twice, the added time can cost you much in headaches and mortgage payments.

A special note on baths. Because they are such a crucial part of the sales package, quality design is important. People do not want their baths just to be functional; they should have an air of luxury about them. If you do not feel you have the skill for this, hire a specialist such as an architect or bath designer on an hourly basis. The cost will more than come back to you.

Codes and Ordinances

Be aware that every city or town has building and zoning codes and you want to make sure you are not violating them in planning your project. Usually in newer structures this is not a problem, but in older ones it can be. Plumbing has changed a lot in the last fifty years and some items that were installed in the past might not meet today's building codes. Talk to an inspector before you tear out anything, as you may not be allowed to replace it in the same manner.

Sometimes cities have two codes, one for new construction and one that recognizes older properties. This is to allow renovations to be compatible with the existing set up even if they do not meet current code. Check with your local jurisdiction on this point.

Profit and Loss from a Renovation

RENOVATING TO INCREASE THE VALUE OF THE BATHROOM

A home in Oakland, California, was a 1920s Tudor with a tired-looking bathroom—chipped tub, an ugly vanity with lion's head handles from the 1960s, and an old average-looking tiled floor.

There was a little privacy problem, as the bath window looked out upon the neighbor's house. The mirror over the vanity had lost some of its silver and the wall-mounted light fixtures were poor electric imitations of candles.

To renovate this bathroom, the tub was refinished ($250), a new shower curtain installed ($15), and the renovator had a handyman paint the room in an off-white semi-gloss ($100). The renovator also painted the vanity, replaced the knobs with new brass ones ($2 each), replaced the existing outlets with GFCI outlets ($14 each), and replaced the mirror ($45).

A row of Hollywood lights was installed where the candle-like fixtures had been ($42). A new toilet seat was installed ($12) and the vanity top replaced with a new marble one ($59). The renovator replaced the faucet with a brass one ($39 on sale) and finished off by replacing the glass in the window with a beautiful piece of stained glass, thereby solving the privacy issue and also creating a wonderful lighting effect ($60). In addition, the floor was retiled ($400), although this was not really necessary.

The total cost of this renovation was under $1100 because the renovator did most of the work herself. Was it worth the expense? It is hard to break down the sale of a house room by room, but the entire house was renovated for under $20,000 and sold a year later for $50,000 over the original cost at a time when the area was not appreciating much.

INCREASING THE APPARENT SIZE OF A SMALL BATHROOM

Many homes just do not have the room to expand the bath. Yet in order to compete with homes that have larger baths, one must make the bathroom appear as large as possible. Using mirrors, light, and angles, help transform a bath. Figure 10-4 shows a before and after of such a renovation.

Plumbing costs were kept to a minimum by keeping fixtures in the same place. All that was required were slight alterations of supply and drain lines in the case of the vanity and the shower. Mirrors and new lighting helped give the room a more spacious feel, and the angles directed the eye to the longest possible view through the bathroom, making it appear larger than it actually was.

COST OF RENOVATION

New vanity and countertop	$450
New corner shower with doors	$745
New faucets and fittings	$200
Additional plumbing work	$250
Floor tile	$350
Wall tile	$700
Recessed lighting	$300
New window	$290
New mirrors over vanity	$250
New linen cabinet	$300
Miscellaneous	$100
Total cost	$3,935

This may seem like a lot, but if you compare it to the cost of upgrading the bathroom without moving the fixtures or adding the window or creating the fancy angles ($2480), you will find that the unimaginative scheme does not save that much more ($1455) and the creative one will add the needed sex appeal to sell the home.

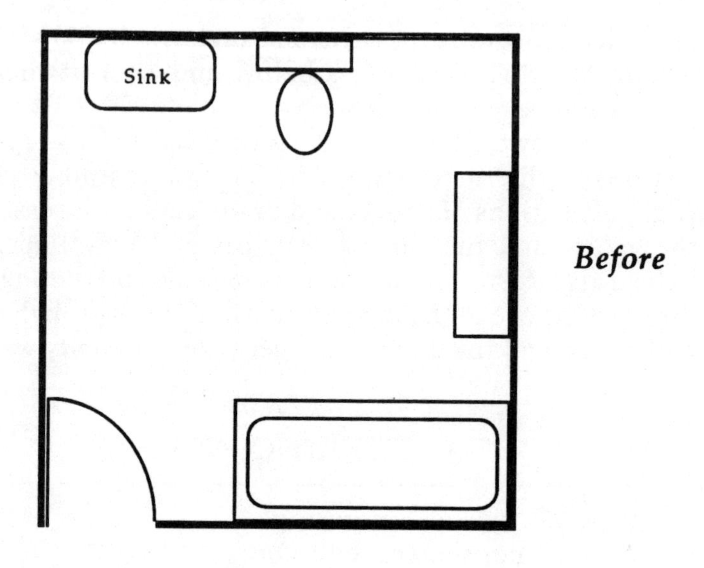

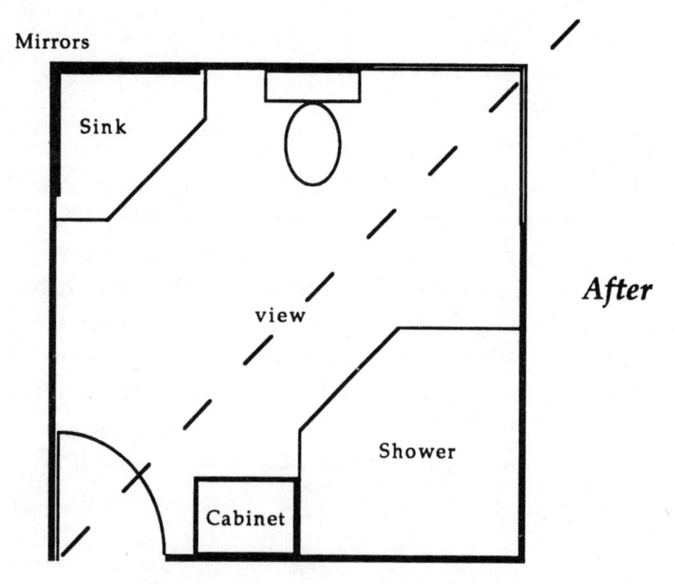

Figure 10-4 *Increasing the apparent size of a small bathroom*

ADDING A NEW BATHROOM BASED ON THE MARKET

In analyzing recent sales in a typical price-stable neighborhood, a seller of a three-bedroom, one-bath house noted that the average sales price for three-bedroom, one-bath houses was $216,512, while the average sales price for three-bedroom, two-bath houses was $283,908, or a difference of approximately $67,400. This is a sure signal that adding a bathroom would be well worth the investment of time and money, even if the return was only half of this spread.

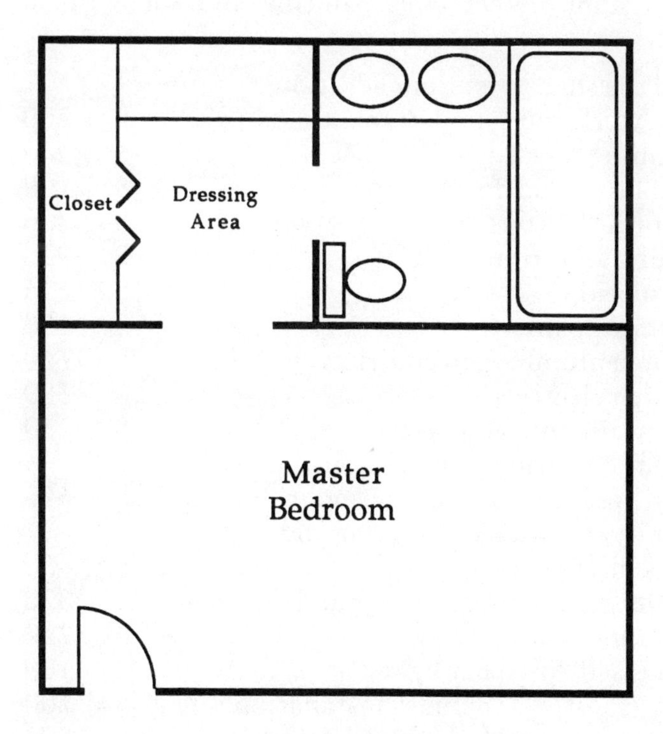

Figure 10-5 *Creating a master bathroom*

Since there is currently only one bath in the house, it would be wise to choose to create a master bath—a private retreat. Try to incorporate a dressing area and some storage into the design to make the room a little more luxurious. Also, the renovator should choose a double vanity, lots of mirrors, and emphasize the lighting.

In this neighborhood, a tub/shower is acceptable, as the neighborhood does not warrant two separate units and the extra cost would not likely come back. In the pricing below, the fixtures are all standard or above-standard grade. It also uses brass faucets and towel bars, which add to the cost but fit into the wants of a buyer in this price range. Figure 10-5 shows the layout of the additional bathroom.

COST AND PROCESS ANALYSIS

(Costs assume owner does painting and some finish work)

1. Build the shell (first floor addition):

Site work and foundation:	$ 1,200
Framing	$ 1,900
Windows and doors	$ 1,100
Roofing/gutters	$ 730
Siding and trim	$ 920
Insulation	$ 625
Exterior paint	$ 150
Rough plumbing to addition	$ 760
Rough electrical	$ 180
Drywall, mud and tape	$ 280

2. Build the interior and do the cosmetics:

Tub (including plumbing and installation)	$ 675
Vanity (including plumbing and installation)	$ 450
Toilet (including plumbing and installation)	$ 320
Mirrors	$ 240
Recessed "high hat lights" (6 @ $30)	$ 180
Tile (shower—includes installation)	$ 700
Tile (floor—includes installation)	$ 800
Cabinets	$ 350

Paint and wallpaper	$ 300
Towel bars, toilet paper holder	$ 60
Faucets and fixtures	$ 250
Other finish, electrical	$ 190
Medicine cabinet	$ 370
Telephone installation ($30 phone)	$ 80
Miscellaneous hardware	$ 50
Miscellaneous labor	$ 200
Total cost:	$13,060

Since the difference in price between the three-bedroom, one-bath and three-bedroom, two-bath house was $67,400, the potential profit is $54,340. It is unlikely the profit would be this great, since there are probably other discrepancies between the houses. Yet, it can be seen that there is room for a huge profit whether you intend to sell the house or just refinance for a new loan.

CHAPTER ELEVEN

Bedrooms

The Master Bedroom

THE MASTER BEDROOM HAS become more than just a place to sleep. It is a place to fulfill one's fantasies. Of all the rooms in the house, the bedroom is perhaps the most personal and private. Our goal is to keep the bedroom warm and inviting but not to offend. We want the buyer to imagine himself comfortably enjoying this bedroom and feeling like he wants this home to be his.

Master bedrooms have given way to master suites complete with retreat areas reminiscent of sitting rooms. These create a private mini–living room within the bedroom. Although you may not have such a setup if your home was constructed some years ago, there are ways you can compete with this new buyer want.

Buying a home is a very emotional experience. The master bedroom is one of the best places to create emotional appeal. Most existing homes have humdrum bedrooms. Your high-appeal master suite will create a strong impression in the buyer's mind.

EVALUATING WHAT YOU HAVE

In a recent study by *Builder* magazine, luxury home buyers across the country were asked "where is room size most important?" and the answer came back "the master bedroom." Similar responses were generated by buyers of townhomes, patio homes, and single-family detached homes.

But buyers want more than just space; they want a place to read, relax, and enjoy some quiet moments. The survey also showed buyers want a sitting area and a room awash with natural light. Skylights were a desired item, as were balconies and patios.

The highest item on the list of features buyers favored was the closet. Walk-in closets were a must. His and hers closets were a close second.

FEATURES

Large master bedrooms are very popular among today's home buyers and are a strong selling feature. So make the room appear larger any way you can, such as by using light paint or mirrors, and avoiding busyness and clutter.

Some of the most appealing features to buyers are those that make their life easier. As more and more families become two-income households, convenience becomes not just a want but a need. For example, buyers like a dressing area with a walk-in closet. Separate showers also score well on buyer surveys. Storage space consistently rates high.

Closets

When you look at an older master bedroom, one of the first things you may notice is the lack of adequate closet space. Closets are now considered very, very important. It is almost required in new homes to have a walk-in master bedroom closet, if not a his and a her walk-in closet.

If your closet space is limited, look at the layout of the bedroom to see if you can possibly steal some space from the room. One idea is to steal about two feet along an entire wall to create a full-length wall-to-wall closet complete with shelves and dividers for all the clothes that would normally go into a dresser.

If you've got enough rooms in your home, you might try converting a room near the master bedroom into a dressing area, complete with closets, mirrors, a makeup table, and various storage areas.

The simplest way to make a room appear to have more closet space is to use better organization. There are many companies currently on the market that sell closet organizers. These may be made from vinyl-coated wire, wood, or one of a number of materials. These organizing systems can literally double or triple the usable closet space in any room. An average six-foot closet can be done for under $100.

A more luxurious closet can have fold-out baskets and drawers. Mirrored closet doors add light and space to the room. Try mirrored closet doors on two walls for extra effect.

Recently, many homebuilders have been installing carousel-style closet storage systems. These are similar to the carousels commonly found in dry cleaning establishments. Although these are not cheap, in an upscale home this is an added touch popular with buyers. The carousel literally adds space to your closet by using areas that in the past would have been unreachable.

Size

There are many ways to enhance the feeling of luxury a master bedroom can provide. Perhaps the simplest way is to make it larger. This can be accomplished by actually enlarging the room (very expensive) or by some less expensive solutions.

If the room needs to be larger, see if you can break through a wall to another room. This extra space will allow you to create a luxurious master suite equaling that found in new construction. However, you lose the other room. If your home has too many bedrooms for the neighborhood anyway, this may be the ideal solution.

Perhaps the new enlarged master bedroom only takes half of the neighboring room. You can convert the other half to a functional use that is lacking in your home, such as another bathroom or a large battery of closets. If your home is unbalanced by today's standards—perhaps you have too many bedrooms but not enough closet space or baths—balancing it will increase its worth even if you lose a bedroom in the process.

If you have the room to do so, creating a separate sitting area within the master bedroom will help enhance its apparent size. By creating more perceived uses, you make the room more appealing to a buyer.

Another way to enlarge the bedroom is to add a deck or balcony. French doors leading out to this deck will bring the outdoors in and the buyers to you.

You can add a skylight to brighten the room. Or you can use the attic space to create a two-story master suite. Create a cathedral ceiling and add a staircase or ladder up to your new second floor. This room can be used as a study, a library, or a retreat.

You can just vault the ceiling by removing the existing ceiling and going to the attic. This will increase the height and apparent size of the room although no actual square footage increase is achieved.

Other ceiling treatments attract attention, too. You can easily create a coffered ceiling—a flat ceiling high in the center but lower along the edges. Or you can create a high ceiling and break up the height with various planter shelves or ledges.

You can add a private bay to the room, decorating it with different lighting to create a sitting area. This is not a large addition yet it will seem large when completed.

You can break up a larger room, creating a dressing area through the use of screening. Perhaps the best screen, which also increases your storage space, is a "bed wall." This is a screen wall perhaps six or seven feet high, which serves as the bed's headboard. It can contain bookshelves, cabinets, or any other storage necessary. On the other side of the wall is clothing storage or a dressing area.

WALLS, FLOORS, AND CEILINGS

Wall-to-wall carpeting is the most common flooring for the master bedroom. It is warmer to the feet than wood and less expensive. Make sure it's clean and free of stains. If it shows signs of excessive wear, it should be replaced. Warm, cozy feelings are what you want to generate in the bedroom.

Wood floors, although not as warm physically, are warm visually and bespeak a higher-quality home. A shag throw rug or other small carpet will add a nice touch to the room while helping to muffle sound transmission.

Wood floors need not be dull. They may be bleached for effect (this works well in modern homes) or perhaps surrounded by an elaborate inlay (these can be purchased in preassembled strips ready for installation). Nor must all floors be one-inch oak. You can have a wide plank floor (country or colonial look) or a floor made of another wood such as maple.

One key to leaving a good impression and getting a better price is making a room appear more than it is . One simple technique that's recently gained popularity is stenciling floors. If you have a cheaper wood floor, such as softwood planks, stenciling a pretty pattern can make it appear full of country charm. Some of the most opulent and exciting floors give their effect merely because of the quality stenciling. Although labor intensive, all you need are two good hands and a creative mind.

Area rugs and furniture can be used to define space and to separate an ordinary bedroom designed for sleeping into one with a bedroom section and a retreat section.

Walls should be painted a light color such as rose or off-white. A contrasting color or white on the molding is desirable. Make sure all cracks are filled and any imperfections in the walls corrected.

Walls need not be painted a solid color. They can be marbled, sponged, dragged, or painted with any number of techniques. Although not noticeable from a conscious viewpoint, a room done up this way tends to leave a more elegant impression. An excellent book on different painting techniques is *Paint Magic* by Jocasta Innes.

Wallpapers and wall fabrics can make a room look expensive and add distinction to an otherwise featureless room. But caution is the word here. Your taste in paper may turn someone else off. Paint is safer. However, some wonderful work has been done with the use of wall coverings.

The ceiling should be checked for cracks, stains, or mildew. If there appears to be a leak, its source should be checked. Otherwise, all cracks should be filled and sanded, all stains should be covered, and a fresh coat of paint applied.

OTHER ELEMENTS

The current trend is to make the master bedroom as luxurious as possible. One of the simplest ways to transform a bedroom into a sumptuous retreat is to add a fireplace. This is not as expensive as it sounds. With the fireboxes now available, no masonry support is needed from below. They can be easily installed and a new mantel built for under $1500, with many being several hundred less.

Install dimmer switches. They help provide texture and elegance to a room. Few rooms should be lit at the same intensity for all occasions. With dimmers, you may set different moods for different times of day.

Creating a room full of natural light rates high on the list of buyer wants for the master bedroom. Skylights are an easy and relatively inexpensive way to create this airy, open feeling.

A bay window with a window seat is a way of both gaining more light and increasing the apparent square footage of the room. It also creates a sitting area, a highly desired item.

Adding a wall containing bookshelves, cabinets, and lighted niches to display artwork will increase the appeal of an otherwise bland room.

Master Baths

The master bath seems to be merging more and more into the master bedroom. Newer homes sometimes don't even put a door between the two rooms. Since the rooms are so intertwined, we feel it is appropriate to make a few comments regarding the bath here.

Ceramic tile for the tub and shower is high on buyers' lists as they look for the luxury the master suite affords. It speaks of quality to them. The only item that scored higher than having a ceramic-tiled shower was having two, or at least one large enough for two and with two shower heads. When the drought came to California years ago, "shower with a friend" bumper stickers appeared all over. It now seems that the builder who hasn't taken this desire into consideration may take a bath in lost profits.

Make sure the bath also has lots of vanity storage, lots of natural light, upgraded fittings, and lots of mirrors. A whirlpool tub is a hot item, as are two sinks.

CONTRACTORS

Most work on the bedroom is simple cosmetic work that the average homeowner can do wonderfully with her own hands. Patching and painting, refinishing wood floors, or installing French doors where there was a sliding glass patio door can be done by the do-it-yourselfer.

If you are getting involved in larger projects, such as vaulting your room through the existing ceiling, you should at least get the advice of a professional. Demolition work is easy for the homeowner—in fact, too easy for some. Beware of wrecking your home. If you do tear up the ceiling, use this opportunity to install a new lighting system or some other feature you might desire.

COMMON MISTAKES

A common theme throughout this book is to avoid the use of tired-looking, cheap-looking, or dull materials.

Although you will always be tempted to save money, using these can do more harm than good. This is especially true in the master bedroom. When planning your budget, give this room priority.

Most construction mistakes involve doing the job wrong the first time and having to come back to fix it. As renovations get more complex, such as adding a bathroom and a deck to a master bedroom, it is easy to cover something too soon or to miss a detail. Doing a job a second time will cost you far more than twice as much. It could cost you an order of magnitude more.

The direction of swinging objects such as doors, windows, and cabinets is critical. Be alert for doors that will end up blocking access to the light switch when they are open, or blocking the circulation from another direction.

Before deciding to tear down a wall, check to see if plumbing runs through it. Check with a metal detector and look in the attic to see if any vent pipes run up through the wall you are planning to remove. These can be moved, but it adds cost to the project.

Other Bedrooms

The number of bedrooms is one of the key determining factors in a home buyer's decision to purchase, as evidenced by the prominent location of this information in real estate listings. The number of bedrooms is usually the item that appears immediately after location. Many buyers will eliminate a home from their list of possibilities based on the number of bedrooms, without ever looking at the property. Along with kitchens and bathrooms, the number, design, and layout of the bedrooms plays a key role in influencing home buyers.

One of the most common uses for converted attics, basements, or garages is additional bedrooms. An extra bedroom can add greatly to the value of your home (but check your local market first). The most desired homes today have three or four bedrooms. Adding a bedroom to a two-bedroom home is almost always a good decision. Adding a sixth bedroom to a five-bedroom home probably is not.

OVERALL IMPRESSION

Bedrooms used to be just for sleeping. Now people want to be able to use them for other purposes, too, such as reading, writing letters, or reflecting on the day. If you can provide for these extra activities, you will help to increase the appeal of your home.

WALLS

Once again, clean, newly painted walls give the best impression. A light neutral color is good in the bedroom, although this is one place where a little color can be added. A pastel rose or light blue can warm up an otherwise cold room.

FLOORS

Carpeting and hardwood floors are the two most popular floorings in the bedroom. If you have wood floors, refinish them with a sanding and at least two coats of polyurethane. Place an area rug on the floor to add warmth to the room and to help deaden foot noise. Noisy rooms are not appealing to buyers.

If you have an existing carpeting, make sure it's clean. Rent a shampooer to get out all the spots and odors. If the carpet is old and worn or very dark, it might be a good time to replace it. If you are selling an unfurnished house, this is especially important.

CEILINGS

Bedroom ceilings are not usually noticed. Just make sure they are in good shape. If there is something unique about the ceiling that you'd like to call attention to, use some of the suggestions in the decorating chapter.

WINDOW COVERINGS

Window coverings play a more important role in the bedroom than in other areas of the house. They add much to the warmth of the room, which is very important for what is the most personal room in the house.

CLOSETS

The more closet space the better. Use some of the suggestions in the section on closets to help here.

Mirrored closet doors are popular. They not only act as doors and reflect light, but make the room appear larger, too. Buyers like larger bedrooms.

Closet space is a key concern in all bedrooms, although not quite as critical as in the master bedroom. The key here, if you can't add closet space, is to make it appear you have more through better organization and getting rid of excess possessions.

Empty out all the clothes except those you are currently wearing. This includes storing out-of-season items and getting rid of those items you haven't worn in months. Donate them to charity.

A clear floor will make a closet seem more spacious. Invest in a shoe organizer.

Install a closet organizing system.

Organize your closet within that system. An organized closet seems roomier and leaves a better impression of the closet space and the room.

Install a light in the closet (battery operated ones are available for $10). Your buyers can get a better view and they will like the added feature.

LIGHTING

What type of lighting can enhance a bedroom's appeal? There are two categories—mood lighting and functional lighting. You can create mood lighting in several ways. Placing dimmer switches on all controls allows you to set the intensity of the lighting for different effects. If you have a room large enough for several uses, a separate control for each area will greatly enhance the possibilities. An interestingly lit room can greatly increase its appeal to buyers, since most of the rooms they see are flatly lit.

Functional lighting also plays a role. People like to be able to read in bed. If you have a built-in system, it might be attractive to some, although it limits where they can place the bed. Make sure you have lights in the closets.

DEPERSONALIZE THE ROOM

Perhaps more than any other room, our bedrooms are an expression of ourselves. This is wonderful. However, when you sell a home, it is crucial that the potential buyers can see themselves living in your home and sleeping in your bedrooms. For example, if you have a teenager who has painted his room purple and has Sex Pistols posters up in addition to a couple of *Playboy* centerfolds, it may be hard for a buyer to envision his four-year-old daughter living there. Remove all items to which buyers may not relate.

If a room is particularly tiny, but you want to pass it off as a bedroom or nursery, decorate it as such. Use brightly colored wallpaper and other cues so buyers won't see it as a tiny space but rather as a nursery.

Another way to make a small room pass as a full bedroom is through careful furnishing. To make the room appear larger, make the bed an interesting focal point and minimize the use of other furniture in the room. A small bed with a bright quilt set against a quiet wallpaper, with a floor plant or night table nearby, may be all you need to make the room appear as a bedroom to buyers. When clutter is eliminated, size is not as much of an issue.

If your target market is families with children, decorating a bedroom as a children's room will help stimulate the feeling of ownership. This might include

King-size storage shelves for children's toys

Lofts

Bright colors

Built-in desks or dressers

Children's posters on the wall

GUEST BEDROOMS

Guest bedrooms tend to be a magnet for all sorts of matter. It is essential that you remove the clutter and design this room to make it inviting to guests while still allowing for other uses. Placing a bed in the room, even if you usually use it as your home office, will help signal to the buyer that this is a bedroom.

Renovation Strategy

There are several ways to upgrade the bedroom. Access to a patio or deck is a big plus.

When adding a bedroom, make it of an adequate size. Minimally-sized bedrooms turn off home buyers. A 10 x 10 or 10 x 12 room is usually adequate for a standard bedroom. Perhaps the best way to determine what size a room should be is to imagine the uses and furnishings of that room and to design enough space for them and for an easy circulation around them.

Add as much closet space as possible when adding a new bedroom to the home. This costs hardly anything per square foot but sells well.

CONTRACTORS

Most of the work that goes into upgrading a bedroom is cosmetic and, therefore, ideal for the homeowner. Patching and painting walls, hanging wallpaper, putting up new curtains, and installing closet organizing systems are all small tasks that can be completed within a day or two.

Refinishing hardwood floors is a dirtier task but still an option for the homeowner. Installing carpeting is best left to professionals. Shop around for a good price on installation.

If you need to build a closet or enlarge the opening and install bi-fold doors, some carpentry skills will be required. This is a very basic job and does not require extensive experience. The average handyman should be able to do quite a good job.

Breaking through the ceiling to increase the volume in the room, and installing skylights, are best left to those with more experience. If you will be removing structural components, the work, or at least an inspection of it, is best left to professionals. A good architect can design an appropriate space while maintaining the structural and stylistic integrity of the building.

Building a deck off the master bedroom is a job the handyman can perform, if it is on the first floor. If your bedroom is on the second story, this is best left to a skilled professional.

Lighting and electrical upgrades can be performed by the handyman provided the local jurisdiction allows it.

EXAMPLES

Transforming a Bland Bedroom at Low Cost

Bedrooms can be easy on the budget to transform. Assuming an average size room, the biggest problem most bedrooms have is the lack of closet space and a poor layout of furnishings. In this example, we deal with both issues.

The first issue is to get the closet organized or to expand it. It was decided that giving up eighteen inches of room was a small price to pay for the dramatic increase in closet space that would be created. In order not to create a monotonous wall of closet, and because the existing inadequate closet went into the eaves, we created a large closet and, in the narrow area, built-in bookcases. A mirrored strip was placed between the closet doors and the shelves to help separate them and to provide interest in the room.

Since we are dealing with a stripped version of a 1920s Dutch colonial home, it was appropriate to restore the room to a period look by running a molding along the wall at ceiling height. This helped soften the transition to the ceiling. Since much of the work in making a bedroom desirable has to do with decorating, we also concentrated on the furniture. The furniture was arranged as shown in Figure 11-1.

Note that the bed was placed on an angle to increase the depth perception, making the room appear larger. Also, a large area rug was placed on the floor to help soften the sound of footsteps. It should also be noted that a separate sitting (retreat) area within the room was created by simply arranging a chair, table, and lamp.

This whole renovation cost under $400 for the homeowner, who did the work herself.

Creating a Dressing Room in a Master Suite

Figure 11-2 shows a low-cost renovation. This was a move to modernize the room and give it more of a master suite appearance with a dressing area.

Moving the sink into the "dressing area" freed the bathroom, which allowed one person to shower or use the toilet while the other used the vanity to shave or brush his teeth.

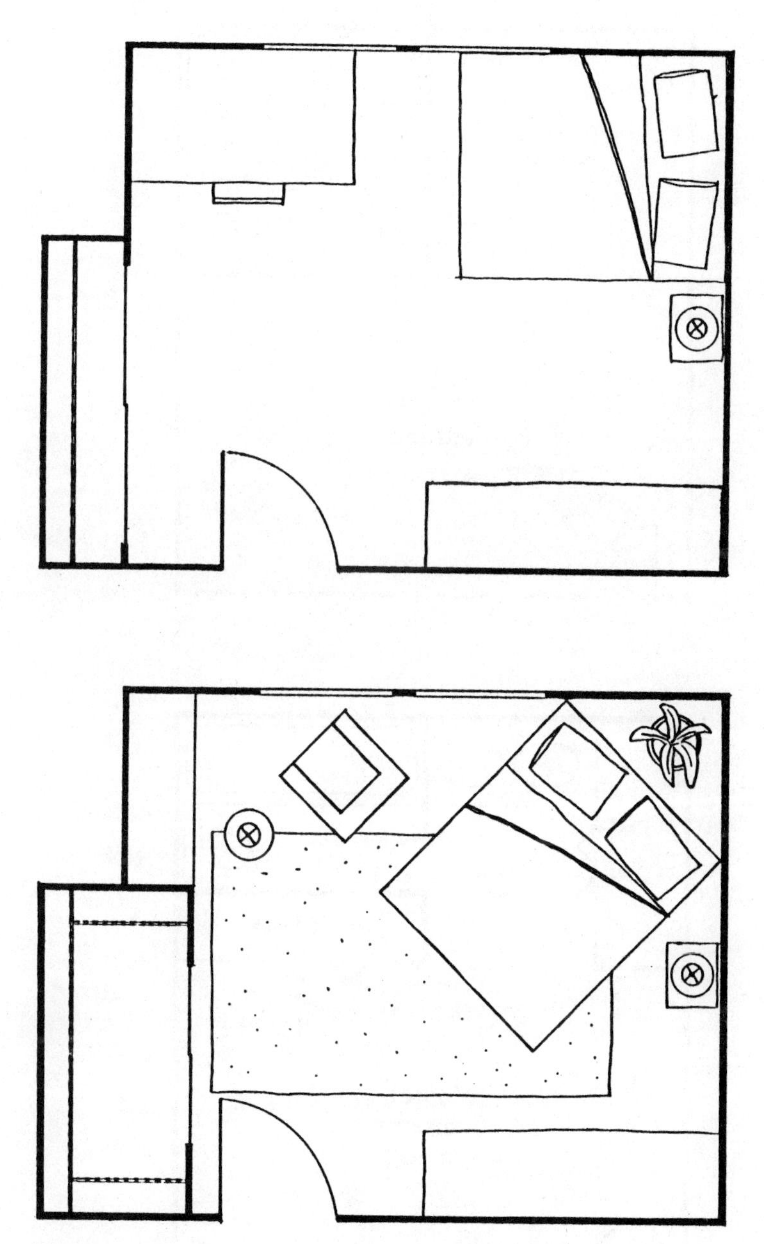

Figure 11-1 *Improving a bedroom with minimal cost*

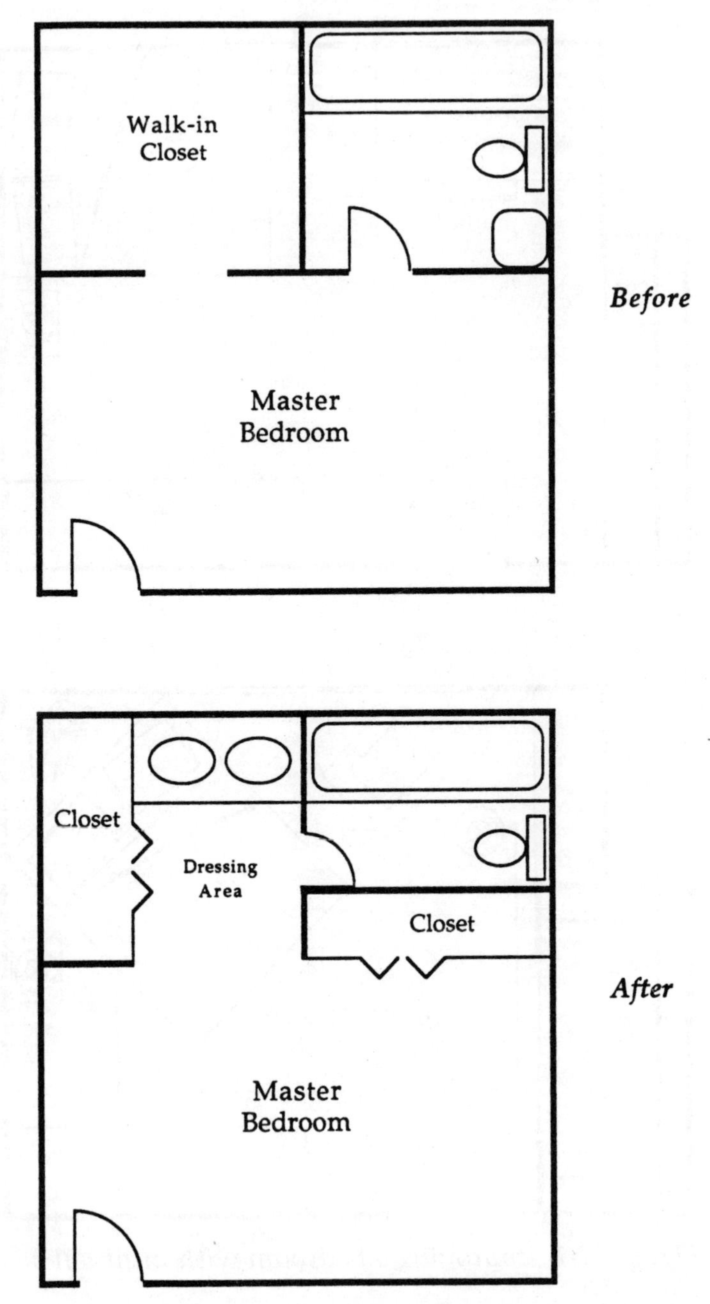

***Figure 11-2** Creating a dressing room in a master suite*

Adding a Bedroom Over the Garage

The idea for this renovation was based on our appraisal of the desired housing in the area.

COSTS

Remove existing roofing, siding; cut opening	$ 1,100
Frame and sheath new floor	$ 500
Frame walls	$ 525
Frame and sheath roof. Construct ceiling	$ 900
Install two windows	$ 900
Install roof	$ 1,000
Install siding	$ 825
Install gutters and downspouts	$ 240
Insulate wall	$ 150
Insulate ceiling	$ 275
Install electrical wiring	$ 160
Install drywall	$ 400
Install carpet	$ 600
Install trim and molding	$ 180
Paint	$ 200
Install door, light fixtures, and miscellaneous	$ 200
Total	$ 8,155
Contingencies (multiply total by .25)	$ 2,039
Expected total cost	$10,194

With our estimate of costs complete, it's time to evaluate the market to see where we stand. Looking through the multiple listing book, we find the average three bedroom two bath home selling for $275,000, while the average four-bedroom, two-bath home is selling for $325,000. At first glance this looks like a good renovation to perform, but we must now check the houses to see if there are any other differences. Many times the four-bedroom homes will be larger all around and of better quality than the three-bedrooms.

Drive around and look at the exteriors of all the homes on the comparables sheet, and also look at every available three- or four-bedroom house on the market in your neighborhood. Eventually you come to the conclusion that it is not just the room that is creating the difference in price, but a combination of many features of the other homes for sale. The idea is abandoned.

You may find that many of your ideas do not work out. The key, when you evaluate your home or any other one, is to brainstorm all possible solutions before you start eliminating some. A day or two of this kind of work can save you many hours or make you many dollars in the long run. If this had worked out, it could have been a good way to make $35,000. You could have literally bought three-bedroom homes at market and converted them to four-bedrooms and still made money. You wouldn't even need to find a bargain (although you should always look for them).

In many neighborhoods across the country, areas that were once full of bungalows are now wealthy enclaves with large homes. Many of the smaller homes need to be upgraded to accommodate the new lifestyle of the area. This is a good opportunity.

CHAPTER TWELVE

Other Rooms

Family Room, Den or Home Office

FAMILY ROOM

THE FAMILY ROOM IS a post–World War II invention and a growing necessity in today's homes. Forty years ago family rooms barely existed. Twenty years ago, you could get by with a basement rumpus room. But today, it has become an important room in its own right. If you have a nice family room and you're competing with neighborhood basement ones, your home should win hands down.

Today the family room is a room for gathering informally to watch TV or for the children to play games. As such, the room reflects an informal character rather than the formality of the living room or dining room.

Decorate the family room to convey an air of informality. Because the room is used for play and takes a lot of abuse, use a carpeting that hides dirt well. Try not to make it too dark, though, because the room should still feel light and airy.

Family rooms usually contain a door directly to the outdoors. This is a desired feature to add if it is practical. Opening the family room out into the yard provides a safe place for children to play inside and out. Another desirable element in the family room is a fireplace. It's nice to gather the family around a cozy fire. It adds to the informality of the room.

People like their family rooms large. So if you are converting a room to a family room, make sure it is of sufficient size.

DEN OR HOME OFFICE

The den can be used for a number of tasks, such as home office, library, or even an occasional guest room. The major distinctions between a den and a family room are size and openness. A den tends to be more closed off and of a smaller size than the family room.

If you have an extra bedroom that is adding little value to your home (you have a six-bedroom home in a three-bedroom neighborhood), one way to add value and make your home special is to convert that extra room into a library or den. People will remember the special room and think of it as an asset rather than just another bedroom in a series of bedrooms.

Home offices are more and more in demand these days, with two working members in the family. People don't want to have to run into the office on the weekends and they like to work out of the home. Creating an attractive secluded space out of your extra room can serve this purpose.

Although nice to have, a den is not a highly desired item on a typical home buyer's list. It is not worth creating an addition to house one.

Usually the den is located on the ground floor of a home. If it is to be used as a home office, especially if one sees clients, having a separate entrance or locating it near a door are very important considerations.

If you intend to use your den as a home office and as a guest room, installing a Murphy bed in the wall will allow you to achieve both purposes and can be a nice selling feature. A convertible sofa also works nicely.

If you don't have the room in the house, you can make a corner of your dining room do double duty as a home office.

REMODELING STRATEGIES

In the family room, walls should be light to help brighten the room. Woodwork is very common in family rooms and usually adds value whether natural or painted. However, if you've got thin paneling with fake wood imprinted on it, it will detract from the quality of the room. See the chapter on renovation tips for how to remove this paneling.

Since size is very important for family rooms, consider opening up the room to increase its actual or apparent size. Many family rooms abut kitchens. By opening up the wall connecting these rooms, you get a space that flows better and seems larger without actually altering the square footage.

The atmosphere in dens can range from old world charm with heavy wood, tall bookcases, and a large oak desk to modern high tech with its whites, personal computers, and bright lights. Whatever the style, keep it consistent.

Built-in shelves are a desired item in the den or home office. A closet is coveted too, for storing larger items. As with the other rooms, remove clutter and organize the shelves and the closet. Displaying an interesting object on the bookshelves can add to the room's appeal.

The den is a good place to display personal collections. It helps to reflect the cultured life-of-leisure style so many people like.

A prefabricated fireplace can be installed for under $1000. This can be made to appear as a masonry fireplace or left in a more contemporary form. A masonry fireplace will cost $2500 to $3000 depending on location in the home and structural support underneath. A typical fireplace is said to add more than $3000, so fireplaces are usually good additions to make.

Basements can be converted to family rooms. This is not as desirable as an above-ground one, but it is much preferable to an unfinished basement. Keep costs to a minimum if doing a basement conversion and use some of the techniques discussed in the basement section to lessen its negative impact.

CONTRACTORS

If you want a den that is full of rich intricate woodwork, unless you are a skilled carpenter, this is best left to a professional. Bear in mind that this is an expensive undertaking.

Most of the work required in a family room or den is cosmetic in nature. Installing wood trim, hanging wallpaper, painting, or changing light fixtures are all easily done, even by a novice.

If you are a handyman and you want to install a patio door where there was none, you should be able to do this without much trouble. Make sure the doorway is raised enough above grade so water will not enter the home even after heavy rains.

New carpet should be installed by a professional installer.

If you are upgrading the electrical system and adding circuits, you may want to go with an electrician to save you the hassle and to prevent lawsuits if the work isn't right.

Tearing down a wall between a study and a family room is easy to do. Check to see if it's a bearing wall first. If so, you might want to consult a contractor. The cost is worth it—if your ceiling appears to be collapsing, few buyers will be interested in your home. Check for any wiring or plumbing that may be in the wall before demolishing it. Cut open the sheetrock first and look.

Garage and Service Rooms

The garage is an everything room. From storage room to tool shed to exercise room to workshop, garages seem to cover every use not defined within the home, even occasionally including storing automobiles.

Although many older homes have no garage or perhaps a single-car detached garage, buyers today want a two-car attached garage. Even in cities, buyers will pay dearly to have a garage. In San Francisco, homes average $30,000 more if they have a garage, and they sell more quickly. If you only have room for one car, an upgrade will help sell your home. It is rare that you will recoup your full investment—75 percent is more usual. If you don't have a garage at all, adding one will usually more than pay for itself.

An electric garage door opener is a feature buyers are willing to pay for.

LAUNDRY ROOM

A separate laundry room is a real asset to a home, even if it's no bigger than a large closet. Many are installed near a kitchen or bath in order to take advantage of existing plumbing. If you have one, it need not be tired-looking. Its appearance can be enhanced in many ways.

Apply a fresh coat of paint.

Install wire shelves and organizers.

Set up a corner as a sewing or ironing room if space permits.

The location of the laundry room is also important. Over two-thirds of home buyers want the laundry facilities in a separate room. The usual locations are off of the kitchen or off of the garage. In some starter homes, the laundry is located in the garage. This works better only in the lower-priced homes.

If you can provide space in your laundry room for sewing and ironing, you will increase the room's appeal significantly. Remember, though, that no one ever bought a home because of the condition of the laundry room. But a negative one will turn off buyers.

The surfaces of the laundry room can be of any material but they should be practical. A vinyl or wood floor works better than a carpet in a utility area. Walls may be painted or wallpapered, but if the room gets steamy, the wallpaper may not be practical. Good ventilation is essential.

RENOVATION STRATEGY

Garages and laundry rooms are less important than other areas of the home. The main concern here is that they should be neat and clean. All can be made more interesting by adding a little unexpected something, such as a nice poster in the laundry room, or sheetrocking and painting a wall in the garage. The surfaces do need to be practical, but a row of bare studs in the garage never turned anyone on.

The garage should look organized, whether it be a workshop, tool shed, or just a place for storage. There are now garage organizing kits on the market. These look like something halfway between a set of kitchen cabinets and a closet organizer system. A neat and clean work area is appealing to buyers.

You can create an organized look even more cheaply by building a series of shelves and cubbyholes out of plywood. The finish is less important than the organization in the look of the garage.

Shelving in the laundry room will help in its usefulness and its appearance. Shelves can be of the wire mesh kind, wood, or any other aesthetically pleasing material. If you don't have room to stand an ironing board all the time, one that folds out from the wall is a feature buyers love.

CONTRACTORS

The laundry room involves plumbing and electrical. If you have a gas dryer, it includes gas lines, too. If you have an electric dryer, 220 voltage is required. In other words, such a small room requires quite a few complex skills. Wiring for 220 voltage should be done only by a licensed electrician. It is dangerous for the inexperienced homeowner. Plumbing can be done by the handyman but is best left to professionals.

Gas lines should be left to a professional handyman. Make sure you test them properly and ensure that there are no gas leaks in the house. Also make sure the dryer is properly vented to the outside.

Most cosmetic work can be done by the homeowner or handyman.

Examples

CREATING THE APPEARANCE OF A HOME OFFICE

With more two-income couples and many people working part-time out of the house, a home office is becoming a highly desired commodity. The problem is many times you don't have the room. Your home just wasn't built when home offices were emphasized and you wisely don't want to give up a bedroom for a home office. (Bedrooms appear on real estate listings, home offices don't.)

There are only two solutions: Make a room do double duty as a home office or create a home office out of any nook or cranny around. An office/bedroom is an easy combination to make. Offices have been made out of hall closets, nooks and crannies in halls, landings of stairs, space under the stairs, the corner of a large room, etc.

ADDING A TWO-CAR ATTACHED GARAGE

Many older homes (built from about 1910 to 1940) were built without an attached garage. Since a garage is a highly desired item in much of the country, the possibility of adding one should be considered as a way to increase the value of the home. In areas where parking is tight, this can be even more valuable.

Because it doesn't require any interior finishing materials, garage construction is very cheap on a per square foot basis. All materials that go into building a garage are usually available locally and at competitive prices. People with fancy automobiles or that want a workshop will bid for your home over the many without garages once you've completed this relatively inexpensive addition.

A workable garage must be sighted on the lot in such a way that cars can get to it easily. Hopefully there are no mature trees or other desirable landscaping features that will be paved over. When you build the garage, care must be taken at the point where the garage roof attaches to the house, as this is a potential point of water damage. Make sure the garage blends in harmoniously with the house and the surroundings.

COST

Site clearance:	$ 200
Grading, form work, and pouring of concrete slab	$ 975
Wall and roof framing	$ 1,010
Sheathing	$ 1,095
Roofing	$ 680
Fascia and soffits	$ 350
Gutters and downspouts	$ 175
Garage door	$ 700
Windows and fire door	$ 1,080
Exterior siding	$ 1,400
Painting and miscellaneous	$ 400
Total cost	$ 8,065
Contingencies (25%)	$ 2,016
Maximum cost	$10,081

Don't forget the cost of the driveway, which should run you about $2–3 per square foot depending on where your home is located in the country.

If houses with garages in your neighborhood sell for about $20,000 to $30,000 more than those without, this is an example of a worthwhile way to increase the value of your home. If the lot already has an existing detached garage, it could be torn down, or it could become a tool shed, workshop, or perhaps even a rental apartment.

COMBINING TWO SMALL ROOMS INTO A FAMILY ROOM

There was a time not too long ago when the family room was relegated to a remodeled basement. That will no longer do. Family rooms are now important to buyers and are expected to be large rooms capable of holding a large group of people. Family members are expected to congregate to watch television, talk, or hang out. With the exception of newer homes, many residences do not contain an appropriate room.

In this example, we have a home that has an inadequate family room and a den. The family room is little more than a large bedroom. By opening up the wall between these two rooms, we create a more flexible space—still allowing for a study, but also giving more potential opportunities to the family room.

In order to give the room the feel buyers want, we need to make it comfortable. Wall-to-wall carpeting helps soften the room, as does a warm-toned neutral color paint. The room is furnished casually so a buyer can imagine taking his shoes off and relaxing. In order to sell the room fully we installed a fireplace (prefabricated—cost $1000). The prefabricated fireplace was hidden behind a custom mantle and looks like a site-built masonry fireplace costing $4000 or more.

An inexpensive way to increase the appeal of the room is to install atrium doors with large expanses of glass, allowing an unobstructed view and access to the backyard and garden. Adding a patio in the rear visually expands the usable living space and creates the type of family room buyers want.

CHAPTER THIRTEEN

Outdoor Spaces

Decks and Porches

DECKS HAVE REALLY CAUGHT on nationwide. More people are entertaining at home than ever and leisure-oriented rooms are becoming increasingly important. The deck is an extension of both the house and the yard. It is a place for both formal and informal entertaining and relaxation.

A deck is one of the easiest and most economical additions you can make to your home. It's like adding an extra room for a fraction of the cost. It also can improve the yard by making usable space out of an area that may have been too steep or small.

A deck does not have to be the simple rows of planks of days past. Increasingly, people are adding fancy touches such as turned rails, built-in planters, and interesting angles to make the deck a real showpiece. A deck like this can upgrade a simple home far beyond its cost to you.

Deck construction is simple compared to other rooms of the house and, if you have the time, can be performed by the typical homeowner. Anyone with a degree of carpentry skill can turn out a beautiful deck that will significantly add to the perceived value of a home.

SITE PLANNING

If you're building a deck where one doesn't exist, or significantly enlarging one, some of the items to consider are

Are there trees that frame or block any views?

Can the deck be used to increase privacy or capture views that the house alone cannot?

Can the deck be used as an extension of the rooms it touches?

Can the deck (or porch) be used to increase the curb appeal of the home?

Do you have a small yard that a deck can make better use of? Remember outdoor space appears larger if more uses are perceived. A small plot of grass will seem smaller than a two-tiered deck covering the same area.

Decks can include privacy screens, trellises, and other architectural devices to upgrade their appearance. Depending on the house, they can be left natural or painted to blend in with the main structure.

If you have an existing deck but want to upgrade its appearance, the following are some key elements to consider.

RAILS

You can change the rails from simple horizontal runs to a variety of shapes, such as vertical posts or 45-degree angle runs. Or you can attach lattice work to some rails and create a screen. Planter boxes or benches can also be used as rails.

FLOORING

The pattern need not be a single run of planks parallel to the house. Herringbone and other patterns are not much more costly to design, but can add character to a basic rectangularly-shaped deck.

FINISHES

Decks can be finished in a number of unusual and striking ways. You can bleach the floors, stain them, paint them, or apply a clear varnish or polyurethane. These can blend in with the home to expand the perceived size of the main structure.

OTHER

A trellis can add character to a deck, as can a little gazebo area in a corner. A place for a barbecue can also be constructed. Level changes can make a deck seem larger or can gently glide the user down to the rear yard. If the entry to your deck is from a basement room, a tiered deck can help ease the transition up to grade.

Decks are a greatly desired outdoor amenity, second only to mature trees. Buyers are especially enthusiastic about homes with decks if the deck is easily accessible from the kitchen or family room. If your home is located in a temperate area where people will spend much time outdoors, the deck is a great asset. If you are in an area where the deck is unusable most of the time, do not build one.

Decks are a good investment. According to most surveys, they return between 70 and 100+ percent of their cost. These are decks designed for the average homeowner's lifestyle wants. Include such items as hot tubs and wet bars in an upscale neighborhood and such a market-oriented deck will return much more than cost as it upgrades the yard and the rooms to which it's connected.

Also, since decks are relatively easy to build, a deck that might return 80 percent of your investment if you paid a carpenter will return you 200 percent to 300 percent if you do the work yourself.

Patios

Many of the concepts of good deck design go into patios, but because of the inherent differences in materials, there are some variations. In general, people prefer wooden decks to patios.

Remember, living areas need not be confined to the house, especially in mild climates. If your living room looks out onto the yard but doesn't connect, the construction of a patio can add pleasure to your life and enhance the overall resale value of your home.

Brick bordered by concrete makes a desirable flooring, as does flagstone. Building a trellis or other cover provides a sense of closure and transition from the inside to the outside. The problem with many patios is that they don't act as transitions and extensions from the indoors to the outdoors. The well-designed patio seems to expand the square footage of the house because it becomes essentially another room even though it's only a floor and some hints of wall and ceiling.

You can build a very nice patio for between $1000 and $2000 in material and labor. If you want to do the work yourself, the cost can be as low as $200–300 for a quality product.

Gates, Fences, and Screening Devices

Gates and fences can do more than designate property lines; they can screen ugly views and create a sense of privacy. They can also upgrade the image of a yard or home. Very inexpensive to build, a new fence can make a home seem more dignified, expensive, or private—all values your buyer will be seeking.

You can wall in an area around the home to make your patio more private and secluded.

Lattice works as an excellent screen, allowing light to penetrate, yet obscuring some of the view. It can be cut into arches or any other custom shape. Lattice installation is a one-day do-it-yourself job that the handyman can easily tackle.

Lattice can also be used as a siding for trellises, creating an oasis of dappled shade in the midday sun. Most lattice is made of redwood and comes in preassembled 4 x 8 foot panels. It costs $10–30 per section. PVC lattice costs a little more ($37) but does not need painting.

Trellises make excellent transitional screens and add a sense of quality to the home for little cost. They can help undo the boxiness of many newer tract homes.

Swimming Pools and Hot Tubs

In some areas and markets a hot tub or swimming pool might make sense. Usually these are upscale areas. But it is the rare case where you would install them as a way to increase the value of your home. One hot tub I saw was built on the roof of a Boston home and had a wonderful view of the city. This was one of the best features of the house and obviously added value. But that is an exception. Many buyers will actually devalue a home with these supposed amenities, viewing them as either another maintenance problem or, in the case of a swimming pool, a potential hazard to little children.

If your home has one of these amenities, it is up to you to present it in the best light possible. A hot tub built on a deck can be given privacy with a trellis or a lattice fence of redwood. Similarly, the chain link fence around the swimming pool can be removed and a nice fence of wood lattice erected. Obviously, you will only appeal to the segment of the market that wants to pay for these items, but at least you can get a premium for them.

In warm areas the addition of a pool will only return about half of its investment cost. In colder areas, it returns even less and is usually viewed as a liability. If you plan to stay in the home awhile it might be worth it, but otherwise stay away from this improvement.

Outdoor Rooms

Sometimes, especially in older urban areas, houses are built close to the property line and a cavernous dark area is formed between buildings. Usually this area consists of dirt, dead plants, or a sheet of concrete. This unattractive area can be turned into a small courtyard that will actually add value to the property.

Courts can be paved of brick, made of wood, or of any other warm material. You want to counteract the cold harsh effect of the space. Dramatic lighting can transform the area more, converting a dark alley to a welcoming entry to the rear yard or side door to the home. If the area is wide enough, it can become a comfortable sitting area off of the kitchen or dining room. The key to creating these courts is to provide seclusion and a useful space, even if it will only be used at night. View this area as a potential asset and see what you can do with your imagination.

Landscaping

If your backyard is nothing more than a place for the kids to play football and a home to the barbecue, it's time to transform it into an asset. Imagine creating an environment with lush plantings affording a pleasing view from within the home and an open-air place to enjoy. You can make a small yard appear larger through the careful use of paths, walls, retaining walls, raised beds, and lawn.

Another technique to increasing the quality of the garden is through the use of texture. Having many different varieties of plants invites the eye to linger as it goes from plant to plant. You can use landscape as architecture and theater, creating focal points, hidden views, and varying enclosures.

Landscaping can cost a lot, so it should be used only where it covers up a true sin or in an area of upscale homes where it's required. Remember, buyers have trouble imagining possibilities. You may have to show them.

Careful landscaping can give the house the dignity and privacy of a home on a much larger lot. Move-up buyers want an upgraded landscape treatment that adds value to the house and makes it feel more established and important.

General Tips

Make indoor and outdoor spaces flow together and they will both be perceived as bigger and more desirable. French doors can open the house to the backyard, while patio pavers can come right inside the house, where they can be used as flooring.

To make the backyard seem bigger, break it up into a series of small spaces, each slightly different. Creating screening effects with plants or construction will allow the mind to separate the spaces into different uses while allowing the eye to flow, connecting the spaces into a large single yard.

Just as you tied the home together with paint to make it flow better, you can make your yard appear more grand by tying in the front and back yards. This is done through consistent use of materials for at least part of the surfaces, such as walks or fences.

Contractors

Most decks are basic structures and the ideal project for the beginner wishing to learn more about construction. Some basic carpentry skills are required. It is recommended that the homeowner work alongside someone with experience.

If you are designing fancier decks with curved surfaces, gazebos, and all the other bells and whistles that turn buyers on, you should probably hire a carpenter or deck building contractor. Hiring a general contractor will probably just add unnecessary cost to the work.

If building a deck high above ground level, such as the projecting decks on hillside houses, use a professional. Safety is a key issue and it's not worth risking your life to save a few dollars.

Fences and walls are also items requiring little skill. A homeowner or handyman can build a nice fence over the course of a few weekends.

Obviously, swimming pools and hot tubs, should you decide to install them, are for professionals only. However, the homeowner can easily do the decking, patio work, fencing, or landscaping surrounding these items. Time is the key factor, more than skill or building experience.

Examples

ADDING A DECK TO THE HOME

This project involves building a ground-level deck with trellis and built-in benches. In addition to adding valuable outdoor living space, this deck ended up expanding the perceived size of the living room, and the sliding glass door connection helped to fill the living room with light.

COSTS

Post-hole excavation and concrete	$ 175
Decking (including posts, headers, etc.)	$ 825
Stairs	$ 50
Rails and benches	$ 400
Trellis	$ 350
Sliding glass door	$ 750
Miscellaneous	$ 200
Total	$2,750

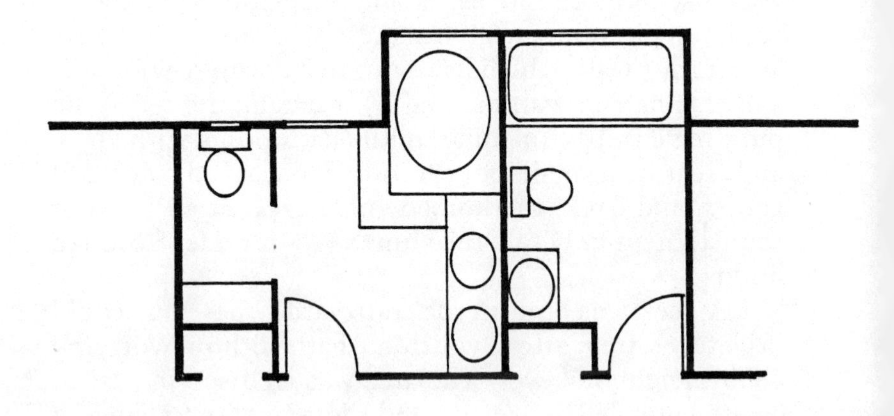

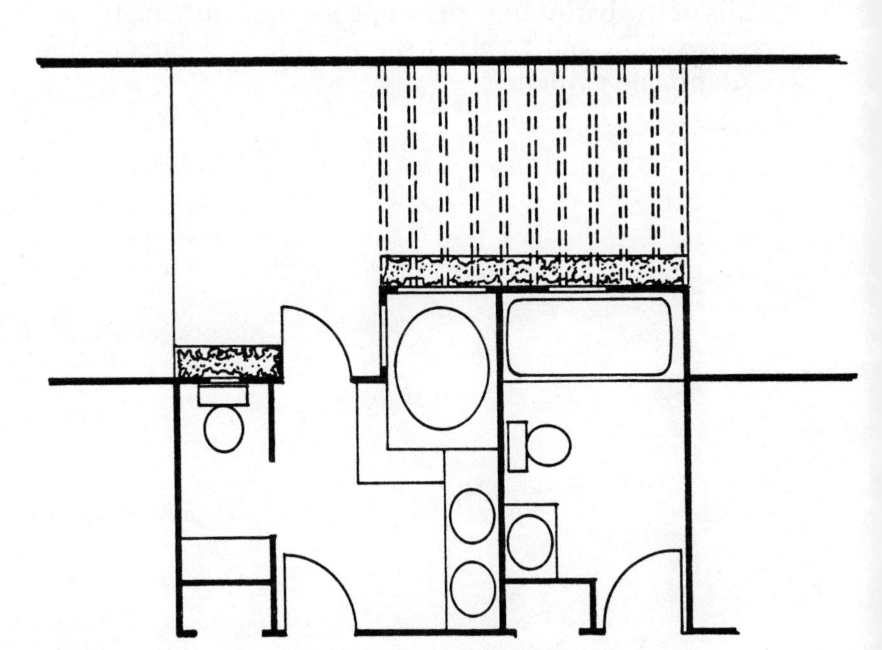

Figure 13-1 *Renovating adjoining baths to create an outdoor room*

CREATING OUTDOOR ROOMS AND DEFINING OUTDOOR SPACE

In Figure 13-1, notice that the existing layout makes a good use of plumbing by having two bathrooms share a common plumbing wall. But these two rooms also share an exterior wall, which leads out to a ten-foot-wide side yard facing the wall created by a neighbor's fence. By building a trellis, opening up the bathrooms with glass, and creating a small, but carefully landscaped courtyard garden and deck, the homeownder created an outdoor room that quickly sold the home yet cost under $2000 to build.

A deck was built in the courtyard, where one could privately retreat after a whirlpool bath without worrying about neighbors' eyes. The area was trellised in part to create a mottled light effect and allow an area for hanging plants. Lanterns were installed on the wall for night use.

Creating this outdoor space made it possible for the walls of the bathrooms to be opened up, allowing for increased light and creating the illusion of a larger bath with private garden.

CHAPTER FOURTEEN

Renovations That Apply to All Rooms

Closets and Storage

CLOSET SPACE IS CRUCIAL to a successfully renovated house. It is a key concern on many buyers' minds. We are a material culture and we all have too much junk—so much so that it's usually overflowing the attic and popping open the garage doors. So any closet or organized storage space you can add will go a long way if it's noticed by the buyer. This includes built-in shelf and storage space.

Every room in the home needs a place for storage. If you can help fill that need you will be rewarded. Consider some of the following storage needs and desires:

The entry hall needs a place for coats.

Bathrooms need linen closets for towels and storage space for toiletries and personal items.

The kitchen or hall needs a utility closet for brooms, mops, and cleaning supplies.

Garages need storage space for tools, ladders, and garden equipment.

CREATING STORAGE

There are many ways to create storage out of existing space. Sunset and other publishers have come up with many projects to add storage space to your home without spending a fortune. Some general ideas are listed following. Remember, people want storage space. If you can show them that your home can hold more possessions than they can imagine, you're a step closer to a sale.

Some ideas are

If it's not being done already, use the space under the stairs as a closet.

Use a bay window to create a window seat with storage beneath.

In the bedroom, create under-bed storage. Build a platform for the bed, and put drawers in it.

Create a storage wall as a screen to divide areas of a room. Half walls can contain bookshelves, or an island of drawers and shelves can be used to divide two rooms instead of a solid wall.

Build a wall shelving/entertainment system along a full wall of the living or family room.

In the bathroom, a floor-to-ceiling storage area for towels and other paraphernalia will only take up twelve inches of the room. Cover the shelves with cabinet or louvered doors.

If you have some attic bedrooms with sloped ceilings, you can create more storage going further into the eaves. Built-in shelving to house a stereo or books adds character and quality to the room. Another part could have a door to an unfinished storage area for luggage and rarely-used items.

A full wall bank of closets is always an impressive item. If you are adding to your bath by attaching the neighboring bedroom, convert the rest to closet space.

If you have high ceilings, space over existing closets or cabinets can be converted to storage for seasonal or rarely-used items such as skis or backpacks.

Convert any unused or underutilized area into storage.

When people look at your home, they are concerned with where they will store all their possessions. The more places they see, the less they'll be concerned that the storage space in your home might be inadequate.

INCREASING APPARENT CLOSET SPACE

Even if you don't even have an extra inch to add closet space to your home, you can increase the efficiency of the space you already have. The closet organizer business has become a major industry today, based on the sole premise of maximizing storage in your home.

For example, a typical master bedroom walk-in closet of 6 x 8 feet has approximately 18 linear feet of storage space. This can easily be reorganized using baskets, shelves, and poles to 48 linear feet, almost three times the amount of usable storage capacity. This works in linen closets, garages, kitchens, or anywhere that storage has been carelessly laid out.

In the master bedroom, an upgrade appearing more and more is the closet carousel, similar to that found in many dry cleaning establishments. The carousel, because it rotates, allows you to access normally unreachable areas. This is an expensive feature, but if your master bedroom lacks an adequately-sized closet, this can help make up for it.

Another idea is to improve the accessibility to closets in older homes. Replace the small paneled doors with a method to create a full frontal opening. One way is with the use of accordion doors. Another method is the familiar sliding closet doors. The look of these has improved recently, although many still lack any degree of character or quality.

Making the storage space look good is also important. Mirroring the closet doors or replacing old flat ones with paneled or louvered doors upgrades the perceived quality of the storage space, making it a luxurious addition, not a forced necessity due to the inadequate size of your house.

In the kitchen, mini-pantries can be installed to reduce the amount of floor space necessary to store critical items. Pot racks can be placed over the island, or unused kick space under the cabinets converted to useful drawer space for flat items.

Most homes are laid out very inefficiently. Taking a foot here or there from a room can actually make it appear bigger through the organized use of space.

People want storage space and will pay for it. If two equal houses come on the market but one has more storage space, it will usually sell first. One of the primary things many people look at in homes is the available storage space. The few feet of space you take from an oversize room and convert to closet space will pay itself back many times over when it comes time to sell the house —not to mention the convenience you'll have while you live there.

Fireplaces

You can add class to any room by installing a new fireplace. Modern prefabricated zero-clearance fireplaces can sit on a standard framed floor and do not require the extensive structural support of a true masonry fireplace, yet most people can hardly tell the difference.

Fireplaces are a high payback item. Surveys show that you can get anywhere from 70–200 percent return on your cost by installing one.

One way to get double use out of the cost of installing a fireplace is to install two, back to back. This could be in two bedrooms, perhaps the master bedroom and master bath, or the living room and dining room. The list is endless but the key is to make the services do double duty.

If you want to add a true masonry fireplace, you will have to add it on an exterior wall to keep the cost down. Unfortunately this is the least efficient use of the fireplace from an energy standpoint.

There are many ways to improve an existing fireplace. The keys to focus on are overall style, built-ins and other items surrounding the firebox, and the materials of the fireplace itself.

Fireplace renovation can be quite inexpensive. Refronting an existing fireplace with a material such as unglazed gray tile can give a contemporary look to the firebox for no more than the cost of a countertop. Many times, just upgrading the hearth (the brick or tiled floor area in front of the fireplace) can make the whole room look nicer. A little marble here and there adds elegance (for only $12/foot) and upgrades the home.

In many homes, a solid wall surrounds the fireplace. Niches, shelves, or cabinetry can be placed in these areas to upgrade the room. Depending on the price level of your home, you may want to go with the cheaper niche (just make it out of sheetrock) or with some fine custom cabinetry.

Drywall detailing over the fireplace can create the equivalent of a planter shelf with recessed lighting below focused on your art or flower arrangement ($250). Little touches like this add pizzazz to the room.

The installation of a fireplace may seem formidable, but with the right conditions it can usually be accomplished by the handyman. The most highly skilled task in fireplace installation is the masonry work. If you use a prefabricated fireplace, most of this work is eliminated. Remember, though, the attractive brickwork around the hearth and firebox will require someone skilled in masonry, as this is what buyers and visitors will see.

Most of the tasks involved in fireplace installation consist of cutting holes in the ceiling and roof, framing around the flue, and flashing the roof around the new chimney. These tasks require careful attention but since they are not cosmetic, the skill required for fine detail work is not necessary. Installing a masonry fireplace should be left to an expert.

Halls

In most new homes, hallways are kept to a minimum. This is because it is space that buyers don't want to pay for. Most people can imagine paying extra for another bedroom, bathroom, or an upgraded kitchen, but for more hall? You've got to be crazy.

However, halls are a fact of life and although buyers will not pay extra for a hall per se, creating a dramatic passageway will add significantly to the overall impression of the house.

Halls do not have to be merely circulation. They can become places in their own right. It's easy to transform your hall into a mini–art gallery by lining one wall with paintings, photos, or posters and setting up a track light aimed at them. This creates a nice effect and makes people forget they are in a hall.

Light is another way of making corridors more pleasurable. A skylight can draw your eyes upward and make the hall seem more spacious. In fact, any natural light will have a significant impact on the warmth and friendliness of the hall.

A long hall can be made to appear shorter through the use of vertical elements in the siding or wallpaper. Another way to change the perceived length is through lighting. Two skylights or dramatic fixtures will help break down the long single hall into two subareas.

Halls and stairs can have their appearance greatly enhanced through the use of a wainscoting and other molding tricks. Paint or wallpaper can also enhance the appearance.

Insulation

In terms of selling the home, energy efficiency doesn't have the selling bang it did a few years back. Sadly, this falls under the old adage that buyers want to see what they're getting. However, if you can make them see how much they'll save on their heating and cooling bills, energy efficiency can be used as a selling point.

According to several studies, the average return on insulating cost is about a six-year payback period in energy savings. This is slower in temperate climates and faster in extreme climates such as North Dakota or south Florida. If you insulate the attic and walls, add new storm windows and doors, and caulk and weatherstrip the major air leaks, you can get up to 38 percent off your energy bills annually.

However, on resale value, insulation does a bit better. A recent study by *Remodeling* magazine showed insulation bringing a return at resale from a low of 29 percent of cost in Sacramento, California, to a high of 120 percent in Austin, Texas. When energy prices rise, the value of an insulated home rises with them.

Foundation

Foundations do not add value to a home in the usual sense. People have bought a home because of the nice kitchen or the beautiful wood siding or even because it was well insulated. But no one buys a home because of the quality of the foundation. It's a Catch 22, however, because they will refuse to buy a home because of the lack of a quality foundation.

Correcting a foundation problem is a very costly venture, but sometimes it may be the only way to sell your home. Many properties have languished on the market for months or years due to a faulty foundation that made the repair uneconomical. The only way to get around a problem like this is to convert the liability into an asset as economically as possible.

For example, in many areas of San Francisco, parking is at a premium. Many people have made money by buying a home with a distressed foundation, lifting up the house, replacing the foundation and building a garage under the house, and lowering the house again. Although the foundation work may have been a $50,000 job, the garage may have added $30,000 or more to the value of the home, mitigating the cost.

Perhaps the neighborhood has changed and you are no longer in an area of only single-family homes, but one where there are some duplexes and triplexes too. Since you need to jack up the house to replace the existing foundation anyway, why not raise it nine feet more and create a separate apartment underneath? The value gained from the apartment plus the rental income will mitigate the cost of the foundation repair, if not actually making it profitable.

Sometimes a neighborhood has changed significantly and what was once a community of bungalows is now an area filled with large expensive homes. A small cottage with an unrepairable foundation is better torn down and a new home built in many cases.

Repairing an existing foundation is a job best left to experienced concrete contractors. Even pouring a new foundation can be tricky, let alone trying to do it while crawling on your hands and knees under an existing house. Foundation repair is a very expensive job. Most of that expense is labor involved in breaking up the old foundation, carting it away, digging the area for the new foundation, and laying the forms. If you can find a way to cut down on this preliminary labor cost, you should be able to reap substantial savings.

Roof

Roofs are of particular concern to buyers and their inspectors. As with foundations, buyers won't give you any money for a good roof but they will deduct for a bad one. There are some ways to keep the cost of roof repair low.

Look at the characteristics of what causes roof decay. It's usually sun and wind. Usually, one side of the roof tends to get weathered more quickly than the other due to its angle to the sun and its wind exposure. It might be possible to replace only this one side of the roof, thereby halving your costs.

If you have a shingle roof, you might be able to replace only the damaged shingles. However, if replacing individual shingles will create a spotty appearance, that entire section of roof should be repaired at one time.

If you have an asphalt shingle roof, you can paint the roof after you've made the repair to hide your patch without having to redo the entire section of roof.

If you're doing a major renovation of your roof and home's exterior, creating a roof overhang where there is none can add much to the appearance of the home.

When observing your home, check to see if you have two layers of roof. If there is only one, you have an inexpensive roof repair. All you need to do is nail the shingles right on top. If you already have two roofs, you need to tear off the whole covering and start over.

Because sun is the major cause of roof deterioration, you can extend the life of a flat roof by painting the black, heat-absorbing tar with a reflective paint. This shows care. However, if your roof has already deteriorated, your painting it could be construed as a cover-up unless you disclose the condition of the roof to the buyer.

If you need to replace the whole roof, studies have shown you will recoup anywhere from 25 to 100 percent of value. One way to get maximum value for your investment is to use roofing materials that appeal to buyers. There are now imitation shingles that look like high-cost materials such as slate. These appeal to more upscale buyers.

Remember, the last thing a new home buyer wants to worry about is having to come up with the money to replace the roof or other major structural item. If you have a roof that needs replacing, it is better to do it before you put your home on the market if you want to appeal to the most buyers. If you enhance it with a warranty that can be transferred to the buyer, you have an added selling point.

Water Heater, Heating, and Air Conditioning

Because these items are not high visibility items, they tend to have less effect on a home's value than, for example, a nice new set of kitchen cabinets. However, they are very important in extreme climates and could make the difference in selling your home. A house without heat in a Minnesota winter is not worth anything to most home buyers.

Most home buyers leave the inspection of the mechanical systems to the home inspectors. Their concern is whether or not the home has heating or air conditioning and they will give it a quick glance. But there are some trappings of these mechanical systems that can appeal to buyers and we will explore these.

The first is to keep them looking clean. Clean all filters, oil squeaky belts, and dust the exterior. Look and smell for exhaust leaks. Convenience is a major concern. Buyers don't want to think their mechanical system is likely to break down at any minute.

Try improving the ventilation around the hot water heater and the heating system. Exhaust fumes smell bad and are unhealthy. This won't directly increase your home's value, but a home that smells of gas will scare buyers away.

Check the hot water heater. Is it adequately sized for the home? If not, before a home inspector comes through is a good time to replace it. The new water heater might impress your buyers. Do you see water underneath? If so, your water heater may be leaking and will have to be replaced anyway. Clean off your water heater to give it its best shot. Beware of cleaning off the corrosion on pipes should there be any. That could be construed as trying to cover something up.

Check the furnace. If you have a gravity furnace that needs replacing, installing a more compact forced-air system can free up needed space in the basement.

Buyers are concerned with how many rooms are being heated. If you have a six-bedroom house with only one wall heater in the entry, that will be noticed. The cost of installing a system will probably end up being deducted from the price of your home anyway. So you may want to consider updating the heating system, for your own comfort in the meantime if nothing else.

High tech thermostats impress buyers and can be highly efficient energy managers of your home. Just replacing your old thermostat with a new computer-controlled one can add sales appeal and also reduce energy costs up to 20 percent by regulating different temperatures at different times. Buyers like the digital displays and other trappings of the "smart" home look.

Some thermostats can be timed to go on just before you come home or just before you wake up. This is a great selling feature and costs little to install.

Modern thermostats can also control ventilating fans to keep the house cool in the summer without the cost of turning the air conditioner on all the time.

Window air conditioners can detract from a home's appearance. They appear added on to an inadequately designed home. If the expense of installing a central air system is not justified, install your portable air conditioners in the wall. This frees up your windows for light and adds more of a sense of permanence to the air conditioning unit.

Another method of "air conditioning" that adds value is the ceiling fan. Aesthetically pleasing and also energy efficient, ceiling fans are a coveted item among home buyers.

Many times it's the humidity factor that makes a home uncomfortable, not the temperature. If your home feels uncomfortable, try eliminating humidity in the summer and adding it in the winter.

Windows and Doors

Stylish, good-looking doors and windows are increasingly demanded by today's home buyers. Richly carved wood doors, doors with leaded or etched glass inserts, and doors with sidelights continue to be favorites with homeowners.

Many homes built since World War II have flush hollow or solid core doors. In some of these homes, this is an appropriate style, although it won't turn on today's buyer. However, many older homes were remodeled during this time period and these lifeless doors replaced the rich textured ones that had existed. Take a good look at your home and see the effect your doors have on the room. It may behoove you to replace these perfectly functional doors with paneled doors and some quality door hardware.

Many rooms will appear richer after a simple door upgrade. Replacing an aluminum-framed sliding glass door with a pair of wooden French doors can totally transform an entrance to the backyard or patio. A new front door can change the initial impression your home makes. Make your new doors reflect the style of your home.

In addition to looking good, a door has to feel solid to buyers. It should glide easily on the hinges and have some weight to it. Also, a solid door closes with a solid click, not the dull thud of a hollow core door. A quality door should open and close easily. You shouldn't have to give it a little extra push to get it into or out of the frame.

Many doors are now being installed with three hinges instead of the usual two. This causes the door to glide more smoothly and feel more solid. If you are replacing doors, adding another hinge will not cost much more but will add significantly to the quality feel of the door.

When installing interior doors, you can buy prehung sets, which are cheaper ($30–100) and easier to install than the custom kind. Prehung sets containing higher-quality doors are a little harder to find but they do exist.

Upgrading the door knobs and other door hardware will give you a good return on your investment. Also replacing a wood door with a glass one can sometimes upgrade a room substantially for the small cost.

Replacing exterior doors and windows in general will give you about a 50–70 percent return on investment. Because of increased energy savings, if you stay longer in the home, that return will be higher. However, replacing specific windows and doors can give you substantial return. Doors and windows that affect curb appeal fall into this category.

Check the garage door, too. Many garages today make up a substantial portion of a home's street facade. In order to keep your home ranking high in curb appeal, the garage door should look good, too.

But looks aren't everything. Garage door openers are a desired item for which more than half of today's home buyers would willingly pay extra.

WINDOWS

Let's make window shopping respectable. A smart purchase will add both beauty and value to the home. There are many good reasons to purchase new windows. They include

Sound insulation—if you're on a noisy street, new triple glazed windows can seal out the noise and increase your home's value.

Replacement of rotting windows.

Increased light through enlargement of an existing window.

Creation of a new window where none existed previously.

Correction of earlier bastardizations of remodeling.

Creation of a uniform appearance from the interior or exterior.

Upgrade to the front of the house.

There are numerous varieties of windows (double hung, casement, etc.) made of numerous materials (wood, aluminum, vinyl). In general, home buyers prefer wood to aluminum. The downside to wood windows is the cost and the maintenance. The recent introduction of vinyl-clad wood windows has made the maintenance issue moot. The cost of wood windows may be initially greater, but if that is what buyers want, the money will be returned to you at resale.

You can also enhance the appearance of existing windows through the use of shades, shutters, screens, blinds, and other window dressing. Figure 14-1 shows some ideas for window coverings.

If a window needs major repair because of weathering, termite damage, or just general abuse, it will probably be cheaper to replace it with a new one of the same size. If you have to replace more than one window in a room, it's a good time to reevaluate the type and style of window you have to see if you can create a more luxurious room without any additional cost.

There are many styles and designs of windows to choose from, as shown in Figure 14-2. You may decide to change the size or shape of your existing windows. Use discretion in doing this. You want to make sure the renovation will fit the character of the house and that it is a desirable style and material for today's market.

Before making the decision to replace old windows, thoroughly check their condition. Most times, the deci-

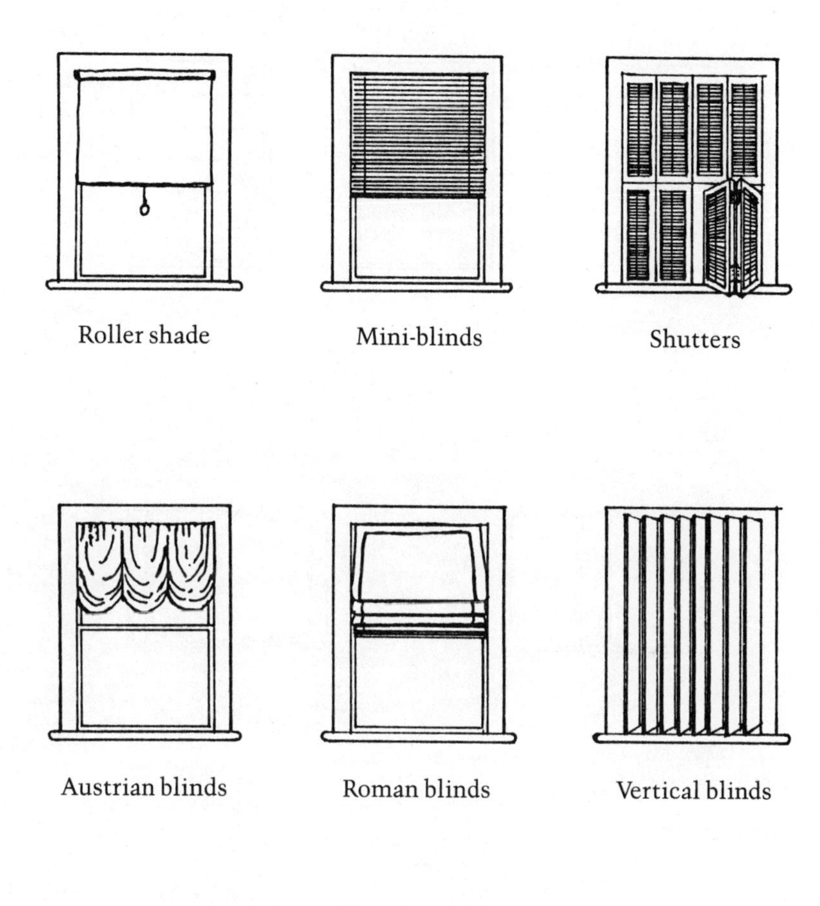

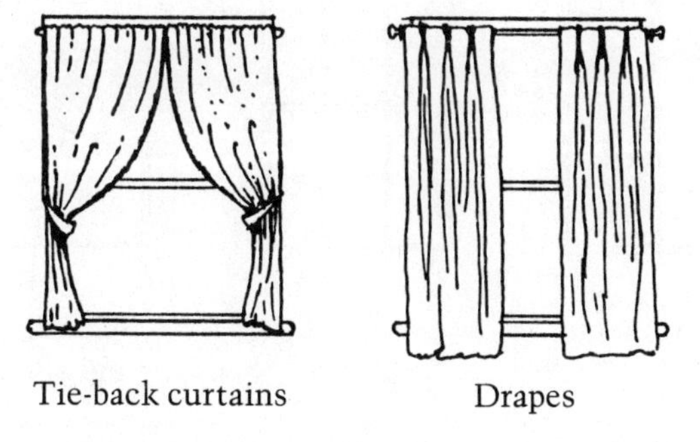

Figure 14-1 *Window treatments*

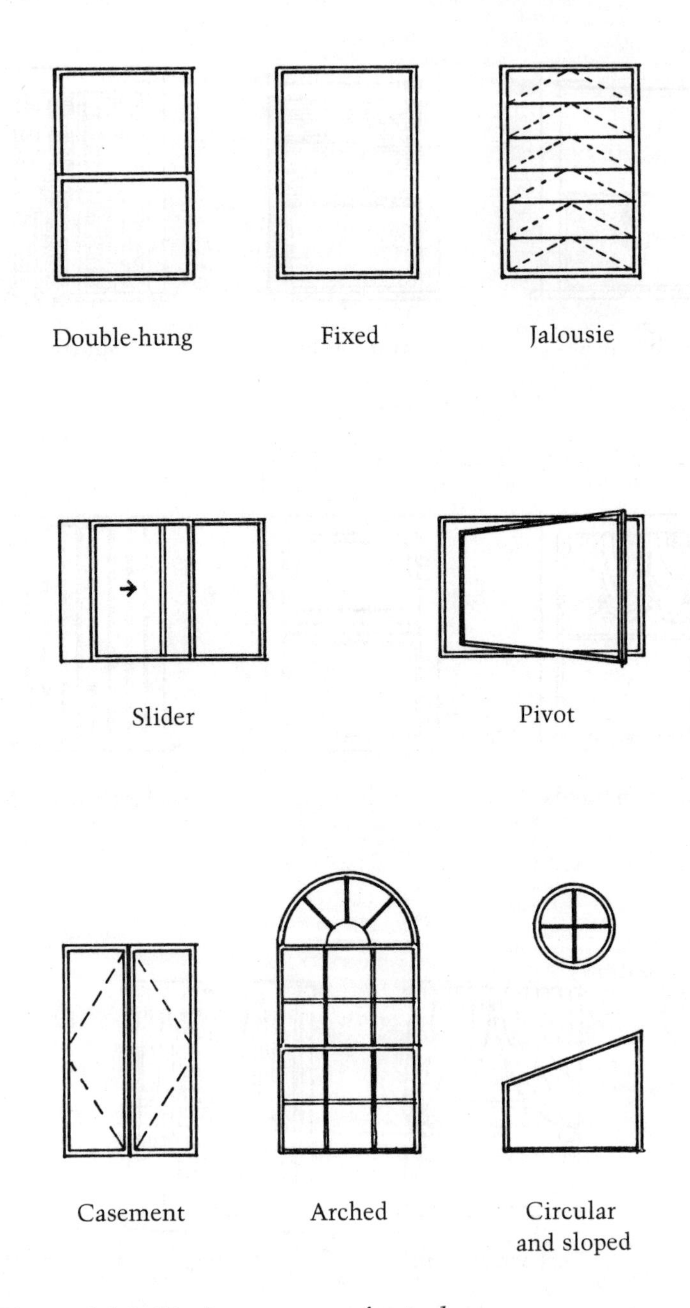

Figure 14-2 *Various types of windows*

sion to replace an entire window is due to a rotted sill only. A rotted sill can be easily replaced at minimal cost.

Some items to consider if replacing windows are the change of character, switching from wood to aluminum, and panes to paneless (divided light to solid).

If you must replace wood windows with cheaper aluminum ones because of budget constraints and the value of homes in the neighborhood, there are several considerations that will help mitigate any potential resale and aesthetic damage.

> Keep wood windows facing the street. Cheaper windows can go on sides and rear of house. This is what many builders are doing in newer homes.
>
> Use anodized aluminum windows.
>
> Put wood trim around new window that fits the character of the house.
>
> If your windows are double hung, replace with double hung aluminum windows. Avoid the side-to-side sliding type. They look cheap.

Windows per se rarely add value in themselves. But the effects they create are the value enhancers. If you add a window to a dark bathroom and suddenly it's awash with light, the window added value. The same is true in any room where the size, style, or placement of the window creates a strong positive change in the room.

One type of window that usually produces a good return is the installation of a greenhouse window in the kitchen (at a cost of under $300).

SKYLIGHTS

Skylights can brighten up dull rooms and add sex appeal to a home. They also can be energy efficient by bringing more heat into the home. Like fireplaces, skylights have improved to the point where they are no longer energy drains but can make a positive contribution to the heating bill.

Skylights can provide a source of natural lighting, improved ventilation, and a feeling of spaciousness to the home. A dark and dreary living room, bedroom, or bath can be transformed into a bright and airy space by installing a skylight in the ceiling.

One relative of the skylight that is quickly catching on is the roof window. These are an improvement over standard skylights because of their operability. They can be cleaned from the inside so you don't have to climb onto your roof to wash your window.

Statistics show that skylights are a popular item among both home buyers and homeowners. Sales of skylights nationwide have more than quadrupled since 1983. A skylight is an easy way to lighten and update your home.

Electrical System

An electrical system won't directly increase the value of your home but it will allow for many other upgrades that will. If you have an inadequate system, you won't be able to upgrade your kitchen (adding a dishwasher or disposal), nor will you be able to do room conversions or many of the other added value renovations. It is vital that you know the existing condition of your system and what you can do to improve it.

The condition of your electrical system may first be detected by looking at your home's electrical panel. This may be a fuse box or, more likely, circuit breakers. Check the amperage coming into the house by looking at the main breaker or fuse. Is it 30, 50, or 60 amps? If so, you have inadequate electrical for today's needs. A 100-amp service is a minimum by modern standards and 200 is preferable. Don't panic, though, if it's inadequate. A new service to the home generally costs under $1000.

While you're at the service panel, check to see the voltage coming into the house. If you have two wires, you have standard 110-volt service. If you have three wires, you have 220-volt capacity. Electric ranges, dryers, and many heaters need 220 volts. Otherwise 110 is adequate.

Many people get confused at the difference between voltage and amperage. The best analogy is to think of electricity as water flowing through a pipe. If you increase the diameter of the pipe, more water can flow in. That is equivalent to increasing amperage. You're allowing for more electricity to enter the home. If you keep the pipe the same diameter but increase the pressure, that's equivalent to increasing the voltage. So a 220 circuit needs a higher electrical "pressure" to operate.

An ideal electrical panel should be of adequate amperage, have a main switch, and have some room for expanding. This is to allow for added circuits (such as to new rooms in the attic). If the only item lacking is room to expand, its easy and inexpensive to add another subpanel nearby.

When running new wires through the home, use 12 gauge for all outlets and 12 or 14 for lights. Outlets should have at least a 20-amp service per circuit and lighting circuits 15.

The most expensive part of upgrading an older home's electrical is not in the main service but in the interior. Snaking wires through existing walls can take ten times the amount of time and energy it would take to wire an open wall. In fact, much of the cost in wiring has to do with tearing up and/or patching walls. So if you're tearing the plaster off a wall to do some work, think about any wiring you might want to add before covering up again.

Use any upgraded wiring to install GFCI outlets in the bathroom and kitchen. Try to take advantage of any added wiring you've done. Remember, it is not necessary to redo the wiring that is already in place unless it is dangerous.

Add any outlets necessary. Code minimums are one outlet for every twelve feet of wall. Look around. If you have extension cords all over the place, it's a sure sign that your home has inadequate outlets.

Make sure all switches work and that they turn on something. If a buyer walks into a room, flips a switch, and the light goes on, he won't give it a second thought. But if nothing happens, you've just set off a series of negative reactions. Check all switches before showing your home.

Plumbing

Plumbing costs more than electrical to upgrade. Replumbing an average home can cost from $1800 to $4000 depending on complexity. Your goal is to leave the pipes alone if they are adequate. It's only when they're deteriorated to the point that it's affecting the home that we take action.

It's a consolation to remember, when undertaking a plumbing project, that the plumbing system is really three systems—the supply, the drain, and the vent. All three need not be replaced in all remodeling. If you have to replace all three, you might want to walk away from the building. That will never pay for itself.

Supply problems usually take the form of lack of adequate pressure or leaks in the supply pipes. Drain problems tend to show as clogs or backups. These can be leaks, too. The vent problems will usually appear in the form of a rotting sewage smell in the house. This is a sign of deteriorated pipe that must be replaced.

Buyers tend to be more concerned with the electrical system than the plumbing, although an extreme problem in the plumbing will be cause for alarm.

Most buyers, when looking at homes, are concerned about what they can see. A dripping faucet that needs a five-cent washer replacement might cause more concern than the fact that the entire home contains 25-year-old galvanized pipe that is at the end of its lifespan. Make sure all leaks are corrected and all drains are flowing properly.

You will also notice that many buyers are more concerned with how the faucets and fixtures look than with the plumbing behind them. For some reason, a $100 faucet seems more important than a $2000 plumbing repair. For maximum effect, update every plumbing item the buyer sees.

If you need to do plumbing remodeling, find out the full range of materials with which you can work. Many, such as plastic pipe, are much easier, and thus cheaper, to work with than the old cast iron. You want to do a quality, code-accepted job but to minimize the time and effort required.

Other Hints Around the Home

Sometimes views are a good reason to make exterior changes. Opening up the home with windows and skylights can look good from the inside and the outside.

If adding wall sconces, use quality ones. The cost of the fixture is low relative to the installation. Remember, you don't save by cutting back on what the buyer sees. Saving a few dollars by buying ugly cheap fixtures will cost you more in the long run.

If your home just doesn't have the potential to be a quality home, concentrate on the landscaping and on how you can get views to the exterior from within the home. Many a shack has sold because of lush landscaping.

CHAPTER FIFTEEN

Summary of Room Renovations

THE PURPOSE OF THIS book is to show you what is necessary in order to get top dollar for your home. All the suggestions in the book will gain you value in your home; however, not all are applicable and not all should be weighed equally. Here we present a summary in the order recommended in renovating your home to get maximum effect on a limited budget.

The first and most important task is to get people to want to buy your house. You can only do this by getting them in to look at it. Thus the impression your home conveys from the street is of number one importance. This impression is known as curb appeal. It may only take cleaning the exterior of your building and trimming the hedges to bring your home up to top form, but it is vital.

Next is the front entryway. Once again we want to make a good first impression on the buyer. This is merely an extension of the curb appeal concept but now the buyer is up close to your home and can see the detail. Make sure this area conveys the message you want to send. By starting off on the right footing with a buyer, we will be coloring her impression of the house in a favorable light.

If we start off wrong, it will take more effort to turn her impression around.

Next is the kitchen. Experts agree this room is the single most important room in terms of selling the house. It's so important that an entire multimillion dollar industry has formed just to remodel kitchens. A kitchen renovation does not have to be costly, but even a costly one will probably return more than its cost. An exciting kitchen has been known to carry an otherwise bland house to a smooth sale. Make your kitchen cook.

Next is the bathroom. Bathrooms have only recently come of age in terms of the variety and quality they offer. Serious buyers know this. The whirlpool tub, once a high-end upgrade, is now standard in most new homes. Buyers want to relax after a hard day at work and if your bath provides that sanctuary, you're halfway to a sale.

Finally, on the list of musts, we have the basics of light and cleanliness. You could have built the biggest closets, the sexiest deck, and the warmest fireplace but if the home is dirty your buyers won't even notice them. It's sad but true that sellers with homes with wonderful features have not been able to get top dollar simply because their homes were dirty or cluttered and were not perceived as quality homes.

The other items mentioned in this book are all important in enabling you to get top dollar for your home with the lowest cost in renovating and should not be ignored. It is the entire home which sells itself. But these few rooms and considerations should be first on your mind when renovating with a limited budget.

You may have read many surveys in magazines which tell you the returns you can get from certain rooms. Don't believe them. Although in general you will get more benefit from kitchen remodeling than the installation of a swimming pool, once you get within the structure, a general survey like that is pointless. The average patio returns 40 percent of its investment cost, but if it is the item that makes your home appealing, it may return 200 percent or more. Keep an open mind when reading those surveys.

The following is a general checklist of items you probably want to consider before you do your renovations. It is meant to be a general guide.

Item	Condition	Comments	Priority	Estimated Cost
EXTERIOR				
Lawn				
Landscaping				
Fence				
Walk				
Driveway				
Paint				
Front				
Rest of house				
Siding				
Roof/ chimney				
Mailbox				
Windows				
Hardware				
Front entry				
Doorbell				
Light				
Railings				
Other				
GARAGE				
Paint				
Siding				
Roof				
Doors				
Windows				
Hardware				
Other				

Item	Condition	Comments	Priority	Estimated Cost
OTHER EXTERIOR				
Trash area				
Patio				
Floor				
Rails/walls				
ENTRY				
Walls				
Ceiling				
Floors				
Trim				
Light fixtures				
Closet				
Hardware				
Stairs				
Furniture and decorating				
Other				
LIVING ROOM				
Walls				
Ceiling				
Floors				
Trim				
Light fixtures				
Hardware				
Windows				
Doors				
Heating and cooling				
Furniture and decorating				
Other				

Item	Condition	Comments	Priority	Estimated Cost
DINING ROOM				
Walls				
Ceiling				
Floor				
Trim				
Light fixtures				
Windows				
Doors				
Heating and cooling				
Furniture and decorating				
Other				
FAMILY ROOM/DEN				
Walls				
Ceiling				
Floors				
Trim				
Light fixtures				
Hardware				
Windows				
Doors				
Heating and cooling				
Furniture and decorating				
Other				

Item	Condition	Comments	Priority	Estimated Cost
BEDROOM (MAKE A SEPARATE LIST FOR EACH BEDROOM)				
Walls				
Ceiling				
Floor				
Trim				
Light fixtures				
Windows				
Door				
Heating and cooling				
Closet				
Size				
Condition				
Furniture and decorating				
Other				
BATHROOM (MAKE A SEPARATE LIST FOR EACH BATHROOM)				
Walls				
Ceiling				
Floor				
Windows				
Lighting				
Toilet				
Sink				
Tub or shower				
Sink faucet				
Tub/shower faucet				
Medicine cabinet				
General tidiness				
Other				

Item	Condition	Comments	Priority	Estimated Cost
KITCHEN				
Walls				
Ceiling				
Floors				
Appliances				
Stove				
Refrigerator				
Dishwasher				
Disposal				
Microwave				
Sink				
Electrical				
Counters				
Cabinets				
Size				
Quality				
Light				
Exhaust fan				
Faucets				
Hardware				
General tidiness				
BASEMENT				
Walls				
Floor				
Storage				
Dryness				
Stairway				
General tidiness				
ATTIC				
Floor				
Storage				
Insulation				
Vents				
General tidiness				

CHAPTER SIXTEEN

Expanding within the House

ALTHOUGH WE'VE TRIED TO keep the costs outlined to minor or moderate renovations in this book, there are times when more space is needed. If you are going to live in your renovation, you want to know what additions will add value over cost, which ones will just pay for themselves, and which ones are simply a consumption item designed for your lifestyle and have a minimum payback value.

Certain rooms can dramatically increase your home's value over their cost, such as an added bedroom or bathroom. The number of bedrooms and bathrooms both appear on real estate listings and are key numbers for buyers in determining whether or not they even want to look at your house. In general, the more bedrooms or baths you have, the less value an added one gives. Thus, adding a second bath to a two-bedroom, one-bath home will do much more for its value than adding a fourth bath to a six-bedroom, three-bath home. However, no rules are absolute and you must investigate your local market.

Utilizing Wasted Space

Many times there is space within the house that is being underutilized. This may be an unfinished attic or basement, unnecessary halls, or an awkward layout of rooms that would produce higher quality and quantity of space if reorganized.

Hallways are one of the biggest wastes of space. People do not want to pay top dollar for circulation. You might be able to reorganize the rooms in such a way as to steal part of the hall into another room without impairing access or circulation. Any space that is converted from wasted circulation to rooms or closet space will add value to the home.

Attics, basements, unfinished garages, rooms that are too large, and inefficient floor plans are all potential wasters of space, and places where you can cheaply "expand" your home. However, not all of these spaces are suitable to convert to valuable living area. That depends on the structure and layout of your home, the market in which your home is located, and your home's value in relation to your neighbor's houses.

ATTIC EXPANSION AND RENOVATION

Attic expansion is one of the least expensive ways to add extra rooms to the home, assuming your home has the necessary existing structure. Many older homes have large underutilized attic spaces. This can be made accessible for storage simply by the addition of fold-down stairs. You can even sheetrock parts of the attic, put a few doors and closet bars inside and create a showplace closet and storage space that may help sell your home.

If the space has good access and a high enough ridge to make it usable as living space, it may be a prime candidate for the addition of those extra bedrooms, baths, or study that will increase the sale price of your home.

Code requirements for attic rooms are a minimum ceiling height of 7 feet 6 inches covering at least one-half the room and a minimum ceiling height of 5 feet along the outer edges of the room. Most codes also require that habitable living areas generally be at least 7 feet wide and 70 square feet in area. Not all attics can meet these requirements. Even if yours seems like it might qualify, check to see if the floor is thick enough to hold your weight. You may have to raise it, losing valuable headroom.

If the ridge is high enough but there's not enough space to house a room, the addition of dormers will increase the available square footage at reasonable cost. A shed dormer is the cheapest approach but, depending on the style of your home, may not be appropriate. There are also other styles of dormers that cost more to build. We talk more about that later.

Insulation in the attic takes on a more critical importance than in other parts of the house, as it butts directly against the elements on all sides but the floor. You will need to insulate the attic space well, providing vapor barriers around the walls and ceiling and ventilating the attic space above the finished space and on each side. The last thing you need is condensation and the wood damage it brings. Fans inside the attic are good for increasing cooling capacity and airflow within the finished space and preventing condensation.

When planning your attic conversion, make sure there is enough space on the floor below for a flight of stairs. The usual straight-run stair requires a space 3 feet wide and 10 feet long plus a 3-foot space for a landing at the top and bottom. There must also be a minimum overhead clearance of 6 feet 8 inches at any point on the stairs. If space is tight, spiral stairs may be a solution, although most buyers don't like them (they know how hard it is to get furniture up and down). Some codes won't even allow them. If there is another way to get furniture up and down, spiral stairs may be allowed.

There are also fold-down stairs, which you pull down when you need them and fold back up into the ceiling when done. Although many times more practical than spiral stairs, an appraiser may not consider the rooms above as real rooms, but rather as attic rooms, a less desirable category when it comes to getting a bank loan. Your buyers may reach the same conclusion.

Even if you already have stairs to your attic, they may not be up to code. Many older stairs are too steep, provide inadequate head clearance, or turn too tightly around corners. In order for you to do your renovation and in order for buyers not to think you've built a shoddy addition, make sure the stairs provide what the law requires.

Adding skylights can significantly alter the feel of the attic. The best ones to install are operable. Also called roof windows, they allow for ventilation as well as light.

You might find that you get wonderful views you never knew existed by adding windows in key locations in the attic. Climb out on the roof (be careful) to get an idea of the possibilities.

Convert the attic into a retreat or home office if it doesn't work as a full bedroom. To get higher head clearance, you can box in the collar ties and make them part of the room design.

CHECKING THE STRUCTURE

Transforming an unfinished attic into salable, usable space can be a simple matter of installing a finish ceiling, walls; and a floor covering. However, it will often require adding a shed or gable dormer for more space or for natural light and ventilation. Dormers also add to the charm of the room and can provide wall space for windows and doors.

The major structural concern is the adequacy of the floor joists. Although adequately designed to hold the ceiling below, they may be inadequate to carry a full floor load. It is best to get professional advice on this point but many times one can make the floor serviceable simply by doubling the joists.

The usual choices in dormer construction are shed, gable, or double gable dormers. These are shown in Figure 16-1.

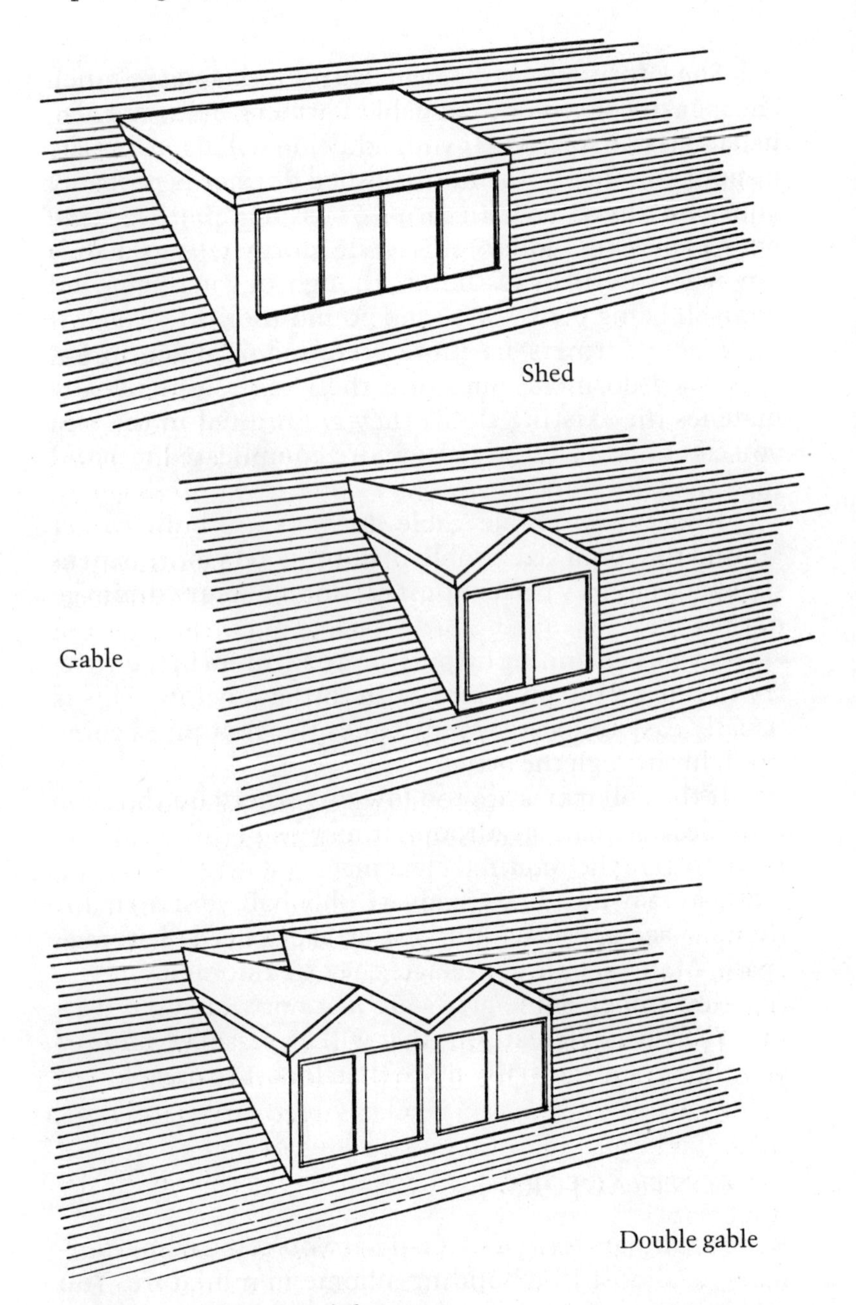

Figure 16-1 *Types of dormers*

Shed dormers can be made any width and are much cheaper to construct than gable dormers. They are also usually less attractive. If your addition will be facing the back or the side of the house a shed dormer is probably your best alternative. In terms of usable square footage per renovation dollar, this style dormer wins hands down. Be careful of aesthetics, though, or you might find yourself being penny-wise and pound-foolish.

Gable dormers are more preferred on older homes than shed dormers, but since their roof slope usually matches the existing slope, they are limited in the size you can build. They are also more complicated to build than shed dormers.

Sometimes double gable dormers are built to get around the room size problem, but this gets more expensive and requires better construction to assure drainage of the roof.

If you're planning on putting a bathroom in the attic, try to line up the plumbing with the bath below. This is usually easy to locate. Many times the vent pipes come up right through the attic.

If the collar ties are too low but otherwise the attic provides adequate headroom, it may be possible to raise them to give the required clearance.

You may decide to renovate only half your attic for living space and leave the rest as badly needed storage space. Many people appreciate the extra storage.

Remember, some attics are just not worth renovating. The key is to create one that will increase the value of your home substantially more than it cost to create.

CONTRACTORS

Renovating an attic, especially if you're building dormers, is almost like building a home in miniature. You will have jobs ranging from roofing to carpentry to interior finish work. Depending on your skill and experience, you should be able to handle anywhere from only a few tasks to being able to do much of the renovation yourself.

Building the dormer is generally best left to professionals, especially if you are building a more complex shape than a shed dormer. You can let the contractor build and close in the attic area, allowing you to do much of the interior work yourself.

A primary consideration in doing attic work is accessibility. Remember, you will be carrying lumber, plywood, and sheetrock up there. So get some help. You need to figure out where to build the staircase. Figure in that cost, as well as the loss of living area below.

If the attic floor joists are inadequate to meet current code, you may have to call in a professional to beef them up, especially if it involves an esoteric approach such as bolting steel members to the joists. Also, your stair building is best done by a professional carpenter as stairs need to look good as well as meet code. An exception to this is if you are using a stair kit with premanufactured parts. A handyman or skilled homeowner should be able to assemble this.

Systems such as plumbing, electrical, and heating and ventilation are best left to experienced workers. Running wiring is not hard, nor is extending plumbing across open studs but you must know the codes if you are to attempt it yourself. Delays are costly and in a project as large as this can add up quickly.

Interior work such as hanging sheetrock, and finishes such as wallpaper installation and painting are easily handled by the average homeowner. If you are adding a bathroom in the attic, see the chapter on bathrooms for advice as to contractors.

Skylights and roof windows are a common element of attic renovations due to the slope of the ceiling. A skilled homeowner can install skylights, but a professional carpenter will be able to handle quantity installations better.

Finally, you probably should hire an architect if attempting a renovation this large. An architect will help you to best utilize the space and will find an appropriate placement for the stairs. Also, attics give the potential for creating a dramatic space, such as a master suite, which may end up being the selling point of the house. Having professional design advice will help ensure the best conversion possible.

Basement Refinishing

An unfinished basement may be one of the easiest places to expand. However, finished basements are not as popular as they once were. Just nailing up some cheap paneling from the local home improvement store won't convince your buyers that you've got a real room down there. All it will convince them of is that a shoddy job of renovation was done. Care must be taken to get rid of any association of the room being a basement.

Two of the main disadvantages to basement rooms are dampness and lack of natural light. Dampness in the basement can be partially overcome by the installation of vapor barriers on the floor and walls. The lack of illumination can be tackled in a number of ways.

One way is to cut larger windows into the basement and then landscape a sunken area (held back by retaining walls) outside of the window. This will allow much more light to penetrate and will also get rid of that feeling that you are below ground. To reduce the feeling of an imposing wall, step it down slowly, perhaps with plantings and patios along the way.

You might go one step further and create a little sunken outdoor patio accessed by French doors from the basement room. You will be creating a small private oasis and ridding the room of the basement stigma.

The best place to add windows is the south wall, as you get more light for your renovation dollar. Obviously, if the south side is your street front or if there is some other obstruction, you should use an alternate appropriate wall. Do not use the north side, though, as it never gets the direct light so needed to brighten a basement.

FINISHING THE BASEMENT

Basement finishes should match that of other rooms described in previous chapters. Brightly-painted drywall, mirrors, and reflective surfaces are probably the best finishes, as they reflect a lot of light. However, certain special techniques may be required before you put up your first stud.

Keep in mind that basements tend to be damper than the rest of the house, so a system of dehumidifying is recommended. Also, basements tend to be cooler, so you'll want extra ducts in your heating system to go down here. An auxiliary system of electric heat may be an inexpensive way to solve the heating problem.

Check your home for potential moisture problems. Check the gutters and downspouts to make sure they're in good working condition and make sure the grade slopes away from your foundation. See if there are any areas where water tends to puddle. It's best to wait through at least one rainy season before deciding to do any work on the basement, to give all potential problems a chance to show themselves.

Many times the source of leakage in your basement is the joint between the floor and the wall or small cracks in the foundation. These must all be filled with an epoxy cement.

You may need to waterproof your basement with tar or some other method. The worst thing to have is a musty smell. Negative smells have a stronger impact on home buyers than almost anything else about your house. Increasing your ventilation will also help, even if the ventilation is mechanical.

Other problems you may run into are exposed pipes and ducts. Most can just be covered up, but if they block the room or prevent proper head clearance, check with a professional about the practicality of moving them.

FLOORS

Concrete basement floors can be covered a number of ways. The cheapest way is just to carpet over the concrete. This can provide an nice finish and no one will ever suspect concrete is just below. If, however, your floor is cracked and uneven or damp, a vapor barrier can be installed and then a false floor built on furring strips. This wooden floor will feel better to the feet and stay warm and comfortable. Do-it-yourself books explain the furring technique.

If you are creating a bath area, tile and linoleum can also be laid directly onto concrete.

WALLS

Walls may be as simple as painting the concrete or leaving the exposed brick or stone. If your basement is made of one of the latter, it may add charm to leave a wall or two exposed. Usually, however, covering up the wall with sheetrock is the best way to go. It allows you to wire and plumb behind your false walls and also provides an added level of insulation from the cold, damp earth. The false wall should come out from the original wall only the minimum amount of space necessary, as windows should appear normal and not too deeply recessed into the wall.

There now is a product out on the market that can be used to cheaply and quickly transform concrete basements into finished walls. Called Flexi-Wall, it is a gypsum-coated fabric that is rolled onto the walls creating a smooth or textured surface as desired. It is used in many poured-concrete commercial buildings as a way to give them a warmer feel.

If you have exposed pipes in the ceiling, it's best to encase them in sheetrock. Box them in or, in architectural terms, create a soffit. What you are trying to do is to make them look like planned architectural elements of the room rather than a mechanical system cover-up.

Finally, you still want storage and easy access to the mechanical systems. It is desirable to design your basement rooms to allow for direct access. If you need to go through a bedroom to get to these areas, it leaves a worse impression and may not even be allowed by code.

As a final note, before covering up any pipes, it's a good idea to inspect the entire plumbing system. If any pipes are leaking or if you notice signs of corrosion, take care of these problems now. Covering them up will only cause larger problems later and may get you sued by a new owner.

CONTRACTORS

Much of the work in bringing a basement up to a livable space can be done by the homeowner or handyman. Insulating, furring out walls, and hanging sheetrock are just some of the tasks a homeowner can do. Since, in general, a basement area is going to be perceived as having a lower value than some other parts of the house, professional craftsmanship is not as critical here as on the main level.

There are a few areas where the professional can be very crucial, though. One is in building stairs to the basement level. Even if you have existing stairs, they probably feel like "basement stairs" (shoddily built, too steep, or no banister, just a cheap rail). If this is the case, rebuilding them may add value to the whole conversion. Stair building requires precision cuts, many times working with expensive materials, so you don't want to leave it in the hands of amateurs.

If you are excavating on the exterior in order to create a garden or patio area, depending on the condition of your soil and the depth of your basement, you may want to call out a concrete contractor to pour the patio and retaining walls.

If you have moisture problems, call in an expert to help you evaluate the scriousness and extent of the problem before proceeding with your interior finishes. You may find that you need to do more than merely apply a sealer to the wall.

Electrical and plumbing can be done by either the homeowner or a professional, depending on skill level, wants, and code considerations.

Garage Conversion

Another inexpensive way to expand is into the garage that is built as an integral part of the house. If the garage is well built, the only work necessary is to do the finishing. This is much less costly than adding onto the house. You can then add a garage to another part of the house. Perhaps you had an old one-car garage. This will allow you to create more livable space and then to build a modern two- or three-car garage that will blend harmoniously with the house. Since the garage is usually near the kitchen, some of the more obvious conversions might be into a family room or a home office. It could also be converted into additional bedrooms or become a second apartment.

A variation on garage conversions is to build a few rooms above the garage. This can serve as a separate apartment, a home office, or an art studio. These extras can increase the desirability of the property. Don't overimprove for your market.

Some attached garages step down from the main house. If ceiling height warrants it, build a wooden floor to make it level. This will have the added benefit of a warmer and softer floor. You will usually have to add some windows and insulate the structure.

The best wall to do the work on is the one that contains the garage door. Remove the garage door and then frame in your doors and windows as required. You will still have the driveway coming up to the wall. To mitigate this, create a planter area with flower boxes and potted plants. You might even want to remove the asphalt near the house to disguise the fact that the room was a former garage.

Most of the work of a garage conversion can be handled by the homeowner. Much of it is interior finish work and installing insulation. The items that a homeowner might leave to the professional are installing any exterior doors and windows and, if the garage floor is cracked or uneven, installing a raised wooden floor.

Sun Rooms

Enclosing a porch or adding a nook off the kitchen can significantly increase the apparent size and amount of living space of your dwelling for less money than a standard addition. Both these areas are ideal for becoming "sun spaces," rooms with glass panels on the walls and part of the ceiling.

A small living room can appear larger with the addition of a sun space and breaking through the walls. Although many sun spaces are prefab units, there is now enough variety to make them appear custom. You can also create custom spaces, though this will cost more. A sun space essentially allows you to add a room to the existing structure without having to compromise light to the interior rooms. Thus you get more square footage and a lighter house overall.

Sun spaces can serve solar heating functions, too. A south-facing sun room can collect solar heat, which is absorbed and stored in the concrete and quarry tile floor until needed, then reradiated into the living space, reducing the heating burden on the mechanical equipment. Thus you can get increased square footage and reduced heating bills—a win/win combination. The key is it must be south-oriented and follow basic solar heating principles. This topic is too extensive to cover here but there are many good books on the subject available at bookstores and libraries.

Perhaps the sun space's best use is as a breakfast nook or dining area off of the kitchen. Many postwar kitchens are of an inadequate size for today's buyer, who demands a larger airy kitchen. A sun room allows for a reorganization of the kitchen by moving the dining area into the new space, freeing up valuable kitchen space. Structural problems are overcome by building a dividing island with posts between the two rooms. If you use a similar flooring material and wall covering, the two spaces will tend to blend into a single unit.

Prefabricated sun spaces in general only return about 50 percent of cost, when installed by a contractor, on a quick resale, but if they positively affect the other rooms of the house, this return can be substantially more.

Note that sun spaces make for a beautiful and energy-efficient space when properly located. Ideally, this means a southern or western exposure. East is less desirable and north is unacceptable. Also, it is preferable to protect the sun space from direct wind. Wind can accelerate heat loss when the sun goes down and a protected corner can mitigate this.

If you are enclosing an existing covered porch, this can be done at minimal expense and will probably return more than its cost to you. Even if done by professionals, the work shouldn't cost more than $3000–5000. A homeowner can usually do it for half of this.

A sun space kit requires some skill and experience to install. The main expenditure of energy and skill is in the construction of the foundation and knee wall on which the sun space sits. Because the foundation and knee wall must be leveled and fit precisely with the dimensions of the premanufactured sun space greenhouse, mistakes can be very costly.

The homeowner or handyman can install the flooring, any interior or exterior sidings, and the finishing work.

Enclosing an existing porch into a sun room is a much easier operation mostly because the foundation and floor framing have already been done. All that is required now is the walls and windows and then the interior work.

Adding Another Story

If your home is significantly smaller than others in the neighborhood, jacking the house up and adding a new ground floor may be the least expensive way to increase the square footage of your home significantly. It's also an easy way of adding a second unit to your home to help pay the mortgage. Many small older homes have inadequate common areas—the living room may be too small for modern needs, etc. An easy way to change this is to convert these rooms into additional bedrooms and then build the larger, grander public rooms on the new first floor.

This idea is one of the ideal examples of using a needed repair to your advantage. The skilled renovator will take a foundation problem, a strong negative, and mitigate the problem or make it an asset, as in this example. If the home has a faulty foundation that needs replacement, and you have to jack up the house anyway to replace the foundation, you might as well get an economic benefit by adding a story below containing much needed livable space. Of course this is not appropriate for every situation, but it shows how, with creative thought, you can capitalize on what others perceive as problems.

General Rules for Additions

If space requirements cannot be met utilizing available attic, basement, or garage space, or if the floor plan will not allow these areas to be used effectively, the only alternative left may be to construct an addition. Be awarc of zoning regulations restricting height and regulating setbacks for your addition.

The market approach to adding rooms is to design additions for your most critically needed space. If you need more bedrooms, but you would also like a much larger living room, maybe the present living room can be used as a bedroom and a large living room can be added. If you want a large modern kitchen, think about adding on a new kitchen and converting the old kitchen into a utility room, bathroom, or hobby room.

Some important things to remember when planning additions to your home are

Zoning setbacks may have changed since your home was first constructed and they may restrict the size or placement of the addition.

The addition should be in keeping with the style of the rest of the house. Rooflines, siding, and windows should all match the original structure as closely as possible.

The shape of your addition influences its cost. A square is the most practical shape in terms of usable square footage per linear foot of exterior wall.

General Renovation Tips

Focus your efforts. Concentrate on the areas with the most remodeling potential. Keep the renovation manageable and within the budget.

Use architectural tricks. Vary the ceiling heights. Let a room explode in volume. Use flooring patterns to extend connections between rooms.

Keep circulation space to a minimum. No one likes to pay for halls. All too often, passageways prevent you from fully using your potential square footage.

Use fewer partitions. Open up interiors by removing any walls that aren't necessary. Half walls or columns can define spaces while maintaining a spacious atmosphere and allowing light to penetrate farther through the house.

Think quality. Even if your home is only a thousand square feet or less, it needn't be boring or confining if it's an attractive, well-thought-out space. High-quality finish materials make the positive difference.

Other Room Additions and Conversions

One of the simplest ways to update a house and add extra space is through the use of nonbearing partition walls. Some older homes have huge rooms that are not being properly utilized for today's lifestyle. Dividing such rooms into two rooms can instantly create value in your home. Be careful to match all architectural detailing or else redo the whole room with new detailing. Your home will be listed in the multiple listing book with more rooms and, especially if the added room is a bedroom, its appraisal value will be increased.

Sometimes value can be added even by reducing rooms. Some older homes have a multitude of tiny rooms, none of which has the feeling of spaciousness or the character people want in their homes today. Tearing down these partitions can allow you to create dynamic, light, airy spaces that people will die for. The open plan came into use early in this century and has become the dominant mode of housing in the United States. It fits into people's wants, expectations, and desires. Figure 16-2 shows some examples of floor plans improved by opening them up.

Removing a partition involves the tearing down of walls, and alterations to the floor and ceiling. However, if it's a load-bearing partition, something must be done to take up the missing support. If attic space is available above the opening, a supporting beam can be placed over the ceiling joists, allowing the joists to hang from the beam, creating an unobstructed space below.

If that's not possible, you will have to keep a support beam in the room where the wall used to be. A way of

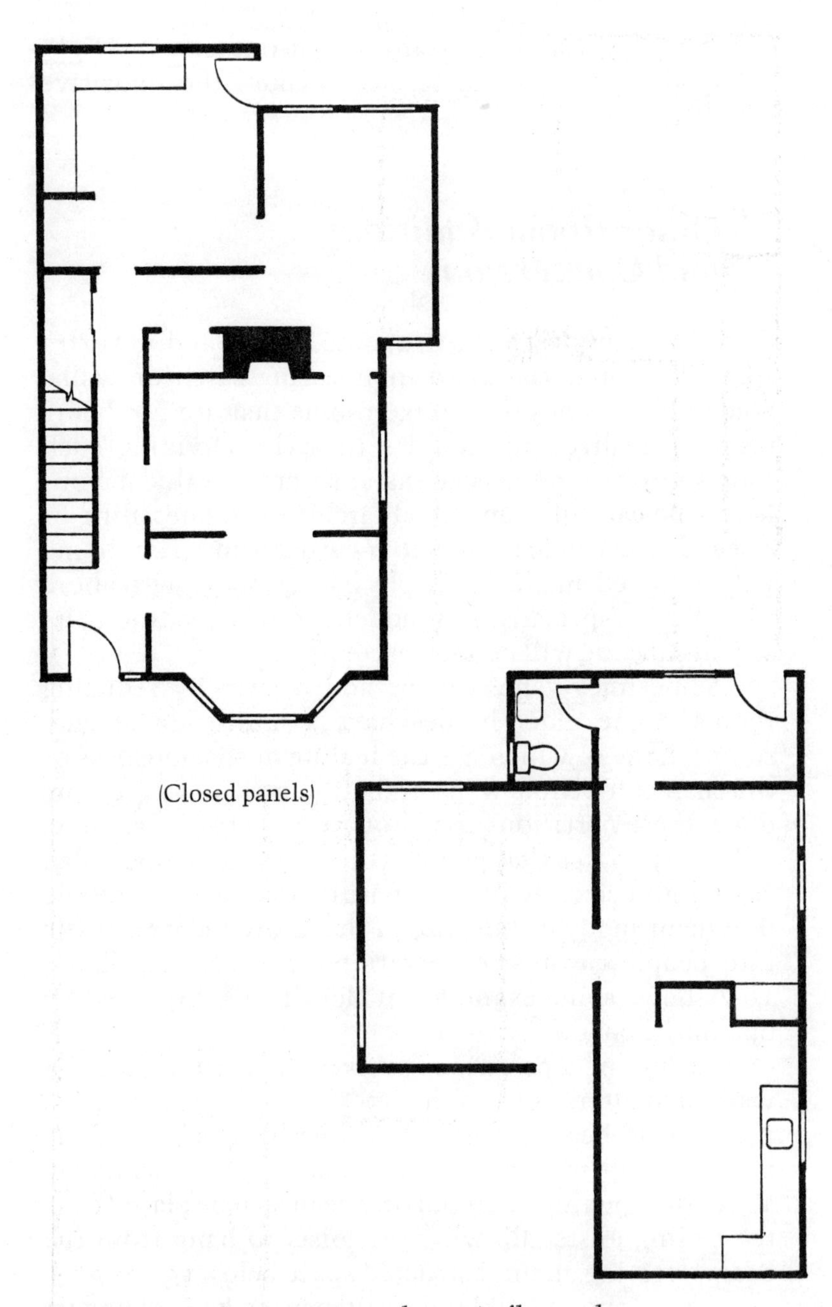

Figure 16-2 *Opening up a home's floor plan*

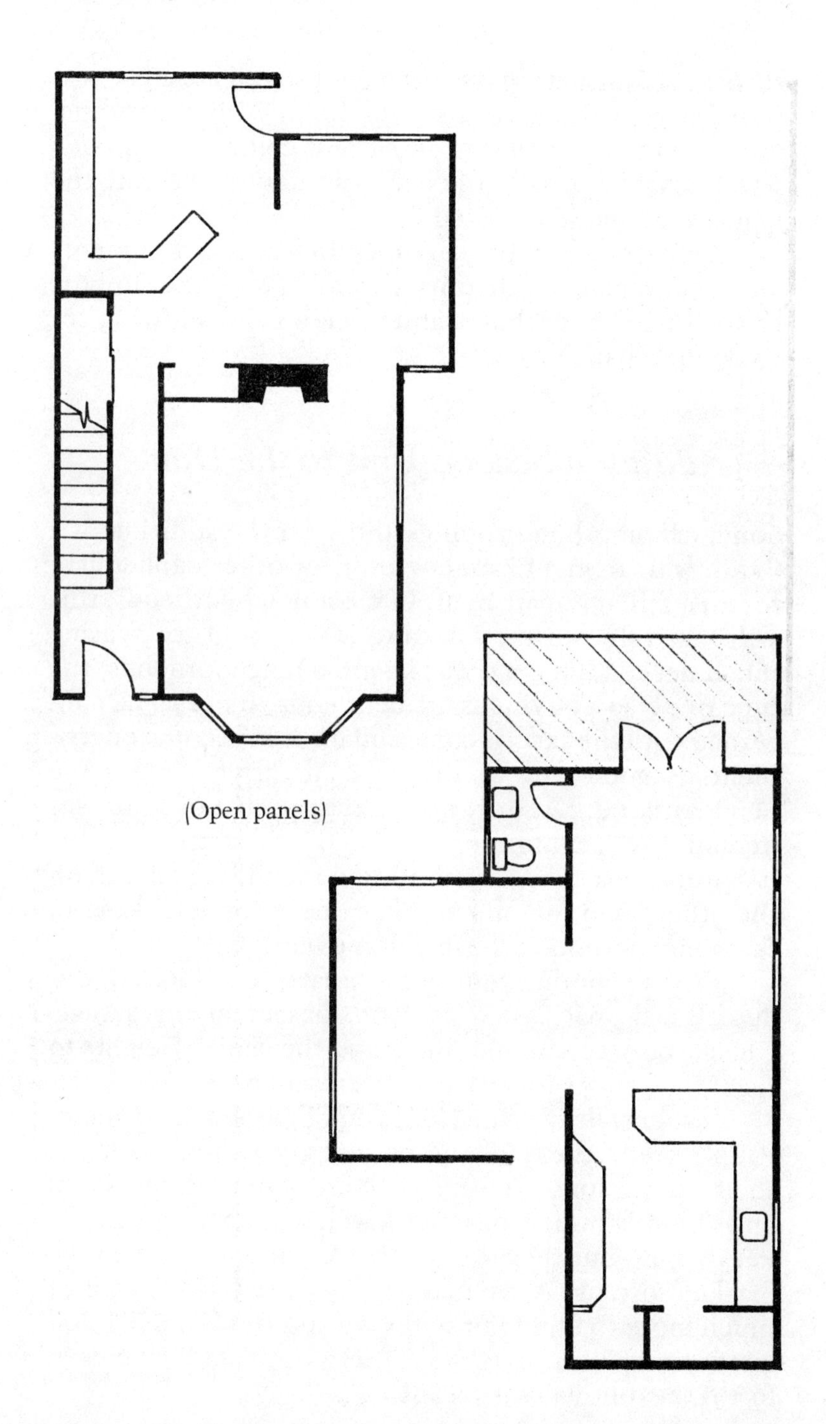
(Open panels)

turning this situation into an asset is to create a fake exposed beam ceiling, if this style fits in with your home. You will thus be creating an elegant ceiling and no one will know that one of the beams is actually bearing the load a wall once supported.

Sometimes columns or other architectural elements are used in place of the former wall. These can support the ceiling above while framing views and allowing for an open, expansive feeling.

Adding a Second Unit to the Home

Some neighborhood zonings allow for the addition of a "granny apartment," in-law unit, or other euphemism for an auxiliary apartment. In most neighborhoods, this will add value to the building in addition to creating much needed housing. But in some neighborhoods, the type of person buying is affluent enough not to be concerned with the extra income and it could become a detriment. A good rule of thumb is to drive around the neighborhood, carefully noting the number of addresses or mailboxes per building. If several have auxiliary units, it's probably a good neighborhood for adding one. If, on the other hand, no one else has one, people looking in that neighborhood probably don't want one.

When planning your in-law apartment, look for underutilized space such as attic, basement, or garage. Check the access to plumbing and the ceiling heights to see if the project is workable at a reasonable cost.

If room allows, construct a one-bedroom apartment. People prefer these to studios as it gives them room for their possessions. Too many apartments are too small and shoddily built. These work well while a housing market is tight, but they are the first to sit empty when the market softens. A well-constructed unit will not cost much more to build but will save you thousands of dollars long term in rents that otherwise would have been lost if the unit had sat vacant.

Determining Market Value with and without the Apartment

Before you start your construction project, you want to be sure it's worth the effort. Call up your local real estate agent and get some comparable sales for properties sold with second units and for ones sold as single-family homes. You may find that the unit adds no sale value to the home, just rental income. Thus you must see if the rental return justifies the cost. One real estate expert feels that if the payback period is three years or less on rental properties, it is worth doing the project (this assumes you'll own it at least three years). Otherwise, save the money and just sell the potential to the next guy. He may be looking for a home with in-law potential. It may help your building sell faster.

One of the simplest ways to determine what the apartment is worth is to calculate the income it will produce. Check the newspapers. See what the going rate is for an apartment similar to the one you propose to build. You should probably go and see these apartments, too. Either be up front about why you're looking or pretend you're a potential renter. Get a sense of the market. What is the going rate? What type of apartments are desired in your neighborhood? Check size, quality, and layout. Notice which ones rent right away and which ones languish for weeks or months on the market. Try to determine the important variables in order to plan your apartment.

Now how much will it cost to produce the apartment? If it's going to be financed, you must figure in the loan payments in your calculations. Once you've estimated the cost of the apartment to you, there are two ways to calculate its value. Note that cost and value can be very different. That has been the basis for this whole book.

The first method is the comps method talked about earlier. This is where you compare the values of buildings with accessory apartments to those without. The second is to capitalize the annual rent received. This method is useful if you intend to own the building for awhile, as it shows you the return on your investment.

To determine value by capitalizing income, you first find out what the Gross Rent Multiplier (GRM) is for your area. This is done by asking real estate agents or appraisers. This is a number that determines the value of your apartment based solely on the rent it can produce. For any given region, the GRM will be a higher number in better neighborhoods than in worse neighborhoods. Thus the same apartment will be worth more to a buyer.

An example calculation for capitalizing income is

	MONTHLY	ANNUAL
Rent from your apartment	$ 400	$4,800
Less loan payments	($ 252)	($ 3,024)
Tax deductions (depreciation, etc.)	$ 90	$ 1,080
Net income	$ 238	$ 2,856
Times Gross Rent Multiplier (7.3)	$1,737	$20,848

The value according to the capitalization-of-income system is thus the annual rent times the GRM or, in this case, $20,848. Assume that when you compared the value for houses with and without an apartment, the difference was $35,000. This means that the range of value for the apartment is $20,848 to $35,000. When calculating your costs to build, try to stay toward the low end of the range.

Even in the best neighborhoods, many homes could use an extra apartment, commonly referred to as an au pair unit.

COSTS OF BUILDING AN IN-LAW UNIT

The cost of building an in-law apartment can range from $8,000–20,000 with extreme cases being more or less. One of the main considerations is the layout of your home and the location of plumbing and other utilities. If you have to reconfigure some of the rooms in your house to make up for the space lost in the formation of the apartment, that will add to your costs. The need to install a separate entrance will add to your costs, as will having to rebuild stairs or do cosmetic work on the exterior to integrate the second entrance gracefully into your home.

Where your apartment will be located in the home affects your cost. If you need to refinish an attic, it will cost more than taking the rec room and converting it.

Obviously, the quality of the materials you choose and the quantity necessary will affect your costs. But again, you will make much of that back in having a unit that is seldom if ever vacant, and an asset at time of sale.

As with any building project, you must beware of incidentals that will add to your costs. In the matter of second units, there are some special considerations. Many communities require a separate off-street parking space for the added unit. If you don't have the room, it might get expensive to alter your floor plan to provide it. You might be able to have this restriction waived by making your unit accessible to the handicapped or restricted to the elderly.

Another cost is pleasing the neighbors. They can make your project costly with delays or bad publicity. One way to reduce this friction is to work out major problems with the neighbors ahead of time. Another way is to make sure your design fits into the neighborhood. If they are all single-family homes, yours should look like a single-family home, too. The only thing that should give away the fact that there is more than one unit is perhaps two doors and two mailboxes. For sides of the home that are not seen from the street, blending in is not as crucial.

Finally, the amount of work you do yourself will have a great bearing on the final costs of the new unit.

When designing the apartment, remember not everything needs to be house scale. A full 10′ x 12′ kitchen is way out of place. Make rooms appropriate to a small apartment. Many of the building and decorating items discussed in other chapters can be applied to in-law apartments. Also there are special magazines dedicated to apartment decorating.

Remember, although you get increased living space, if you have to give up rooms to create your second apartment, you are decreasing value on the one hand while increasing it on the other. It is the net increase that must be large enough to justify the cost.

The cost of building a separate detached structure is almost always greater than renovating within an existing shell. With new construction, you've got four exposed walls, a new foundation and a new roof to add to whatever costs the apartment interior creates.

Laws and Zoning

Before doing any of this work, check the zoning for your parcel and for your neighborhood. It will tell you if second units are allowable. If your parcel is not currently zoned for two units but many of the other ones are, you could either apply for a variance or go through a total rezoning. This will increase your property's value.

Many properties lie in areas where zoning has changed. This usually means that certain types of property would no longer be allowed although, because they already exist, they are allowed to remain. These are called nonconforming uses. In general these are less valuable because they contain a use that is out of favor with the city. This may be a commercial building in a residential zone or apartments in a single-family home zone. However, depending on how you present it, this can also be a prime selling position if you have the only apartment complex in a good single-family neighborhood.

Renovating a Home for Office Use

In many towns and cities across the country, older neighborhoods that were predominantly residential when they were built have become integrated with an expanding commercial area. Also, many streets that were once wholly residential have given way to commercial uses due to street widening or a change in zoning. Many of these homes are beautiful, large Victorian or Edwardian structures and will make charming professional offices for lawyers, doctors, counselors, real estate agents, and property managers. These offices can sometimes be rented for a premium because of their charm, but there are a few issues to consider.

BUILDING AND OCCUPANCY CODES

If the use of the home is being changed to office or commercial, a whole new, more stringent set of codes comes into play. Sprinkler systems, seismic upgrades, and the banning of certain materials are just a few of the issues in converting from a residential building code to a commercial one. Bear in mind that many of these structures would not even meet current residential codes and you will realize that the cost in creating a commercial renovation can be great.

Equally great, though, can be the rewards. You might be able to buy one of these buildings at a discount since few people want to live on a noisy street near a commercial area. You can charge more rent while you own it. It is not uncommon for commercial rents to be two, three, four, or more times what a residential rent would be. When it comes time to sell, commercial buildings in general are more valuable than residential.

WHAT COMMERCIAL USERS WANT

Commercial users want the efficiency of a modern office and the charm that your building brings. You must be able to demonstrate that your building has both.

The majority of what you will be selling is the charm. Most lawyers and doctors are bright enough to know that a modern office will be more efficient. But what they want is the uniqueness of your building. Because of this, curb appeal and the entry are both very important. This is what their clients are going to be seeing first.

ZONING

In order for your building to be used as offices, it must be legal to do so. Check to see if the zoning is for office or commercial or, if it's still a residential zone, if these commercial uses are allowed.

If not, there are two changes to the zoning you can get: a variance or a rezoning. If you can get the property rezoned, you can usually add a lot of value, even if you did nothing to the building, because commercial zonings in general are worth more to people. But you must know your local market to see if this will be so in your particular case. Rezoning a piece of property if the rezoning makes no economic sense will not raise its value. If you rezoned a piece of farmland 200 miles out of town from agricultural to commercial, its value would not change.

CHAPTER SEVENTEEN

Buying a House to Renovate

BEFORE GOING OUT TO buy a structure to renovate, you must decide what it is you want. This can be broken down into two categories. The first is how much time, effort, and challenge you want to undertake. The second is what you intend to do with the property.

The first category can be broken down as follows:

Want to add value though cosmetic renovations only

Want to add value through altering floor plan or adding needed amenities

Want to add value through change of use

The first of these, adding value through cosmetic renovations only, is the true gem when you can find it. It's the type of property all the "get rich quick through real estate" books tout. This type of building has no problems—it's just tired-looking. In reality, it does have one problem—finding it. Most sellers and agents are aware of the potential improvements new carpets, paint, and drapes can make and will be asking top dollar even for tired-looking properties if their potential can be seen.

Even if the seller doesn't see the potential, many real estate agents will and they will buy this type of property before it ever really hits the open market. This is especially true in hot real estate markets.

The second type, major alterations, is the best chance for renovation in the 1980s and 1990s. It's what we've talked about when we mention developing the renovator's eye. Most people are looking for the first type of renovatable structure, the cosmetic renovation. They've read books or attended seminars telling them how to make a fortune in "don't-wanter" properties. But few are looking for, or have developed the imagination for finding, a gold mine of a renovatable structure—the type where you create the value through your vision.

The third type, change of use, is what is often called recycling of homes. It involves looking at transitional uses and adding value through change of zoning or through maximizing to the current zoning. For example, there may be a large old home that might function better as two apartments due to the changing demographics of the area or due to affordability. It's a lot easier for two families to buy a flat each than for a single one to afford a large house. Many of these renovations have gotten a bad reputation due to shoddy development and planning. Quality jobs can be done.

The second consideration in buying to renovate can be broken down as follows:

Want to renovate and rent

Want to renovate and turn over for a quick resale

Want to renovate and speculate in an area that's on the rise

Each of these three requires a different strategy. The best renovations combine all three. For example, you can buy a house, fix it up, and rent it. Ideally, you should earn rental income while you are holding it, you should make a premium on the renovation if you decide to sell today, and third, if you hold it for awhile, you should make money on the neighborhood's appreciation.

Different Renovation Strategies

RENTAL

These homes are usually in the lower price categories. You need to find a home cheap enough so that the rent you must charge to cover your expenses and make a little profit is no more than the market will dictate for a competing apartment. Once you start getting into higher-priced rentals, you compete for people who have enough money to make a mortgage payment. Given the choice, they will probably buy, unless your property is in such a unique and desirable location that they will prefer renting to ownership.

You need to calculate a return on your investment. If you put $40,000 into a house and, after renovating it, you're only getting $50 per month positive cash flow, you probably will do better to sell it. Unless you're holding for appreciation, expecting that the neighborhood will increase in value, that $40,000 is worth more in the bank. It's fine to hold for appreciation; history has shown that properties tend to rise in value above the inflation rate. Just realize that this is not truly investing, it is speculating.

BUY AND SELL

This is the easiest to comprehend. All that is required is that you purchase the property at a low enough price so that the original cost of the house plus the cost of your renovation plus your desired profit will allow for a sales price that falls within the current market range.

Don't forget to calculate all the "soft costs" of renovation—the financing costs, title and escrow fees, permits, plans, and other expenses that are not actually part of the renovation. These costs can turn a project that looked profitable into a loser very quickly.

BUY AND HOLD

This requires some knowledge of the local real estate market and some luck. Most people are looking for this type of property. It's what people would call "investment" property. This type of property is located in an area where homes are appreciating faster than other assets and faster than the rate of inflation. The best place to find these properties is in marginal neighborhoods that border good, established ones.

Because you're earning a profit on your renovation and not necessarily on the neighborhood, if you guess right and the market value of the area happens to increase, you can make a lot of money. But whether this happens or not, you'll make money. Most other people need the area to increase to make their profit.

When looking at properties, you must make offers that allow you to turn a profit on your work—otherwise why do it? Many people buy "fixer-uppers" only to discover after the cost and effort of the renovation is through that they would have done better just to buy a home in good condition already. You don't want to pay for the right to work on a house you want to be paid for your effort. Make sure there's enough profit potential before you start.

Judging a Neighborhood

One of the keys to getting the best house for your money is the neighborhood in which it's located. We may be able to alter rooms, change the landscaping, and even scare off problem neighbors, but we can't move the property. Ten years ago, you could buy a house anywhere and it would appreciate in value. The market was hot and inflation was high. But times have changed and if you want to make money today, you've got to take the extra care to research the neighborhood and view your house with the eyes of a seller instead of a buyer. Remember, you *make* your profit on the purchase, you *realize* that profit when you sell. If you buy wrong, you're playing catch-up the whole time.

Look for a neighborhood that is changing. You can usually tell them by the exterior signs. If one house is being renovated and the one next door has a car up on blocks in the front yard, it's probably a good neighborhood for finding bargains. Some people like to use a rule of thumb that if 25 percent of the homes are renovated or in the process of renovation, it's a neighborhood to investigate. Transitional neighborhoods require a longer holding period than good established neighborhoods to get full value. The world has to realize that the neighborhood has changed. This could take two to five years. But the profits can be worth the wait. Many transitional neighborhoods have some of the nicest architecture in town and will be worth a great deal once the neighborhood has turned.

If you don't want to work in transitional neighborhoods, top quality neighborhoods are also good sources of value (relative to your expected sales price). It may cost more for a house in a top neighborhood, but the profit potential is greater. Many times people in higher income brackets want a house they can move right into. They don't want to have the hassle of improving their new home and they can pay top dollar for what they do want. Also, you'd be amazed at how little imagination people seem to have when looking at homes. They cannot visualize what could be there. You are paid a premium for that skill, and you'll be paid more for it in upper-income areas.

One warning: Beware of neighborhoods in decline. Some transitional neighborhoods are on the way down. An easy way to spot those is to look at the visible signs: Are they widening the streets? Are businesses moving into areas that were once wholly residential? Is nothing new being built or renovated?

Is there a fashionable neighborhood located nearby? It may be getting too expensive and buyers will be spilling over into your affordable neighborhood. See if much activity is going on. Check recent sales. Are prices increasing? Is the neighborhood gentrifying?

Is there a master plan for the area? If so, what type of growth is projected. Talking to a planner at the county courthouse or city hall could be one of the best uses of your time. They can tell you of major projects and plans for the area and of what type of project is likely to be approved or denied. You want to know if proposed zoning changes usually get granted or denied and if there's a strong neighborhood organization.

If you're buying a single-family home to renovate in a mixed economic area, a good strong neighborhood organization can be your best friend. They will make sure the neighborhood stays single-family and that you won't have a gas station go up right next door to your house. Also, working with the neighborhood association to improve the area will raise everyone's property values, including yours.

Talk to the building department, too. They can tell you what permits have been granted and what is in the pipeline. You may find that apartments are scheduled to go in down the block, lowering your single-family home's value.

Although you may only be in the home for a short time if at all, your prospective buyer is going to be there a long time and is concerned about many life issues. You must view your purchase through his eyes. Think about the things your prospective buyer will be looking for when he comes to see your newly remodeled home for sale. Here are some of the major items.

Are the schools nearby? This is particularly crucial if you plan on selling to a family. You want the home to be near schools but, in general, at least one block away from the actual school buildings themselves. How is the school system in the neighborhood? What percentage of students drop out? What percentage go on to college? You can find out these things from the local school board.

You want to be near convenient shopping (but again, not right across the street). Also find out the makeup of the neighborhood. Is it white-collar, blue-collar, yuppie, or an unofficial retirement community? Are there old established families or is the area generally transient? What is the proportion of renters to home owners in the area? For a home, you want the proportion of renters relatively low.

Check access to supermarkets, movie theaters, shopping centers, and the like. Is there public transportation nearby? Is there convenient freeway access?

You should also determine the location of the fire station, perhaps even where the dump is located.

Are new jobs moving into the area? Of what type are they? A booming local economy is sure to drive up values.

Does the city or regional jurisdiction have any major plans for the area? Is your street about to be widened into a freeway on-ramp or will it retain its quiet character?

Much of the information you'll need to judge a neighborhood can be gotten from local real estate agents and from the chamber of commerce. Local bank officers also are a good source of information about neighborhoods and property values, as they have to make loans on homes in those areas. The key is to gather as much relevant information as possible. Property values can change drastically from block to block just because homes may happen to be in a different zip code or because the school district boundary falls between them. You need to know the unseen borders that divide neighborhoods of value from the others. People want to live in a good neighborhood. It's up to you and your research to determine where the neighborhood boundaries lie.

Degree of Renovation

As you start your search for a renovatable structure, you must first decide the degree of renovation you are willing to attempt so you can be on the lookout for that type of property. There are basically five types of properties on the market. You will be interested in only two or three of these if you wish to make money. The five types are:

- The pride of ownership (real estate agent phrases "decorator's dream" or "wonderful family home," etc.). This is what most buyers are looking for. It is a nice, well-kept house in a good neighborhood. At worst, it may have some flaws, but nothing an average couple wouldn't be willing to fix on weekends. You don't want to buy this type of home. This is what you'll be competing with when you sell.
- The cosmetic renovation (agent phrase "needs TLC," "charming"). This is the gem we talked about earlier. If you can find one that is not overpriced, buy it. These require little effort, are perfect for the beginner, and can yield excellent results.
- The visionary renovation (agent phrases "needs TLC," "handyman's special," "diamond in the rough"). This is what we focus on. You must analyze the market to see if it's worth the effort. You may have to go through many homes, but these are out there. Some things to think about are

    Can I profitably add a bedroom or bath?
    Would a skylight help here?
    Is the attic expandable?
    What if I moved the living room to here and converted that to a bedroom . . .

- The contractor's special (agent phrases "needs TLC," "handyman's special"). Beware of major structural and systems work. You must be able to buy the property cheaply enough to make it worth your while.
- The loser (agent phrases "handyman's special," "contractor's delight," "has charm potential"). Stay away. This house is functionally obsolete—small rooms, inadequate wiring, an unrepairable foundation, etc. This should be torn down.

Finding the House

Drive through the neighborhoods in which you're interested and try to get a feel for property values. Go into as many open houses as possible. Talk to real estate agents. Look at the dumps and the renovated homes, but especially the renovated ones, as you want to get an idea of the future value your renovation will bring. A note of caution: Don't go by asking price. Find out what properties are actually selling for and how quickly they are selling. People can ask any price they want but they may not be able to get it.

Here are some of the things to be looking for as you search out your potential renovation project:

> Is the neighborhood well landscaped? Are people taking care of their front lawns or do a significant percentage contain overgrown weeds, bottles, or garbage? A lack of concern for appearances is a negative sign and you want to avoid this. Look for a neighborhood of generally well-kept lawns and freshly painted homes.
>
> Do you hear traffic noise as you walk down the streets? People generally want a quieter neighborhood. How about your particular block? Is it noisier than the rest? Is the home located near a nightclub or bar? Is it near a teen hangout?

Be aware the neighborhood character changes at different times of the day and on different days. What may seem like a quiet residential street at 11:00 A.M. may be the major thoroughfare at 5:00 P.M. when all the workers come home. Or your street may become a parking lot for the weekend flea market.

The goal is to buy the worst house on the block with the best potential for renovation. Buying the best house is always a mistake. People who can afford it will be looking in a better neighborhood and people looking in your neighborhood probably won't be able to afford it. The key is to take an okay house and turn it into a nice or even a spectacular house. The worse your house is relative to the ones around it, the more potential it has to rise in value. When it comes time to sell, know that a good house in a good neighborhood will always find a buyer.

Remember, you make the most money by bringing your home up to the average level of the neighborhood or slightly above. You're not likely to recover remodeling costs that take you too far above values in the neighborhood. There's good potential in seeking out homes with one bathroom in a two-bathroom neighborhood. Adding a fourth bedroom in a three-bedroom neighborhood makes it harder to recoup your costs.

As you start your search, you will notice that many streets have one or two homes that have become rundown from lack of proper maintenance. This may be because the owners have gotten old and no longer care for the property, or perhaps it's because of an absentee owner. Sometimes money is tight and the first thing to go is home maintenance. All these add up to potential bargains for you and a chance to increase substantially the value of that property.

Planning

The quality of homes in the neighborhood will dictate what you can do to your prospect and still turn a profit. There are three types of basic categories of houses you will be examining.

> The economy home. There is nothing particularly special about this type of house. This is the lower-priced house geared toward rental or sale in the lower price range. Many older suburban tract homes fall into this category, as do smaller bungalows and cottages in working-class communities. Economy is the key here. You will not be making this into a dream home.

The standard home. This is an older home with some charm and some very nice features that you just don't find in homes any more. However, it also has a number of functional problems in relation to today's lifestyle. Perhaps the rooms are too small or the bathroom is inadequate. The key to this type of home is to keep the best of the old and to upgrade the rest. This type of home is not neighborhood specific and could be located in any area from the best to the worst. In the better neighborhoods, this type of home should be upgraded with some modern features like gourmet kitchens. In not-so-great neighborhoods, the key is to make this a nice, comfortable, functional home.

The grand home. This home is full of beautiful architectural detailing unreproducible today. The key is to restore the classic parts and modernize the rest. Many of these homes are located in parts of town that were once grand but are now run-down. You need to be careful as to how much renovation you can do. If you find one in a good neighborhood, you've got a gem to work with.

Judging the House

The first thing to notice through the eyes of a renovator is the siting of the house on the lot. Which way is south? Which rooms will get the morning light? Which will get the afternoon sun? How is the approach to the house? Is there room for change or improvement?

How far is the house from the property lines? You want to know if there's room to spare from the minimum setbacks. Many times zoning has changed and a home now sits in a setback. You will not be allowed to expand your home in that direction without a lengthy variance procedure. It's important to know what legal limitations will affect your remodeling.

Also, is your potential purchase at risk from natural causes? Observe the lay of the land. Ask questions of the neighbors. You might find out that your potential home is under five feet of water every winter.

Although not a soils expert, take a look and see if the particular type of soil (sandy, rocky, clay, etc.) has had any effect on the house. Has the foundation cracked or settled unevenly? Pay particular attention to a house perched on a hillside. Is it sliding down the hill? If your home is on the coast, be aware of the potential hazards of wind, flooding, and landslides. Try to envision all the different weather conditions that will occur over the course of a year and how they will affect the property.

Notice the drainage. Are there signs of erosion around the foundation?

How is the landscaping? Are there mature trees or shrubs? These are valuable amenities. Many times the element that makes many new suburbs look so unattractive is the lack of mature landscaping. Many a fine old subdivision looked positively bleak when it was first built. It is the mature landscaping that adds grace and character. If you have these elements, even in an unkempt form, it is an asset.

Although this may be more applicable in rural areas, you want to make sure all utilities are connected to the house and to investigate their source. Is the water well water or from the city? Is the house on a sewage system or does it depend on a septic tank? What kind of heating and cooling system does the house have? Does it need to be replaced?

There are many books out on home inspection, and it is recommended you review one. We will only go over some of the key areas to look out for. Also, we recommend that you have a professional inspection ($200–300) to point out any potential costly defects. When it comes to renovating, this is one item that pays for itself. Find a good, appropriate inspector for your concerns. Don't hire a roofing contractor to inspect your cracking foundation.

What you are looking for in the house is its renovation potential. This is the skill for which you will be getting paid. If anything is inadequate, whether it be a small front porch or a dark kitchen, if it is easily correctable and will add considerable value to the house, it is not a problem. Problems are only items that are too costly to correct or will not provide a good return. Bear this in mind as we continue.

We talked earlier about repairs versus improvements. A repair is an item that costs you money. You get little if any return on it. Buyers expect certain items to be in good repair. An improvement, on the other hand, is an item that adds value. A house that needs much improvement but few repairs is a house worth considering.

CHECKING THE STRUCTURE

The first area to look at is the foundation and the structural system. Your whole house rests on the foundation. If it's weak, the house will be weak, and if it needs to be replaced, it can be a very costly job. A $50,000 foundation remodeling is not uncommon.

Stand back and look at the house from all angles. Is the house twisted or leaning a little? Make a note. You can use the siding of the house for clues. Sight along the horizontal lines of the siding. Does it seem to sway? Or is it holding straight? The sway could mean some serious structural problems.

Does the foundation have major cracks? Check the corners first. Look for V-shaped cracks. Those are the ones to alarm you. Remember, there is no problem that cannot be fixed. But foundation corrections can be one of the costliest items of repair and many times will not make economic sense. Get a quote on repair costs before removing contingencies.

Check for drainage. If it's the rainy season, you have no problem. You see the water. However, if it's the drier times of the year, you need to investigate further. Sniff. Does anything smell musty? Look for items, such as boxes in a basement, that rarely get moved and then move them. Do they have water stains?

Check for signs of rot and for termite infestation. This can be a costly item but usually you can get the seller to pay for it. See if there's any fungus or mold growing on the wooden members. These can all point to potential drainage and ventilation problems.

If you are looking at a stucco home, check to see if there are any large bulges in the walls. A bulge can signify a serious problem within the structure. These are the type of problems not worth tackling unless the seller is willing to discount the price of the house substantially.

Look at the attic. Is there room for expansion? What do you judge as the remodeling potential? Is it structurally able to hold another floor? How's the ceiling height? Many people ignore this potential source of increased value when selling homes. They just see it as an attic. After all, it's always been an attic.

Look for evidence of sagging floors or walls out of plumb. These may indicate costly structural problems or they may be minor. Try to determine their cause. Bring a level with you on the inspection to check.

Look at the roof. What is its condition? Look near the edges to see if there's one roof on or two. If there's only one, you can put new shingles right on top, a relatively inexpensive operation. If there are two or more, you need to do a major reroofing. This can cost several thousand dollars. You get no payback.

If the house has a tar and gravel roof, note the condition of the tar. Is it old, brownish, and dried out or dark, rich, and black. Flat roofs can last ten or more years if properly gravelled or painted. You want to know where in the life cycle this roof is, because replacing it is money out of your pocket.

CHECKING THE SYSTEMS

Electrical

While you're outside, look to see what the service is to the house. Modern homes should have a minimum of

100 amperes, although 150 to 200 amps is more adequate. Also, is the home wired for 220 voltage? You'll need it for electric stoves, dryers, or heaters. Even if the main service to your house is inadequate, it may be easy to upgrade. To find the box, follow the wires from the utility line to the house. The service box will usually be nearby. Check the main breaker to see the amperage to the home.

If you are able to, check the existing wiring. If it's aluminum, it may be a sign of inferior wiring. It's not horrible, but copper is preferred. If you notice two-pronged outlets mixed in among three-pronged outlets, check to see if the three-pronged ones are really grounded. Many times homeowners will replace the old two-prong outlets with the newer three-prongs but not upgrade the wiring behind them.

Plumbing

Now check the water system where the pipe comes into the house from the meter. Try to determine if it's galvanized steel, copper, or plastic. Scraping the pipe with a key will usually reveal what material it is. Galvanized steel is a sign of old pipes and will probably have to be replaced. If the main pipe leading into the house is copper, you've already saved some money.

Next you want to determine the pipe size. A three-quarter-inch main pipe is standard for a two-bathroom house. If you want to have three bathrooms, a one-inch main is recommended and may even be required by your building code. So before you intend to add that third bath and make your fortune, see if the infrastructure is adequate.

If your home has galvanized steel plumbing, the age of the home makes a huge difference in the expected condition of the pipes. Galvanized usually lasts about 50 years before it's so corroded it needs to be replaced. Copper is newer and is the usual replacement material for galvanized, as it is not subject to the same corrosion process. One way to check the condition of the plumbing is to check the water pressure with several faucets open. See if any of them appear starved for water. Flush the toilet and see what happens. If the pressure drops substantially, you may have a major cost in upgrading the entire plumbing system—a cost from which you will not benefit.

While you're at it, check how quickly water seems to drain. If just one or two items drain slowly, no problem. If everything drains slowly, it's worth closer inspection. You may have an inadequately sized drain for your needs, especially if you're thinking of adding a bath or upgrading the kitchen.

Heating

A house with a poor heating system may detract from its salability down the road. A new central forced-air system can run from $3000–6000 in a house. This is a sum large enough to eat into your profit.

What type of heat is there? Is it central (good) or separate wall heaters (not so good)? Check to see how many heat registers are in the home. Is there one per room or just one or two for an entire house? Check for asbestos around the heating ducts. Asbestos scares many buyers currently, and although easily encapsulated, it's an issue you will have to deal with when you sell. Perhaps you can get the seller to credit you money to have it removed.

FUNCTIONAL OBSOLESCENCE

Times change, and some items that were appropriate in the past just do not work in today's home. There was a time when indoor plumbing didn't exist. When indoor plumbing became standard, homes that relied on wells and outhouses fell in value. Many other items built into homes during the last century don't work so well today. Although some are alterable, many of these are expensive to change and might cause you to have to say no to a particular house.

Check the layout of the rooms for good circulation. Do you have to walk through one room to get to another room? Or is there a corridor? In the former case, you have fewer renovating options with that room. If the house looks appealing, draw a floor plan. See how you can alter the layout. It doesn't have to be exactly to scale, but a rough plan will let you analyze the house later for circulation problems and options you may miss on the inspection. Some circulation problems can be solved merely by adding a door or two. Your floor plan will allow you to see items that can't be detected merely by walking through the house.

Some Things to Look For

As you walk around the home, be observant. Think about what you can offer a potential buyer when you sell. Are the children's rooms separate from the adults'? Are there views out the windows? Look at the size and type of plantings in the yard. Observe the maintenance level of the neighbors' homes.

Following is a property rating checklist for inspections. You can use this checklist as a general guide to looking at a property, and you may think of things to add to the list as you use it to judge different houses.

Important Facts

List price

Is the location good?

Utility costs per year: High/Average/Low

Property taxes

Number of

- bedrooms
- bathrooms

General Layout and Amenities

Are all rooms of adequate size and shape to take on their planned use?

Does every bedroom have a closet? Are they of adequate size?

Is there a big enough area in the kitchen to eat?

Is there a true entry hall?

Is there a hall closet near the entry?

If not, is there room to build one?

Is there room for a washer/dryer?

Do you have to walk through any bedrooms to get to another room?

If so, which ones?

Is there a formal dining room?

Is there a den or family room?

Is there a direct connection from the kitchen to the dining room?

Can you see the family room from the kitchen?

Is there outdoor access near the kitchen?

Is the kitchen counter and cabinet space adequate?

Are the stairs wide enough?

Are they too steep? (Treads should be 10–12 inches, risers 6–8 inches)

Are the bedrooms separated from the public areas?

Interior Amenities

Can the master bedroom comfortably hold a double bed?

Can the living room wall accommodate a full sized sofa?

Does each bathroom have a window? Can one be cut out?

Is there an attic? Does it appear expandable?

Is there enough closet storage space?

Is there enough long-term storage space?

Is there adequate natural lighting or the potential for such?

Arc there any views?

Exterior and Landscape

Does the home fit in with the neighborhood architecture?

Does the home's size fit in with the neighborhood?

Are there mature trees on the property?

Is the lot as good or as large as others in the neighborhood?

Does the lot drain away from the house?

Is there sufficient parking?

Windows and Doors

Do the windows work?

Are there enough windows?

Do the windows or doors need replacing (for aesthetic or functional reasons)?

Are the doors wide enough?

Do windows and doors open easily or do they bind?

Structural

Foundation:

Does the foundation appear to be in good condition?

Is it damp or leaky in the basement?

Walls and floors:

Are there sagging floor joists?

Does there appear to be any decaying wood?

Is the floor springy or noisy?

Roof:

Are there one or two roofs?

Does the roof need to be replaced?

Are the gutters and downspouts corroded?

Is the ridge line sagging?

Systems and Energy Efficiency

Is the plumbing copper or galvanized?

Is the water pressure okay?

Is the electrical adequate for a modern home?

Is there 220-volt power?

Are there enough electrical outlets?

Is the wiring grounded?

What type of heating system?

Is it deteriorated?

Does the heating system extend into enough rooms?

Can rooms be individually controlled?

Is there an air conditioner?

Does the home's orientation toward the sun make energy sense?

Is the home adequately insulated?

Is the attic well ventilated?

General

Is the circulation good?

Is the house easily expandable? (Is there an unfinished attic, basement, or garage that can be converted)?

What are the three most positive features of this house?

What are the three biggest drawbacks of this house?

How can I transform each of the negative features into positive ones?

Is the house worth pursuing further?

As you go through the house, inspect the overall quality. If the house appears cheaply built, it will have less potential after you've renovated than a soundly built, although perhaps ugly or neglected, house.

Most items such as cracked plaster, peeling paint, and other cosmetic defects should encourage you. These are the very things that turn many buyers off and can give you a bargain. Smells are even better. Professional renovators love walking into a house that smells so bad it almost makes them sick. This is a sure turnoff to the average buyer and it's unlikely the owner has gotten any offers. If you can, locate the source of the odor and make sure it's a smell that can be removed. If its source is a broken sewer line, that can be a major expense. If it just means tearing out the old carpet, you're in luck.

If you're in a colder climate, insulation will be a concern of your buyer. Attic insulation is easy to see. Check the walls for insulation, too. One way to do this is by taking off the cover plates of the electrical outlets and peering into the wall with a flashlight. Make sure the house is insulated. That's an expense that will give you little return. Buyers pay for sizzle—for things they can see—not necessarily for things that make a good house.

As you walk around the interior, notice the location and size of the bathrooms. One should be near the master bedroom and they should all be large enough, or at least have room for expansion to create the kind of bath buyers want.

Look at the kitchen. Is it large enough for a modern buyer's wants? Is there a wasted room you can expand into? You want to find potential others don't see. Is the kitchen light and airy? Or at least does it have the potential to be? How about views? What does it look out onto?

Remember in your inspection to take nothing for granted. Have you visited the house in the rain or after a rain storm? Was there standing water in the basement? Check the air conditioner even if it's winter and the heating system even if it is summer. If they are turned off and you can't check, can you at least get something in writing which states the boiler or air conditioner is in good working order?

Look at the materials in the home. Are there hardwood floors in the living and dining rooms? Are they inlaid? Is there a carved wooden mantle? Many older homes have features that would cost a fortune to replace today. However, their beauty may not be so obvious. Many items are painted or covered over. As you walk around the home judging its potential, look for any gems you can clean up with just some minor work. Much of a home's potential for profit is in its uniqueness.

Look at the dark rooms to see if you can make them lighter. Look at small rooms to see if you can connect them to larger ones or find some new uses for them.

Most of all, you don't want to pay for the privilege to work. You want to be paid adequately for your time and effort. So, even if the property has much potential, if the market doesn't justify the price, walk away from the deal.

Look up at all the ceilings as you go through the rooms. Are there any water stains? Find out if the leak is active. This could be a minor leak or a potential costly repair.

Look for signs of a previous addition to the structure. Does it change the character of the home? Are there different moldings and baseboards? If this appears to be the case, gather whatever information you can and inspect the quality of the addition. Many times they are of a poorer quality than the original structure.

Many older homes have small closets. Is there room for expansion? Is it possible to convert another room into a series of closets and another bathroom? One must look at every defect and see if it can be turned around to become an asset. In many homes this is just not possible, and those homes should be avoided. They are outdated and are not for the person seeking to renovate for profit.

As a final reminder, a professional property inspection is recommended before you purchase a property. The list above outlines just some of the things to look for when judging if a structure is a prime candidate for remodeling.

Condos and Co-ops

If you're buying a condo or a co-op, you must also be concerned with the quality of the common areas and with potential noise problems. Your renovation plans may also be affected.

Common areas are the first impression your buyer has of your unit for sale. If the common areas speak poorly about the building, your buyer may be turned off before he ever steps foot into your unit. Condo and cooperative organizations have boards to handle property maintenance and upkeep but their standards may be too low and your lone vote may not change things. If, however, the common areas look good and it is only the unit which needs work, you have a potential project.

Noise is a big concern among buyers of condominiums and co-ops. Many older units (and many newer ones, too) just don't have the sound-insulating qualities desired by today's purchaser. When investigating a unit, see if you can have someone make noise in the neighboring units and test for sound radiation. If it's too loud—get out. That's a property of the building you just can't alter without a major expense.

If there's central heat, do you have your own control? Or is the heating determined centrally. Check this for noise too. Forced-air fans can be noisy as can steam radiators. Even if it is summer, you want to know if the heaters make noise.

Do the units have individual hot water heaters, or do you have to wait twenty minutes for the water to warm up after a shower? Also check the plumbing. Have someone flush the toilet, turn on the tap, etc. Do the pipes bang? Does the water sound like it's in the room with you even though you're at the other end of the unit? These types of problems are uncorrectable by you.

Also check the legal documentation. Who's responsible for a leak in the ceiling of your apartment caused by the apartment above you? You or the person above? Are you required to buy heavy carpeting and padding that would cover up the beautiful hardwood floors because of a noise restriction clause?

Finally, note that building codes are different for multiresidential construction than for single-family and also that many condo organizations have covenants and rules limiting what you can do to your unit. Perhaps the plumbing can't handle an added dishwasher or disposal or perhaps your wood windows won't be allowed because everyone else's are clad aluminum. Be aware of these issues before you write your purchase check.

Predicting Increased Value

The key in renovating for maximum profit is the art of determining where you can derive value from the house before you ever hit the first nail. This takes in a lot of factors such as

Functional obsolescence—outdated electrical systems or plumbing systems which would need a major overhaul

Style obsolescence—an old corridor kitchen rather than a modern eat-in kitchen or a master bath suite that isn't large enough by today's standards

Neighborhood—is your home the nicest in the area? Who would be looking for a home in your neighborhood?

General state of the local real estate market—how long do homes sit on the market? You need to know this in order to calculate carrying costs.

Times change and items which were once desirable no longer are. Other items have come into vogue and are given value out of proportion to their cost in the house. This can be an advantage to you if you know what buyers are going to look for as you go through a potential purchase.

In Chapter 1 we talked about comparing your home to others in the neighborhood to determine the high- and low-end values. When looking to purchase a renovatable property, you use the same basic method. The only difference is you work backwards.

Let's say you're looking at a two-bedroom, one-bath house that's for sale for $95,000 and needs a lot of work. You know that two-bedroom, one-bath homes that are in prime shape sell for about $135,000, and you estimate it will cost you about $20,000 to renovate. You want to do this investment as a quick resale and you figure it will take six months to do the renovation and probably another three until the house is sold, or nine months total. If you paid full price and you put 10 percent down, your mortgage would be $869 per month assuming a 10.5 percent interest rate and a standard 30-year loan. Multiplied by nine, this equals approximately $8000. The calculations are as follows:

Expected sales price	$135,000
Cost of renovation	$ 20,000
Carrying costs	$ 8,000
Sales costs	$ 9,500
Unforeseen contingencies	$ 4,200
Profit desired	$ 20,000
Maximum purchase price	$ 73,300

This is the maximum price you can bid and still get what you want out of the renovation.

Let's assume the seller won't budge. He says $95,000, take it or leave it. Normally you should leave. There are thousands of properties out there and many of them will meet your requirements. You just need to be patient and make a lot of offers. Many professionals go through 30, 40, 50, or more houses before they actually get one they can purchase on good terms.

But you don't want to leave yet. It is the best neighborhood in town. You have a hunch there's a way to create value even though he's asking too much for the property for what it is. So you do some research and find out that three-bedroom, two-bath homes sell for an average of $215,000. You know it's not going to cost you $90,000 to add a bedroom and bath. So you redo your calculations, figuring in the additions at $50,000.

Expected sales price	$215,000
Cost of renovation	$ 70,000
Carrying costs	$ 8,000
Sales costs	$ 15,000
Unforeseen contingencies	$ 11,700
Profit desired	$20,000
Maximum purchase price	$124,700

This falls above the seller's $95,000 requirement. So it's a win/win deal. You make even more money and he gets the price he wants.

The economics involved are more complex than this, but if you leave in that 15 percent contingency factor, you will have an accurate enough set of figures to work with for an initial offer. As you get further involved, there are other considerations to take into account (such as time value of money, taxes, etc.). See a good book on real estate investing for more information.

Investing in the Renovation Market

Most people start looking for renovation properties by looking through a multiple listing book. This is a catalog that real estate agents use to list all the properties for sale in a given market. It is a handy tool to see how much properties are selling for and to get an idea of what is on the market. Most of the properties in the book will not meet your needs or requirements. The key to becoming successful is to make sure the property has renovation potential and room for you to earn a profit for your effort.

Recently it seems properties are being sold in poor condition but at prices that reflect a mint condition property. You need to be careful. Many people who have watched late night TV real estate shows or gone to seminars on fixer-uppers will try to jump onto the renovation bandwagon for a time. These people, in their exuberance to try renovating and in their hope of making huge profits, don't always think things through and soon properties get overbid to the point where you might as well buy a new home. Keep calm and only bid on properties that offer you what you need. You will lose a few but the ones you buy will more than make up for it. If you're going to overpay, buy a house in perfect condition. At least then you won't have all the hassles involved in renovating.

Because of the increased competition in the general real estate market for fixer-upper properties, the place you should look for properties you can renovate for a profit will be out of the mainstream. Once you get out of the standard multiple listing track, you will find there are bargains out there simply because the competition is less.

FORECLOSURES AND BANK REPOSSESSIONS

One area to look at is foreclosures and REO's (real estate owned by banks). In order for lenders to make loans, they need collateral. That collateral is the property. Sometimes, for various reasons, people stop making payments to the lender and it is forced to foreclose and take back the property. You can benefit from this potential source of bargains by following the legal notices in your area and seeing what is going up for auction.

Bank REO's are properties that have already gone through auction and are now owned by the bank. The properties are usually a bit run-down, as the previous owners rarely maintained them well and the bank is not putting any money into maintenance either. This can be your opportunity to make a good purchase, as banks are not legally allowed to hold onto property for very long and will be motivated to sell to you. (You may have to work at this, though, as few banks like to admit publicly that they had to take back property because they made bad loans.)

Some banks do not sell directly to the public but work through real estate agents with whom they have established relationships with. Your job is to find out who those agents are and to develop a good relationship with them, too, so that you are the one they call first.

Many people have an image of little old ladies or families being put out on the streets by foreclosure after twenty years of home ownership because all of a sudden someone fell ill and couldn't make a payment. Although this has happened in extremely rare occasions, the typical foreclosure home has been owned for less than three years, and a substantial number of them are investment properties.

If you choose to pursue foreclosures, you can get bargain properties that usually have been neglected for awhile and need some upgrading. The seller is motivated. You also have more room to put quality into the home, as you can usually get a below-market purchase.

GOVERNMENT LOAN PROGRAMS

There are many different government loan programs that encourage the renovation of properties in neighborhoods. These range from low-interest loans to outright grants in order to facilitate the government's intentions for rehabilitating certain areas of town.

Urban homestead programs, housing recycling programs, low-interest loans, and community block grants are just a few of the many programs offered through federal, state, and local governments. All of these can provide you with inexpensive properties or fix-up monies to help you make money renovating your home or investment property. To find out more about the many programs available, contact your community's local community development office.

PROPERTY DISPOSITION PROGRAMS

VA, FHA, GSA, and IRS may sound like alphabet soup, but they can be a great source of below-market-value properties for you to buy. As with many foreclosed homes, the ones owned by these government agencies usually have suffered a lot of deferred maintenance. You can buy them, fix them up, and sell them or rent them for a profit.

VA (Veteran's Administration) and FHA (Federal Housing Administration) both make loans to buyers at extremely low down payments (2–5 percent). This causes them to make many loans to people that are not truly qualified and thus eventually face foreclosure. When the government takes back one of these homes, its goal is to sell it. All you need to do is put in a bid on one of the properties. These can be found by contacting your regional VA office, or HUD (Department of Housing and Urban Development) for the FHA foreclosures.

The IRS takes back property in its settlements for back taxes and puts this property up for sale at auction. The opening bid is usually between 50 and 75 percent of market value. Although you rarely can get in and inspect these homes, if you can pick one up for a bargain, you have a lot more leeway in what renovations you can perform.

The General Services Administration usually deals with government surplus property such as old army jeeps and cars, but occasionally sells government real estate at a bargain. Contact them to find out about their sales.

As you can see, the government is a great source of property for potential renovation. The key here is you have a seller (Uncle Sam) who is motivated to sell and you have fewer people bidding in this market than in the standard MLS (multiple listing service) market.

MOTIVATED SELLERS

This is the classic seller that every real estate investment book in the world talks about, yet you never seem to be able to find. They really do exist but perhaps in only one in a hundred homes for sale. This is a person that needs to sell for several reasons. Perhaps he needs the cash to pay a debt coming due. Perhaps he's bought a new home and can't afford to be making two mortgage payments. Maybe there's been a recent divorce. There are as many reasons as there are sellers. Your job is to be there in the right place at the right time.

Many of these people can be found through the newspapers. If you look in the classified section under "Homes for Sale" you will occasionally find ads with headings like "low down payment," "seller must move," "needs some work." All these headings are clues that the house has sat on the market or that the seller will deal in order to dispose of her property.

PROBATE

When someone dies and does not leave a will, it is up to the probate court to liquidate and distribute the proceeds. Many times probate homes will be appraised at a very conservative market value due to their apparent condition. These homes tend to be very tired looking. Usually the previous resident had lived in the home for years and did not maintain it very well toward the end. So, depending on the home's exposure to the marketplace, which is not always the best, and the nature of the local real estate market, a potential bargain can come up for confirmation.

THE REHABILITATION INVESTMENT TAX CREDIT

One of the few real estate investment benefits not gutted by the Tax Reform Act of 1986 was the special tax credits for rehabilitating historic properties. A tax credit is different from a tax deduction in that a credit is taken dollar for dollar off your tax liability, not your income. At a 33 percent tax bracket, a dollar of credit is worth $3 of deductions. So this is a powerful money saver. The credit is really a two-tier credit:

A 20 percent tax credit on costs incurred in substantially rehabilitating a building that qualifies as a certified historic structure.

A 10 percent tax credit on costs incurred in rehabilitating a building that was placed in service before 1936.

Residential property may only qualify for the 10 percent credit, not the 20 percent.

Many properties have been rehabilitated since the credit was established in 1980. Most of these buildings were done by partnerships or syndicators. They had to be of a substantial size in order for these people to make money. What is left are many smaller properties, which the individual investor can take advantage of to earn money. By renovating historic properties, you not only make money on the improvements while helping to preserve the nation's historic stock of buildings, you get a partner in the U.S. government, which allows you to deduct part of the cost off your income tax.

Getting Started in Buying for Renovation

Remember to think before you act and to give yourself all the advantages possible. Here are several ways to ensure your success.

Find a bargain location. This is an area where your house will increase in value substantially just because of where it is. Look for those borderline areas near good neighborhoods.

Maintain a positive cash flow. This applies especially if you're just beginning. You may want to sell right away, and you probably will make more money in the expensive parts of town, but if you have a house that would carry itself rented out, you never have to worry about downside risk, as you always have that option to fall back on. Those homes are usually found only in the average to less expensive parts of town.

Target your market. If your home has the expansive appeal that will shine for a move-up buyer, that's who you should target. If it's a beach house and it appeals to a certain clientele, target them. Perhaps location will dictate your market. If you are near a college, military installation, or a large factory complex, circumstances will heavily favor rental housing. Other areas will attract different users. Be alert.

Plan and stay on top of costs. This is the easiest place to lose your profit. Setting up a good planning and accounting system will keep you on budget.

Know the market. Before you buy, know if you are getting a good deal. Don't just go by what the real estate agent tells you. You're the one who's stuck with the property if you made a mistake. The agent has already gotten her commission. A good agent will try to serve your best interests but her interests may get in the way. No matter how good your agent or your working relationship, make sure you feel comfortable before you buy.

CHAPTER EIGHTEEN

Renovating for Rental Use

INCOME PROPERTY HAS A nice ring to it. You have tenants paying off your mortgage while the property appreciates. Who could ask for more? There are some differences in renovating rental properties versus those for home owners. For one, renters will put up with more—they're not paying as much and don't have as big a stake in the property—so your renovations don't have to be as fancy or expensive. On the other hand, the chance of overimproving is greater. There's only so high a rent people will pay before they either move to another apartment or buy a place of their own.

If you are buying a home to renovate as a rental property, you will find that the neighborhoods you can look in are limited. Most single-family areas of America have what might be referred to as a homeowner's premium attached to their value. This premium is the difference between what the house would be worth judged strictly as an investment versus as an intensely desired commodity (a personal residence). The more desirable the neighborhood, the higher this premium. Thus, you might find that a $75,000 home in a lower cost portion of town rents for $800, while the same home in the best parts of town rents for $1600. In the first case, you get a positive cash flow. In the second, the longer you rent it, the more money you lose per month.

You will find that although prices vary tremendously from neighborhood to neighborhood, rents don't vary nearly as much. Thus, you can buy in a decent area and figure you'll get a rent that's not too much lower than the best parts of town.

When looking at lower priced areas, you still want to be in good neighborhoods. After all, tenants are people too and they want to live in the best neighborhood they can. So buy in the best affordable neighborhood. Also determine who you will be renting to—is it families, working singles, or college students?

When researching neighborhoods, check out the schools, parks, and everything else you researched to buy a home. Realize your standards will have to be a bit lower, but they should still bc good. Most landlords never consider this and so have trouble renting their renovated properties.

Do You Want to Be a Landlord?

A key question you must ask yourself before you embark on a program of rental property rehabilitation and ownership is, do you want the hassle of being a property owner? Unlike stocks and bonds, when you invest in real estate, there's a real property that must be maintained and real tenants that must be serviced. It might mean fixing leaky sinks on weekends instead of playing golf, but it also might bring you more money than you're earning on your present job. These are factors that must be considered.

THE NONINCOME APPROACH (PROPERTIES OF TWO TO FOUR UNITS)

Renovating smaller rental properties is similar to renovating a home except you can no longer go top of the line. The people that will buy this type of property from you will usually not be living in it, so they don't want to pay too much. However, the price you get on these properties is similar to a home in that it's not based so much on income as on the physical characteristics of the property such as square footage and number of baths and bedrooms.

In some areas, such as San Francisco, it is common for one of the units to be occupied by an owner. In such a case, it is recommended that one unit be done up as if it were a single-family home in order to appeal to an owner occupant and to open up buyers' minds to the possibilities of the property.

RENOVATING RENTAL HOMES

The exception to the above is renovating a home for rent. Usually homes that will pay for themselves as rentals are not located in the best parts of town. Thus, the amount of money you spend renovating them should not be great. But the difference between renovating a house for rent and renovating a small apartment building is that when it comes time to sell the house, you will probably sell it to a homeowner. Thus, your renovation is going to have to straddle the fine line between rental quality and the quality you will need to appeal to someone who is investing a sizable sum of their money to buy your house and live in it.

THE INCOME APPROACH (PROPERTIES OF FIVE OR MORE UNITS)

Since the value of larger rental properties is usually closely related to the income they generate, your improvements are only important in relation to generating more income and therefore a higher price. But it is not always necessary to improve the property physically to raise income and, conversely, renovating does not guarantee an increase in income if your rents are already above market value.

Many renovators have jumped from doing houses and small rental properties to remodeling larger income properties, only to get burned as they overrenovated or put the money into the wrong areas. The key is to find the market level first. Many renovators have attributed their financial success to their renovation work, when it was actually just that the rents on the building they bought were below market. Find out how much rents can be raised before renovation. Then determine if the renovation will increase rents substantially or not.

In smaller properties, you can get away with overimproving a little bit because many of the buyers of these properties will be owner occupants. However, in the larger buildings, the income and expense statement is really the determining factor of a building's value.

Many of the areas that appeal to home buyers appeal to renters, too. Nice kitchens and baths, lots of closet space, a feeling of cleanliness, light, and peacefulness are all qualities for which renters will pay. The problem is you can only get so much. If you put a $30,000 kitchen in an upscale home, you'll probably get back your investment. Do the same in an apartment and you might get $50 more per month. At that rate, it will take you 50 years to get your money back.

In order to attract quality, high-paying tenants, the renovations don't necessarily have to happen within the confines of each apartment. Typically, much higher returns can be gotten by renovating the exterior and common interior areas of the building such as the lobby and hallways. As with the entry in the home, by making a good impression in the building's lobby or public areas, you will be giving the tenant a favorable impression from the start.

When renovating rental properties, you have to keep two different clientele in mind—those who will be living there, and those who will eventually be buying the property from you. Usually they have similar needs. For example, neither one likes to see deferred maintenance. If

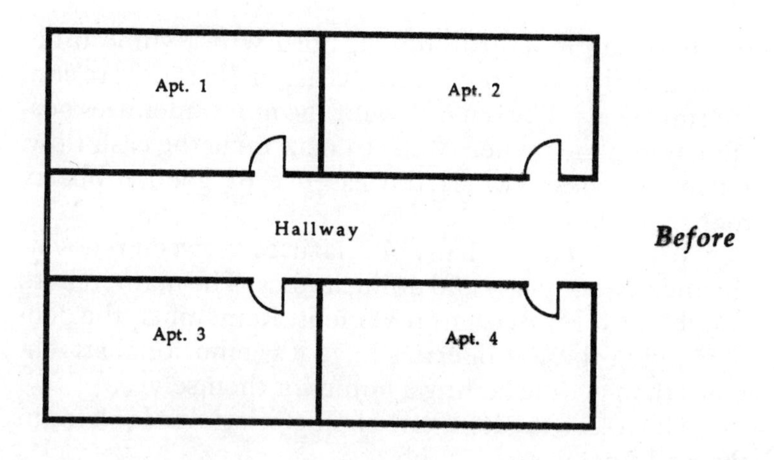

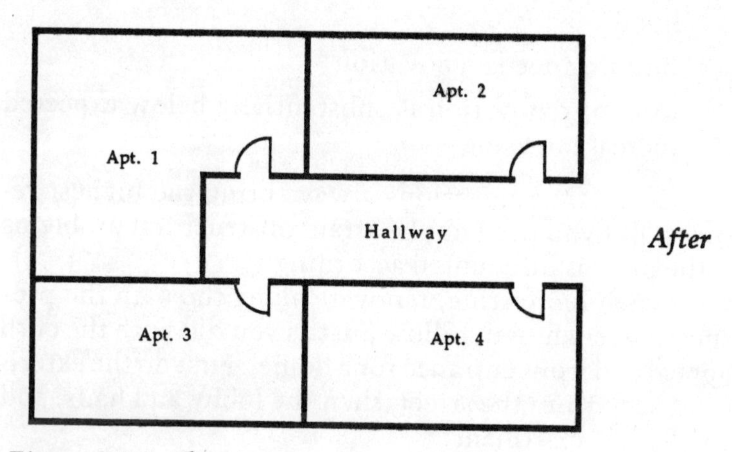

Figure 18-1 *Eliminating excess hallway*

the building looks run-down, both will assume other problems that may not exist. Occasionally there are conflicting needs. The tenants want the most amenities possible while the owners want to maximize the cash flow. Balancing these two is the essence of good property management.

You will notice many similarities between renovating income property and doing homes. The main item to watch out for is overimprovement. Remember, the people buying these properties have less emotional attachment than people buying a home for themselves.

The following items are characteristics to look for in the buildings.

Rents are below market

Building is the worst building in a good neighborhood

Building needs renovation

Cost of renovation is substantially below expected increase in value

Cosmetic renovations always bring the highest returns. But you need not be afraid of structural problems if the price is discounted accordingly.

When renovating, renovate along the path the prospective tenant will follow (just as you did with the curb appeal and front entrance for a home). First do the exterior as seen from the street, then the lobby and halls, and finally the apartment.

Increasing the Value of Rental Properties through Renovation

Since most rental properties' value is based on income, nonrentable areas such as hallways are wasted if they exist in excess of what is necessary. Figure 18-1 shows an example of converting excess hall into rentable property.

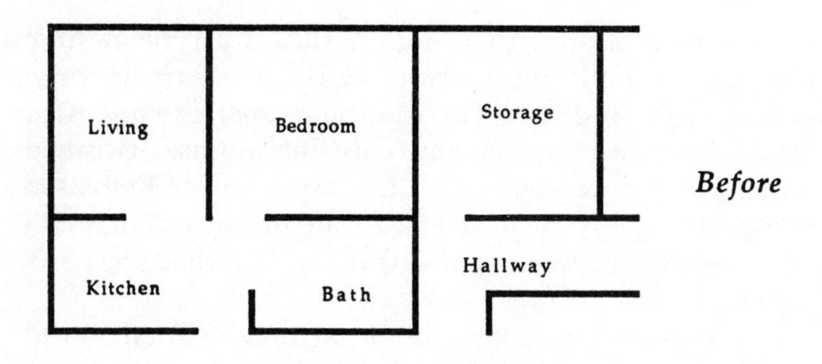

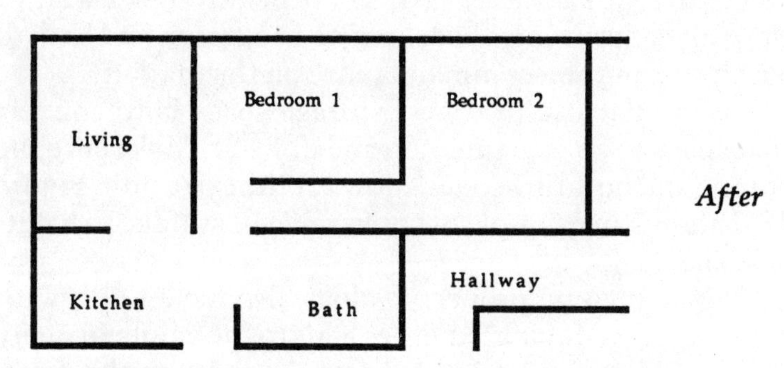

Figure 18-2 *Conversion of storage to habitable space*

The example in the figure shows a typical small apartment building hallway with two one-bedroom apartments and two two-bedroom apartments. After conversion, we now have two one-bedrooms, a two-bedroom, and a three-bedroom apartment. In San Francisco, that could easily mean an extra $300 per month or $3600 per year. With a typical multiplier of ten, that's $36,000 of value.

Another renovation potential in apartment buildings is storage rooms. Most income properties do need storage space, but many have too much of it. Many times this storage space is located adjacent to or below habitable space. It's an easy task to break through a wall or floor and add an extra bedroom or a bedroom and bath to a unit. It can then command more on the market.

A similar use of excess storage space is to convert that space to an apartment in and of itself. Make sure the zoning and building codes allow for the extra unit. Figure 18-2 shows an example of conversion of storage to habitable space.

Since income property values also have to do with net income, reducing expenses adds to the value. In many older buildings, the heating costs can run into the many hundreds or low thousands of dollars per month. Installing insulation and making the building more energy efficient will have a better payback here than in a home, as it shows on the bottom line, a key element for income property buyers.

Another way to increase value is to renovate to the type of apartment most in demand. If your building consists of three-bedroom, two-bath apartments that rent for $900, and you know that one-bedroom, one-bath apartments rent for $500, converting each three-bedroom into two one-bedroom apartments might make sense in terms of the added cash flow.

Sometimes you find that by stealing a room from a neighboring apartment, you will be able to upgrade a premium apartment. Suppose you have two neighboring apartments. One has a view, one doesn't. Perhaps the one that doesn't is larger. By stealing a room and making it part of the view apartment, you can get higher rents overall.

In order to restrain those who might slit their own throats in the effort to maximize rentable square footage, it must be added that certain intangibles such as aesthetics play a large part in the amount of rent you can command for your units. You want to make sure any renovation you do to maximize use of square footage does not have a negative impact on the quality of your building and therefore your ability to charge good rents and receive top dollar at sale.

Tax Benefits

There are many tax benefits to owning income property, from an accessory apartment in your home to a large multiple-unit complex. These include everything from depreciation deductions to expense write-offs. Please consult a text on this for more information. These benefits should be factored into your renovation cost. If you create an apartment in your home or significantly improve a property, some of this will be underwritten by the U.S. government.

Preparing Units for Rental

As you prepare your units, remember you will be appealing primarily to the senses of sight and smell. Make sure everything is clean and in its place. You want to be able to get a good rent and the best way to do that is to have the most desirable apartment around.

You need to do a good basic cleaning. But remember, you will not be living here and chances are, no matter how good a cleaning you do, the tenant will do his own once he moves in. So don't kill yourself over it. Make the apartment smell good. Go over the woodwork with a lemon-scented cleaner, allow the odor of fresh paint to linger, and put a vase of fresh-cut flowers on a counter to add a pleasing scent.

Wallpapering one prominent wall will help add a splash of color to what otherwise might be a drab white apartment.

When painting your apartments, stay neutral. As with home buyers, you want to appeal to the largest audience possible.

Use mirrors, moldings, optical tricks to shorten halls or increase perceived room size, and all the other renovation techniques that you would use on a home.

If you have many units, have one decorated by an interior designer. In order not to waste this potential source of income, provide this furnished unit to the manager. If your manager is a slob, get another manager. If you don't have enough units to hold one empty or have a manager, make arrangements with the tenant in your building with the best-decorated apartment to be allowed to show her apartment as part of your tour with prospective tenants. It will act as a furnished model and you will rent your units more easily.

Repairs and Maintenance

Maintenance is more of an issue in apartment ownership than in preparing a home for sale. You must make sure you pay for durable, cleanable products, even if it costs more. In the long run, this will save you a great deal of money.

Carpets should be steam cleaned before showing. Many times this will update carpets and make them appear almost new again.

Costs are crucial to effective apartment management. Replacing one countertop may not cost too much, but replacing 32 of them adds up quickly.

Burned formica cannot be repaired but that doesn't mean you need to replace the whole counter. You might try cutting out the burned section and replacing it with either a butcher block cutting board or a few pretty tiles to act as a hot plate. Either one will look so good, your tenants will never know they were placed there to cover up a mistake.

If your hollow-core doors are damaged, you can patch the holes and paint. This only works for small holes. If there is a foot-sized hole in the middle of the door where your tenant kicked it, you can cover this up. Cut out a diamond-shaped piece of plywood and fasten it decoratively to the door, covering the hole in the process. You may have to do this to some perfectly fine doors too so that it looks planned rather than as a cheap repair.

Put bright shelving paper in the kitchen cabinets to make them appear new.

If your window sills are constantly deteriorating, try tiling them to make them more resistant to water.

Make sure you check areas that come into contact with water each time a tenant vacates. This includes the kitchen and bath sinks, the tub/shower, and the toilet. It's a good idea to put pressure on the toilet and see if it moves. If it does, reset it with a new wax ring and bolt it again to the floor. This $2 operation will save you hundreds should water leak out and decay the floor.

Tubs should have the caulking checked and should be recaulked if necessary.

Probably the best way to keep repairs to a minimum is to give the tenant incentive to keep the property in good shape. Offer tenants an incentive for keeping the place in top repair, perhaps a rebate if no repairs have been necessary and if your inspection shows no deferred maintenance. You can also give them a gift of a do-it-yourself book on home repairs.

Another way to keep maintenance costs down is to send a handyman out to fix any problems twice a year. That way items can be caught before they become a major problem. The cost of this may end up being less than a large repair later.

Be aware, especially with rental property, that the point of diminishing returns for the work you do happens sooner than with owner-occupied buildings. Don't go overboard attempting to fix every little item. The return won't come back to you and you'll soon burn out.

The best way to have low maintenance costs is to get good tenants. Many property owners slit their own throats in this respect. They keep trying to get top dollar for their apartments, asking above-market rents. Thus, the only type of tenant they get is the one that no one else wanted. This is usually a sloppy tenant, if not a deadbeat. By the time the owner calculates in his maintenance costs, vacancy or collection losses, and headache costs, he's made a lot less money than if he had lower rents.

Remember, it's people and not the property that cause problems.

Selecting Tenants

This is not a book on property management. For that there are many good texts. However, some basics will now be outlined that should help you increase your return on the buildings you renovate and rent.

FINDING NEW TENANTS

The first step in getting quality tenants is to make sure you have the type of building that will attract them. You might try all the advertising in the world, but if you don't have a desirable apartment, the best tenants will go somewhere else.

A desirable property starts with being in a desirable location. Ghetto locations will not attract the college professors and professionals you may want as tenants. As with a home, location is everything.

A desirable rental property, like a desirable home, must have good curb appeal. You can have the nicest unit in town, but if people keep driving by based on the exterior appearance of your building, they'll never know. Remember, even tenants like their home to appear good. It will be what their friends and family see and they want their home to project a good image of themselves.

Obviously, the interior must also show well. Use the methods outlined in this book to improve the apartment. Examine competing apartments carefully and notice which ones rent quickly. You may soon find that certain items are more or less important in your particular housing market. In some areas, a garbage disposal is a must. In others, it's an air conditioner. You must learn your market well.

GETTING THE WORD OUT

Your nicely renovated building is a product and like any other product must be advertised effectively to sell. You need to let as many people as possible know what you have available. There are many available media.

Newspaper classified advertising

Community bulletin boards

Signs

Rental guides

Real estate agents

Other

There is an infinite variety of places and ways to advertise. The key is to target your ad toward the type of tenant you want and can realistically expect to reside in your building.

You can also offer finder's fees and other incentive programs. Offering other tenants a new microwave or VCR for a successful referral is cheap compared to having a vacant apartment. Perhaps the best finder's fee is cash. If your apartment building has a bulletin board, leave a note up offering money off the rent to anyone that brings in a qualified tenant.

GETTING GOOD TENANTS

No one wants damaged apartments, high vacancy rates, and nonpaying tenants. Yet that is what many property owners get because they are not careful about screening prospective tenants. You will have one advantage. By having a physically desirable structure, you will get the cream of the crop of tenants and can choose ones who will aid you in your goals.

There is a method to getting quality tenants. It relies on a number of factors, including the following:

Have a nice unit to show

Show the unit in its best light

Ask a reasonable rent

Prequalify the tenants

Always have prospective tenants complete an application

Read the application

Check references carefully

Remember, selecting tenants is like buying properties, you may have to go through several before you find one that fits your needs. Do not be afraid to reject tenants that don't meet your requirements. But keep the application on file. Some rejected tenants will try to get back at you by calling up a government agency and claiming discrimination. If you have the application on file, you can defend your rejection on its true grounds. Without it, how are you going to dispute their case? A little caution here may save you a lot of headaches down the road.

As you show tenants your building, make a sales pitch, just as you would do to a buyer or an appraiser. But be realistic. If you hide anything, you may have a legal action on your hands or, at the minimum, a vacancy soon after the tenant discovers the offending item. Trust your instincts.

Protecting Yourself

It's a fact of life that in the property rental business, the tenant has the upper hand. She can walk out on you, stop paying rent, damage the building, or a number of other things that can cost you significant sums of money and can quickly turn any cash flow negative. The best way to protect yourself is to check tenant references carefully and to have a well written lease. Do not be content to pull a standard form from a book. Have an attorney draft a quality lease. The cost will be minimal compared to any action you might have to take should a tenant up and move out.

CHAPTER NINETEEN

Decorating for Maximum Profit

ALTHOUGH THE STRUCTURE PLAYS a major role in the look, feel, and sense of a home, furnishings and decorations can go a long way in covering up minor faults and accentuating positive aspects of a home. Builders and developers consistently use furnished models to sell homes and lease space. They learned long ago that the average buyer doesn't have the imagination to visualize all a room can be. So they will spend thousands of dollars on decorating in order to sell their projects. In decorating your home for sale, you need not spend very much. But a little imagination will go a long way.

When decorating for sale, you must imagine your home as a stage set—a place where a drama of life unfolds. You want to create an image, an impression of the lifestyle the buyer wants to live. You can do this through the use of color, the arrangement of your furniture, through small accessories, and by stimulating the buyer's senses.

One key to making a better impression is to be consistent. You want your home to have a definite character, so the buyers can get a good overall picture of your home. Switching from art deco to country kitchen to modern as a buyer goes from room to room makes the buyer feel like he's in a furniture showroom, not his future home.

You need to be careful how you furnish. You want to speak to the lifestyle the buyer feels at home with or wants. If your home is furnished with old Salvation Army specials, you will discourage most upscale buyers looking to improve their image. Some will be able to see through to the potential but many will not.

To get an idea what to do, look around. Take your cues from model home developments and from home and interior design magazines. These are ideals toward which many Americans are striving. Notice how rooms in the magazine photos are arranged, with a book here, flowers there, some elegant lighting in the corner. This is a model for you to emulate in your home. If your mind draws a blank, hire a designer for an hour to help you. The rest of this chapter offers some design tricks used by the pros.

Using Color as an Accent

If you walk into a white room with a white couch on a white rug and there's a cobalt blue pillow in the corner, that pillow will attract your eye. You can use this technique to your advantage. Do you want to highlight the mantelpiece? Put some bright red tulips on it. The new window seat? Put colored seat cushions down. You can direct your buyers' eyes to the best features and they may not even see potential faults.

Color can be a great tool, but don't go overboard. A room full of many different brightly-colored objects becomes a blur to the eye, if not a distraction. You can use color selectively to accent an area, to draw the buyer's eyes to one item at a time.

Using Light as an Accent

Instead of focusing with color, do so with light. If you have a spotlight shining on an object, the buyer's focus will go there. Also, darker areas of a room seem to get less attention. Highlight your features with light.

Controlling Space Perceptions

Lack of adequate space for possessions is the constant complaint of homeowners, yet some homes seem always to have enough. The key is to use the space you have to create the feeling of spaciousness whether you have a lot or not. This can be done with color, proportion, and effective use of space.

Lighter colors recede while strong, dark colors seem to be closer. Patterns also have an effect on our perception of space. A lighter room will seem larger, as will a plain one. To make a room seem smaller, create a continuous band, such as a picture molding, around the room or paint it darker.

If you have a lot of large objects in a room it will appear smaller. The same is true in reverse. In fact, in many model homes in new developments, builders use furniture that is slightly smaller than average, to make the room appear larger than it really is. You don't have to go to this extreme, but putting a king-sized bed in a 9 x 10 room will make it seem cramped.

Also, the consistency of the furnishings will affect a buyer's eye. If all your furnishings are of a similar height, the room will appear larger. If they are a hodgepodge collection of tall and short, large and small, the room will appear more cluttered and smaller. You can use this concept to create a focal point in the room—having one tall thin object among a room full of low horizontal furnishings.

Consistency can be used to enhance space in other facets of the home, too. Separate areas seem to blend into one another when kept the same color. A good way to give all the rooms in your home a feeling of harmony is to paint them the same color. The consistency will register at a subconscious level.

Similar window treatments, hardware, carpeting, light fixtures, and more all lay a subtle consistency to the home and make it feel larger. Many a large home has seemed small because of inconsistent finishes and small rooms. If the home is perceived as larger than it is, people will pay more.

Effective use of space also enhances the apparent size of a home and, consequently, the price buyers will pay. Arranging furniture in rooms to create different zones will enhance the usefulness of the room and raise its appeal.

A common example of this is the living room/dining room of many homes. Many homes built in the post-World War II era do not have truly separate living and dining rooms. It is through the way the furniture is arranged that we differentiate the rooms. You can use this technique to create a study out of a nook or to make the kitchen double as a home office.

You can make better use of little nooks and crannies in your home, freeing up valuable space in the main rooms. Creating a bookshelf under the stairs frees up wall space in the dining room. Organizing your closets frees up more area for storage. The list is endless. Look at your home creatively.

As has been pointed out several times in this book, mirrors are great space enhancers. You can make a small room appear bigger through mirroring a wall. Mirrors are also good for psychologically evening out unusually shaped rooms. A long, narrow room can appear more square by mirroring the long wall, thus making the room more marketable to a buyer.

Hanging objects all the way up a wall will emphasize the ceiling height of a room, while a horizontal strip, such as a picture molding, will help lower the effective ceiling height.

Paint

Paint need not mean plain white walls. Paint can play with the senses, creating a warm, cozy space or a cold, hard room. Paint can be used to emphasize the best parts of a room or to minimize a room's blemishes. Painting can be used to connect rooms visually or to separate them. It can make a wall flat or appear to have texture and depth.

Most of us have painted our walls and ceilings at least once, usually a single color of flat or semi-gloss. Recently, home painting has undergone a renaissance, with books appearing on the many different techniques that can be used to create a variety of effects. Sponging, dragging, stippling, and stenciling can all create illusions in what might have ordinarily been a routine room.

Beware of the darkness of the tones you use. Light, color paint schemes brighten up the home and make it a more inviting place to be. It also makes the home look larger.

If you have a Spanish-style home, you can get away with some darker, earthy tones. But keep the overall feel light and upbeat.

Consistency of color helps the house flow from room to room.

Depth Perception

If your home has low ceilings, it can be made to seem more spacious with the emphasis of vertical lines. This can be done with vertical wood strips or wallpaper with vertical lines.

The same idea works in visually widening narrow rooms. Use horizontal lines on molding or wallpaper.

You can make a home seem larger by increasing the eye's processional effect as it journeys through the room. Creating framed views from room to room will make the whole house appear larger. Also, using mirrors will create a depth to the room that a flat wall cannot.

Traffic Flow

Part of making a room feel spacious is to have enough room between the furniture for people to walk around.

Many people will pick up all the clutter and leave too many furnishings in the room, just because that's what they're used to. However, if your buyers have to walk through the rooms single file in order to avoid your furniture, they are going to feel cramped and they're going to have a hard time believing your home is the spacious one they want.

It may just mean the rearrangement of your furniture. You might like the couch in the middle of the room because you can see the TV better from there. But you should move it so your rooms appear larger. Pay particular attention to exit and entryways and make sure nothing is intruding upon them. You might want to also have doors open already, and open all the way. There's nothing worse than a buyer opening a door too far and it bumping into one of your grandmother's heirlooms. You're upset and they don't want to buy the house.

You can focus attention through formal design elements like symmetry. If you have a particular direction you would like the eye to travel, flanking that area symmetrically on both sides will pull the buyer's view there. On the other hand, an informal grouping will tend to diffuse the focus.

Furniture Groupings

To make a room stand out or appear to be more than it is, one of the easiest ways is to group the furniture to allow for several functions. For example, in a family room, perhaps a few chairs are grouped in one section as a conversation area, or maybe a little workstation is set up in the corner. Many a master bedroom just has a single desk and chair in a bay window, giving it the impression of a separate mini-room.

Ask yourself what makes a room inviting. Whether it be a game of chess set up in the family room or perhaps a guitar leaning against a corner of a room, you want to convey a lifestyle that the buyer either feels comfortable with or wants. People aren't just purchasing a home, but a lifestyle. It is your opportunity to give them what they seek in a physical form. As you set up the rooms in your house before a showing, think of it as setting a stage. You're going to convey a way of life without having to spell it out.

Rooms should be furnished sparsely. This makes the room appear larger. Clutter will make a space seem smaller.

Big paintings can compensate for a lack of architectural detail. They will draw the interest of the eye.

Do not get mentally caught up in room names. Just because something is labeled "hall" doesn't mean it can't be an art gallery. Just because another room is labeled "living room" on your building plans doesn't mean the furniture can't be rearranged to create both a living room and a dining room in that space.

Compose "tablescapes" on your horizontal surfaces. A barren tabletop is unappealing. Bring life to it. Books, flowers, or stationery will add interest to featureless surfaces. As you place items on your tables or shelves, keep in mind scale and proportion and compose the arrangements to feel harmonious and ordered.

Plants can be used as furniture, screens, or decorating devices. Scale and proportion are key in the use of plants for design purposes. A single large plant can help soften a harsh room. Many small plants help add cheer to a greenhouse window in the kitchen. Big plants can look especially elegant with quality background lighting on them. Remember that plants are living things and require different amounts of light. You should know fairly soon if the spot you chose is appropriate for your plant or not.

Use items that suggest the specific use of the room. If your house is the fifth someone has seen that day, they may need visual clues about what is the living room and what is the dining room. Give them a feeling that the house has many rooms with particular meaning, and that you as a seller have found the perfect use for each room. Specific furniture and decorating suggestions follow.

ENTRY

Remember, this is the first part of the house that potential buyers will see. Plan it accordingly. There should be a bench or chair and a table large enough for parcels, letters, or magazines if room allows. Place some fancy candlesticks with candles on the table and perhaps a potted plant. Place a nice print or painting on the wall. If you have a lot of light, large palms or other plants will cheer up the area. Be sure to have an umbrella stand in the rainy season.

BEDROOMS

The bed is the dominant piece of furniture in the bedroom and thus should be given special attention. Buy new attractive sheets or linens to give your bed the look of the department store advertisements in the Sunday paper. If you have an expensive comforter or bedspread, take it to the cleaners to eliminate odors and to give it a new look.

If storage is a problem in your bedroom, you could create a platform bed and store the extra items underneath. There are also many premade beds like this on the market. Spend a little, sell your house more quickly, and take the bed with you to your next home. You'll gain a nicer bed and a quicker sale.

Some other items that make a bedroom more appealing and help a buyer visualize her place in the room are:

Breakfast-in-bed service. Place a tray with folded linens and a single rose on the bed. This helps add a little interest.

A telephone in the master bedroom, set up near a comfortable chair or some pillows signifies a relaxed place to chat.

Stationery, perfume bottles, and other items on the dresser will keep the room from looking like an empty motel.

Lots of pillows on the bed.

A pair of slippers on the floor near the bed.

Some interesting books by the headboard or bed nightstand.

Remove anything that might offend or is of too personal a nature. Religious and political items especially fit into this category.

BATHROOM

Flowers and plants help place a nice scent in the bathroom. A copy of *Metropolitan Home* or some similar magazine denoting an upscale lifestyle should be in view. A plush towel folded and placed on the edge of the bathtub or graciously near the sink softens the room and implies use.

Place most toiletries and personal items out of view, although a cologne or perfume bottle conspicuously placed helps the buyer imagine herself in the room. A telephone on the vanity will get interesting reactions. Conch shells or plants are acceptable bathroom ornaments.

KITCHEN

Place an open cookbook on the counter. Place a container with wooden spoons and other traditional gourmet tools on the counter. Flowers on the counter add cheer and color.

Brightly-colored dish towels add cheer. Some neatly organized ceramic or glass containers with coffee, flour, and rice look nice. A bottle of wine with some glasses or a nice tea service are subtle suggestions to the buyer's desired lifestyle.

DINING ROOM

A vase full of flowers on the mantelpiece or on a hutch will give cheer to the room, as will a bowl of fresh fruit in the dining area or kitchen. Use draperies and other window coverings to soften and add elegance to the room.

Set the table, either formally or for an informal brunch, depending on the time of day you plan on showing the home. Candlesticks in the evening are almost required and a vase of fresh-cut flowers is usually well received.

Keep a consistent look, whether it be country French, modern, or some other style.

LIVING ROOM

Set up a partially completed chess game. It may sound corny, but it gives the room definition. Place some art books on the coffee table. Open one. A grand piano or some fine antiques in the room will help play to the buyer's desired lifestyle.

The living room is a good area for showcasing some art or collectibles. Bookshelves can easily become display shelves or a mantel can hold some treasure. Arrange books neatly in the shelves and try to avoid paperbacks.

It's better if everything does not match perfectly, although a general theme or style is desired. You want to project a warm yet elegant room. A sterile room is never inviting.

FAMILY ROOM

Set up a board game such as Monopoly to convey informality. Decorate with casual, comfortable furniture. A stereo system is also nice here.

OUTDOORS

Redwood planters with flowering plants strategically placed on the porch or deck will soften its lines.

Setting up a patio set with table and chairs helps buyers visualize using the deck. Even better is to place a pitcher and glasses out there, bringing memories of thirst-quenching iced tea to mind.

Walkways can become a place to be, not just one to pass through with the strategic placement of a park bench.

MISCELLANEOUS

You can create a room out of nothing using furniture, lighting, or other personal objects. The more useful spaces the buyer perceives, the larger your home will appear to her psychologically, even if she consciously knows your home is small. For example, an ordinary bland hall can be transformed into an art gallery, or a nondescript nook under the stairs can become a mini-drafting area. Even corners of rooms can become other "rooms" to a buyer. As long as you avoid the appearance of clutter, you will be stretching the value of your home.

Don't forget window treatments. Whether they be soft billowing tufts of cloth to soften the windows in a bedroom or vertical blinds in the living room, window treatments can have a profound effect.

THINGS TO AVOID

Sometimes it helps to point out some things that will turn buyers off to show the contrast. For example, do not put a double bed in a small dark room. If you already have such a situation, take out the bed and put it in storage. Also, be very cautious of odors and mildew smells. An over-scented room is better than a room with a bad smell.

Conclusion

The key to decorating the home to maximize its appeal is like the age-old problem of dissecting the onion. It appears simple on the outside yet is in reality composed of many layers. We can cut the onion apart, but all we are left with is a pile of onion skins and no record of the whole. Instead we must slowly build layer upon layer to bring about the desired effect. No single layer or combination of layers is the whole onion. The total is greater than the sum of the parts. The look and feel of your home must be more than just a few cookbook steps if you want it to give the maximum impact. As you follow the guides in this chapter and this book, use your intuition. It will probably be correct.

CHAPTER TWENTY

Tricks of the Renovation Trade

Painting

EXTERIOR FINISHES

LETTING UNFINISHED WOOD WEATHER naturally is by far the easiest of the exterior finishes. Some woods, such as redwood and cedar, weather well when left unprotected although they will gray or brown in time. Unfinished woods are also more susceptible to warpage, but their beauty is unmatched on many homes such as craftsman-style bungalows.

There are a variety of finishes that can slow the weathering process and allow the building to retain its original look. These are usually water repellent and help protect the wood from cracks and warpage. The application is cheap and easy. They go on just like paint.

If the wood appears too light or you are trying to match new wood to old, there are penetrating stain finishes. Because these finishes penetrate the wood rather than forming a film on top (like paint does), they are especially suited to rougher surfaces and you never get a problem from cracking or blistering. To match a color may require several coats.

Finally, we have exterior paints. Untreated exterior wood should be primed before painting. Exterior paints come in both oil and latex. Oil-based paints are especially good for north sides of buildings and other portions susceptible to dampness. Some states no longer allow their use due to disposal problems.

When you paint the exterior, the architecture of the building should give you clues as to where to apply accents and where to remain with the base color. Remember, darker colors recede while lighter ones will appear closer. If you want a bay window not to pop out from the surface of the building so much, you will paint it darker.

In general, painting darker colors at the base and lighter colors higher up on the building will appear better than having the lighter color at the foundation.

INTERIOR FINISHES

While exterior finishes have weather protection as a major function, interior finishes are more for aesthetics and ease of maintenance. Most finishes mirror the exterior ones, with stains, varnishes, and other finishes for natural woods available.

A key to remember about paint is that flat wall paint goes on the walls and ceilings and semi-gloss paint goes on all the woodwork and trim, including doors, cabinets, and windows. The exceptions to this are the kitchen and bathrooms, where semi-gloss is used all over, as it is water repellant and easy to clean.

Although you should take care to prepare all surfaces properly before painting (i.e., patch all holes, fill all cracks, and make them smooth), paint can go a long way to cover defects. A solid surface in a continuous color of paint tends to cause the eye to glide over it, missing patches and small cracks that might be apparent on closer observation. A mottled paint job, such as a sponged application, can even go a step further in this process.

Sponging, dragging, marbling, and other mottled paint applications can hide surface defects in a wall. Because the eye cannot tell if the change in surface appearance is caused by the paint or the wall, the brain will not register minor plaster flaws as a negative. You may want to use these effects to save yourself some of the preparation time and energy that usually goes into readying a wall for painting.

When choosing colors at the paint store, remember that the colors as they appear on the color chips are not exactly how they will appear on your walls. You should always buy a test quart and paint a patch to see how it looks in reality. In general, colors will come out darker in the interior than they appear on the chips and will appear lighter on the exterior than the chip would indicate.

If you are painting radiators or other objects that get hot, there are special heat resistant paints which should be applied.

Wall Finishes

No matter how nice or new the home, cracks in the wall spell trouble to the uninitiated buyer, even though they may be perfectly benign. If the cracks do not hide anything serious, fill them with spackle and repaint to produce a smooth, new finish. This is probably the simplest repair item in the home.

If you have a problem with cracks in areas that expand and contract a great deal, try using a paintable caulk instead of spackle. Be careful in the application, though, and smooth caulk immediately with a sponge or your finger, as caulk does not sand.

Repairing minor cracks in walls can usually be accomplished easily by patching with spackle or Fix-All and then painting or wallpapering. Sometimes, though, the wall is too far gone to patch well. Following are a couple of ideas you can use in a situation like this.

TEXTURE THE WALL

One of the simplest methods is to texture the walls, to make it seem like all those hundreds of imperfections were planned. Many older homes have experienced settling cracks, have old layers of wallpaper on the plaster, have been patched poorly in the past, and suffer from a myriad of other abuses put on them throughout time. Applying a surface texture will make these imperfections blend together as they now get lost in the thousands of bumps and textures in the wall.

If you look at most new housing developments today, you will see they use textured walls as a standard item. This is to hide imperfections and sloppy workmanship in the quick construction of their walls. Notice the type of texturing they have. This is what you will want to create.

One method to create this texture is to float on a layer of topping compound (available in most hardware stores), hit it with a damp sponge to create peaks and valleys, and then lightly pass over the surface, perhaps at a height of two-thirds the peak height, with a taping knife in a constant direction. After a few attempts at this, you'll soon have the knack of creating textured walls.

Texturing this way is a labor-intensive process and requires some drying time. But in many cases, especially when you have elaborate moldings you don't want to remove, it's quick and inexpensive compared to the alternatives.

Another way to create a textured surface is to use a roller specially designed to leave large bumps, instead of using the sponge, then let dry and sand lightly with an electric sander, leaving a textured surface.

Adding sand to the paint is another method of texturing, although it produces a less attractive surface. It is extremely easy to apply. Just pour some fine-grain sand into the paint, mix, and roll it on as you would normally paint. The sand will be distributed within the paint and produce a rough texture. This is used to hide imperfections in the walls or ceiling.

ROLL ON NEW PLASTER

There are products on the market that are literally a roll of plaster-soaked paper. The paper is rolled onto the damaged wall and smoothed like wallpaper. Because of the paper's thickness, bumps and imperfections get smoothed out and the finished product looks like a new wall. One company that produces this is Flexi-Wall Systems in Liberty, South Carolina.

NEW WALLBOARD

Another method, if the wall is hopeless, is to tear off the old plaster and/or wallboard and hang a new layer of sheetrock. You will then have a perfectly smooth new surface on which to work. Sheetrock is very inexpensive and easy to work with. Tearing off old plaster can be a messy job. Be sure to wear a mask over your nose and mouth. Most do-it-yourself books explain the process fully.

You can also cover the existing wall with a new layer of sheetrock without removing the existing finish. This is used mainly where removal would be impossible or where the overall surface is flat, but just covered with many cracks. This does have the effect of shrinking the room by about a half inch. Remove all moldings first, then replace them onto the new wallboard.

REPLACE WITH NEW MATERIAL

If you have walls covered with an unattractive material such as cheap veneer plywood, removing the material will often leave a very uneven surface. In a case like this you should either replace the whole wallboard or cover

over the existing surface and start fresh. If you are going to wallpaper, this may not be necessary. Use a product like Flexi-Wall to smooth out the surface and fill in the cracks of the wall.

If you have a concrete wall, such as in a basement, you will have to fur it out with thin strips of wood to create an even and easily nailable surface on which to place the wallboard. Do-it-yourself books explain the furring process.

Sometimes, a painted plaster or sheetrock wall isn't the best use of the wall and the room would have a better effect with some other material such as real wood paneling or a quality veneer material. These may require less underlayment preparation.

Molding can act as a distraction, forcing the eye to go to it, rather than the flaws that may line the walls. It also serves as a way to build in a natural break for color changes. A rosette on the ceiling can act as a focal point and pull your eyes away from the wall.

WALLPAPER

Wallpaper can have a dramatic effect in a room. Many an otherwise bland box of four walls has been given life through a good wallpaper job. You have to be very careful of the patterns you choose, though. In general, stick to inoffensive basics.

In its application, wallpaper will not let you escape the tedious preparation of walls that goes on before painting, but the effort can pay off well.

Vinyl and washable wallpapers are available for areas that get a lot of abuse or need washing occasionally. This is the type of wallpaper to apply in a kitchen or bathroom where moisture or grease is present. The downside of some of these papers is their obvious sheen.

Heavily textured wallpapers will help cover minor imperfections in the wall. This is the paper equivalent of textured paints. Or you can use lining paper—an undercoating paper that will smooth out many imperfections in the wall before the final paper is put on top.

If you have a wall with some serious defects, certain manufacturers are now selling wallpaper premounted to plywood. Although primarily designed for new-home builders to cut down on time, it is an easy way to reduce or eliminate prep time. Your selections of wallpapers are limited.

MIRRORS

If you have a wall with an uneven or defective surface, a mirror might be the ideal way to solve the problem. Not only do you get a smooth surface and hide the defect, but you get all the benefits that a mirror brings, too.

VENEER PANELING

There are some very nice veneer panelings on the market. This isn't the sheet paneling with a veneer of simulated wood found in most "home improvement" stores but is paneling with a true veneer of a quality wood. This is much easier to install than solid wood paneling because it comes in standard 4′ x 8′ sheets and can give a room the warm richness of wood. These panels are available in birch, oak, ash, and additionally in several exotic woods. (Price: $12–20 per sheet for the standard, $24–34 per sheet for the premium woods.)

If you have paneling on the wall and it is damaged, there are a few simple techniques you can use to repair it.

If the wood only contains minor scratches or nicks, going over the marred area with a putty stick or a light stain can usually hide it. For more serious damage, you may have to sand and refinish an entire area. Be careful to feather your work out toward the edges to make it less noticeable and to blend into the remaining wall.

If the gouge is deep, you will have to fill the hole with wood putty. After the putty dries, sand it and stain it to match the finish. If you can find a wood putty that matches, even better.

SOLID WOOD

Solid wood paneling is the next highest level. Much can be done with wood. You can creat wainscotings, board and batten finishes, moldings, and many other quality effects that only expensive homes get these days.

You can create a cheaper version of solid wood paneling. Rather than using widths of quality wood, nail plywood to the wall, then put vertical 1 x 2's or 1 x 3's over it to create a board and batten effect. The surface is then painted. No one will know it was cheaper wood below. For all they know it could be expensive oak.

There are an infinite variety of panels you can create using stock moldings. Whether you use picture moldings, crown moldings, or chair rails, you can create a rich effect. Look at homes you like, at pictures in magazines, or get a book on finish carpentry for some ideas.

You can buy solid board panels of wood. These come in all types of softwood or hardwood, in knotty or clear finishes. The panels are usually installed vertically but you can add interest to the paneling by installing it at a 45-degree angle, horizontally, or in any other pattern. Paneling can be applied directly over wallboard or over furring strips.

WOOD FINISHES

Staining can produce a beautiful finish on wood walls, floors, and cabinetry. Staining can actually be even cheaper than painting, and can produce a finish that people associate with quality. The main reason it isn't used as much as paint is that with stain the surface itself must look good. Stain will not hide imperfections but there are a few tricks that can be done with wood.

There are many surface treatments you can give to wood to produce effects that sell. The first is bleaching wood. There are many texts on finishes that will go into the process. The key is to use it to your advantage. By bleaching the floor, you are lightening the room, which always helps in selling a house. For special effects, you can also bleach the wood first and then apply a stain, thus getting a rich look close to that of stained wood but at a lighter color than would have been possible with the unbleached wood.

Ceiling Finishes

If the ceiling is in reasonably good shape and the damage is confined to a few cracks and holes or just in one area, spackle, Fix-All, or a few sheetrock patches should be all that is necessary. If you cannot get a smooth even surface because the damage is too great, you can use many of the texturing methods mentioned previously.

New gypsum board can be nailed to the ceiling if the damage is too great. See a home improvement book for techniques.

A ceiling can be stuccoed and painted for a clean effect that hides all previous mistakes. Or a rosette or some plaster molding can be added in the center of the ceiling to upgrade the look of a room.

Sometimes the only problem is an old water stain. If there is no damage to the sheetrock or plaster, prime with a stain killer, let dry, and paint. If you don't use the stain killer, the water mark will keep re-emerging through the new paint.

CEILING TILES

Acoustical ceiling tiles will help dampen noise from above. This may be important in condominiums or cooperatives. But these tiles can be ugly if not given a proper decorative treatment.

A suspended ceiling of fiberglass or acoustical panels is a good, inexpensive way to hide ductwork and pipes and to put in new lighting without having to tear out the old ceiling. Unfortunately, it's easy to make your home look like an office with this material so caution is the buzzword here. Usually it's better to box in ductwork and pipes by framing around them and then applying a layer of wallboard and finishing.

BEAM AND WOOD CEILINGS

You can trim out your ceiling in a number of ways as you would do your walls. This can be done cheaply with a plywood base and other woods for trim. If you have ceilings with wood, do what you can to restore them. Do not tear them down.

Beam ceilings are also in vogue. Make sure it is appropriate to the architecture of your home. You can hide structural work or just invoke an English manor in your use of beams.

If all else fails or if you need to increase volume and you are on the top floor, you can tear out the ceiling and create a cathedral, coffered, or vaulted wood strip ceiling. This costs more but the effects are also significantly greater.

If you do any major work on the ceiling, it's a good time to think about lighting design. If your lighting is inadequate or inappropriate, the cost of upgrading is at its lowest if the ceiling is already opened up. The major costs in renovating hidden electrical (or plumbing) work are often the tearing up, patching, and refinishing of exposed surfaces.

Trim and Moldings

Baseboards are a must in rooms. They make a cleaner transition between wall and floor and help protect an area that gets much abuse. The size of the baseboard must be appropriate to the design of the room. Many modern homes use smaller baseboards.

Trim always looks good around doors and windows. There are many styles and thicknesses to choose from. What you choose must integrate well with the overall decor and architecture of the room.

Thin picture moldings can be used to create panel doors out of simple plain ones. Cut plywood or other materials can also be used.

Crown moldings serve a very practical purpose. They help visually ease the transition between walls and ceilings and cover up mistakes. Picture moldings placed about twelve inches down from the ceiling provide a good visual transition and help make a room feel more intimate.

There are many patterns of wainscoting that can be built up from simple stock moldings. These can look casual or formal as the room dictates or tie into specific historic periods.

In older homes, sometimes nonstructural columns can add character to an otherwise bland room. These can be simple box posts or elegant Corinthian columns. Use your design sense to see what would be appropriate. A ranch tract home done up like a Roman bath inside attracts a very limited spectrum of buyers.

Don't Underestimate Sheetrock

Sheetrock can be framed into many shapes, creating elegant curves or niches for your artwork or a pot shelf. You can create interesting details using inexpensive framing, drywall, and some trim. You can significantly change the impression of a room with this simple material. Sheetrock can also be formed into arches to create elegant transitions between rooms.

Floors

Choosing a flooring type is one of the most important decisions as far as the look of a room goes. Besides being a visually powerful surface, the floor must also stand up to wear. Especially if you intend to live in the house a while before selling, you need to concern yourself with a few practical matters in your choice of flooring.

Durability. Halls and entries are especially subject to traffic and a flooring choice should respond accordingly. Beware of footpath formation—those areas of rooms that seem to get worn quickly. When you choose your flooring, considerations like this should be made. For example, for entries both tile and hardwood are good materials. Both are durable and beautiful, and, in the case of hardwood, the area can be refinished again and again.

Maintenance. You don't want to be stuck cleaning all the time and neither does your buyer. White carpets may look stunning and will probably impress a buyer at first. But if they start thinking maintenance issues, you might lose the sale.

Warmth and noise. A flooring needs to feel welcoming and comfortable. Industrial floors might be easy to clean but few people want them in their home. Noise is also an issue. That's why carpets are usually a good choice in the bedroom.

Think hardwood. There's nothing like the beauty of a hardwood floor. If you have one, it's a very easy job to make it beautiful again. Usually all it takes is a sanding and refinishing. Floor sanders can be rented for about $35 a day and you can usually get about two good-sized rooms done. Professionals usually charge about $1–2 per square foot to refinish floors.

Small repairs can be made easily by chiseling out the damaged section and nailing down a new piece of flooring. Many problems such as warped or cracked flooring can usually be repaired without removing the damaged piece. However, if your floor is very pocked, burned, or otherwise damaged, you should probably cover it with carpeting as it would be expensive to fix it.

If the problem is just a few dark stains and discolorations, staining it can hide these problems. Removing stain from a floor is very hard. You have to sand down many layers. Even then, it is uncertain that you will be able to get out all the stain. Carpeting or restaining is usually the answer, although you can try bleaching, too.

The easiest way to lighten floors is to bleach them. You can use ordinary household bleach or buy bleaching kits. The kits usually use a two-part process. You wipe on the first chemical with a sponge, let it sit, and then wipe on the second chemical. Bleaching creates a sleek, modern effect that works very well in contemporary homes.

Hardwood flooring is available in many different woods such as maple, teak, or pecan, but oak is the usual choice. Parquets are available in 3/8-inch or 3/4-inch thicknesses, while strips are usually 3/4-inch thick.

Hardwood flooring is easy to install if you have carpentry skill. It can be back-breaking labor, though, if not done properly. There are new flooring systems now available, which come in larger sections rather than individual boards. This saves much in your time or in labor costs.

You can buy hardwood flooring unfinished and then stain and seal it with a finish such as polyurethane, or buy it prefinished. The prefinished floors come in individual planks or assembled sections. Either way, they save you the hassle, mess, and fumes of refinishing the floor.

The type of finish you use is important for looks. Don't use a wax finish in a kitchen as it will spot from drips or spills. Water won't harm a polyurethane finish but it will eventually show its wear and tear by scratching.

To save money, you can buy hardwood floors that are not solid oak but are plywood laminated with a veneer of oak. These only come prefinished.

Putting in a fancy border takes a little skill with a router but will add significantly to the appeal of the floor. Woods for this purpose include rosewood, ebony, and ironwood. Also available are pre-made borders that will dramatically frame your floor for a small premium.

These factory-assembled pieces can be nailed or glued down to the subfloor. You save tremendously on time and labor.

As far as the old taboo about mixing wood and water, that can finally be broken. There are plastic-like finishes that can protect the wood. So don't be afraid to install wood flooring in the kitchen or bath.

You can also install wood in a parquet pattern. These wood blocks usually come in 12-inch squares. You need a very smooth subfloor to lay these.

Plank and strip hardwood floors cannot be directly installed over concrete slabs (there's no place to nail). But parquet squares can be glued down with a mastic. The key criterion is that the floor be flat.

CARPET

Wall-to-wall carpeting is one of the quickest and easiest materials to have installed and can transform the look of a room instantly. Although easy to install, unless you have special tools, it's usually recommended that a professional do the work. (You won't be paying too much for his time.) Carpet comes in an infinite variety of colors, textures, and quality. When carpeting for resale, you need to balance cost with quality.

First establish the demands placed on the area you are carpeting: A hallway merits a more durable fiber than a guest bedroom. Different quality carpets will wear significantly differently. In determining quality, a carpet's pile is more important than its depth. You can even carpet in light colors today without fear. There are special treatments for carpeting, such as antistatic or soil resistance. Remember, they work better if they are part of the fiber itself rather than applied after the fiber is manufactured. A light-colored carpet can easily brighten a room.

The feel of carpeting will be greatly influenced by the padding underneath. Good, thick, quality padding will even help cushion carpet against minor unevenness in the floor.

You can combine carpet with hardwood to achieve a beautiful effect. Either place an area rug on top of a hardwood floor, or install the carpet on the subfloor and have the oak strips installed around it, creating a border where both materials are at the same level.

VINYL

Vinyl flooring, linoleum, or resilient flooring are all descriptions of the same thing. The flooring comes in sizes from 12-inch tiles to 12-foot sheets. The flooring is relatively inexpensive and, in the case of the vinyl tiles, is easy to install.

If you have damaged flooring, it can be repaired if there is some extra around the house. Beware of discoloration that may have occurred. Vinyl flooring tends to look tired after several years of use and usually dictates replacement if damaged.

If you are installing new flooring, make sure the underlayment is perfectly smooth and clean. All imperfections will show, even nail heads. After you've installed it, use a rented or borrowed floor roller to get out all the bubbles and make a perfectly flat floor.

TILE

Ceramic tiles are a beautiful and durable way to upgrade your floor. They offer an almost unlimited number of colors, patterns, and textures for your choice. Different finishes work best for different uses. A smooth glossy tile works well in the bathroom, as it is easy to clean, while a nonskid or matte finish works well on a kitchen floor, taking the constant abuse of feet, spills, and dropped pots and pans.

Perhaps the least expensive way to create the most enhancement with a tile job is to create an appealing pattern in the work. This costs no more in materials than a single-colored job and rarely much more in labor. Figure 20-1 shows some examples of tile patterns.

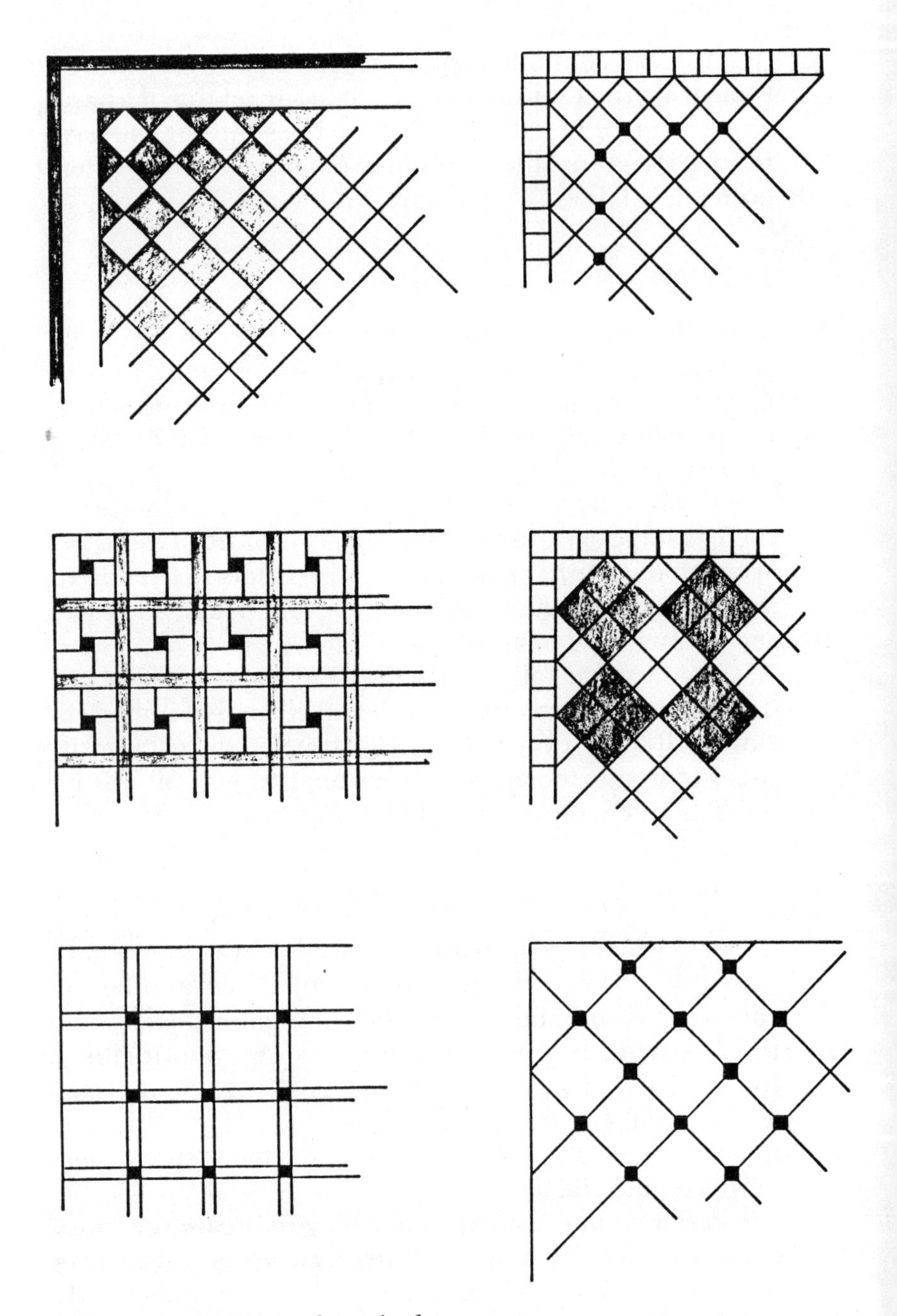

Figure 20-1 *Examples of tile patterns*

When setting your tile pattern, view it from the doorway first. That is how a buyer will approach it, so you want to present the best possible view from the entry.

Tiling can be done by the homeowner if it's done with care. It is necessary to pay attention to detail or your lines may not come out straight. Once the mortar is dry, there's little you can do to correct it. Plastic spacers are available to help minimize this problem.

The quality of the subfloor, the preparation, and the method of installation will significantly affect the durability of the floor. Ceramic tiles can be installed over almost any sound, dry, clean, level surface. Thus you can upgrade almost any surface in your home where tiles might be appropriate simply by putting down a mastic and placing the tiles on top. If the surface is not of the required quality, the tiles will tend to pop up in a relatively short period of time.

If you have a home with cracked or loose ceramic tiles, before you replace them check the surface underneath. A very common cause of loosening tiles is moisture. You'll want to correct the problem before replacing the tiles.

Sometimes the tile is in good shape but the grout detracts from the look of a tile job. This is easy to correct. Scrape out the old grout with a special tool available in hardware stores and then put new grout in. A different grout color can have a strong effect on the look of the tile surface.

If you have just an occasional cracked or missing tile, substitute a contrasting color tile in a regular pattern around the floor. It will look planned.

One item to remember when laying ceramic or marble tile floors is that when you encounter a molding or door frame, it is the wood that gets trimmed to accommodate the tile, not the other way around. This avoids the frustrating and time-consuming task of cutting tiles.

OTHER IDEAS

Raised floors (platforms) can bring life to an otherwise dull room. Whether it's an entire room, such as a raised dining room, or only part of a room, such as a study area in the living area, raising the floor can visually make a "room" out of just a little bit of floor space. Building a platform floor is also very handy for hiding plumbing in a new kitchen or bathroom if tearing up the walls is not practical.

In many homes, you will find the floor is not level, sometimes significantly so. You must first seek out the source of this problem in order not to scare buyers away. A nonlevel floor scares buyers. The solution may be as simple as jacking up the floor. Sometimes the remedy is to level the floor by building a platform or false floor. But where room will not allow, you can pour a floor from a latex substance (there are several different brands) and feather it out with the existing floor. Then carpet to cover and provide warmth.

Little Touches

The details in the home, such as doorknobs, lightplates, cabinet hardware, or mailboxes, can say a lot about a home. Often, changing these details will help in changing the impression of your home.

There are an infinite variety of details and hardware from which to choose. Brass is the preferred metal. You can buy brass mailboxes, house numbers, doorknobs, etc. By making the detailing consistent, you can subconsciously help to unify a home. Although relatively inexpensive, changing all the detail hardware can amount to several hundred dollars, so put your money where it's most important, such as at the front door, the main entry, and the kitchen.

Of all the hardware, doorknobs are the most expensive. Knobs and locksets come in brass, bronze, nickel, stainless steel, and porcelain finishes. Most doorknobs cost from $12–40, with front door locksets going as high as $200. For the full range of styles available, contact major lockset manufacturers such as Kwickset or Schlage for a catalog. For particular styles to match older homes, there are catalogs of details available from renovator's supply houses.

CHAPTER TWENTY-ONE

Financing Renovations

YOU KNOW WHAT NEEDS to be done to your home to increase its value. Now you just need to find a way to pay for it. There are several avenues you can take to pay for the work. In this chapter we will explore some of them.

Paying Cash

If your plans are to remain in your home for awhile, you could finance the renovation out of your pocket, incrementally, as your financial situation will allow. If the renovation cost is not too great and you plan on doing most of the work yourself, this method could be for you. On the one hand, you pay no interest on a construction loan and, therefore, you're not under the gun to get the project done early. However, you can end up stretching out your renovation over many months or years, during which time you basically live in an uncompleted construction project. This could place a psychological burden on you and your family. Many projects financed this way have ended up with a complete home and an incomplete family.

If, however, you are extremely liquid and can pay for a good part of the renovation costs now, this is the easiest option. Usually, though, you will get a better return on your capital if you finance the renovation.

Borrowing from Family and Friends

If you don't have the capital to pay for the work yourself nor the income to qualify for a bank loan, or you have little or no credit history, the best way to finance your renovation might be to borrow from lenders with lower underwriting requirements—namely, people you know. Even when borrowing from family, you should set up a payment schedule and choose a fair interest rate. Make sure you get a written contract. Few things have destroyed more families or friendships than money disputes.

When deciding on an appropriate interest rate, note that the IRS requires that a certain minimum rate be paid on loans. Otherwise they will impute their rate on your loan and tax your lender appropriately. If you'd rather not take out a loan, make your "lender" an investor or equity partner. You might give them a percentage of the profit as their payment.

Credit Cards

If you have several credit cards and you're planning your renovation, see if you can extend your credit lines before you start the work. Credit cards are an expensive way to finance any work but if you don't qualify for a standard bank loan and you will be paying them off soon from the sale of your home, financing with cards should not be too much of a problem. If you can earn 50 percent return on money you borrow at 18 percent, it's a good return, even if the cost of money was expensive.

Bank Loans

For most people, the best way to finance a renovation is with a loan from a local bank, savings and loan, or credit union. The following are descriptions of some of the more common loans available.

HOME IMPROVEMENT OR CONSTRUCTION LOAN

This loan is based on the bank's perceived value of what your home will be worth after the renovation is completed. The loan can be unsecured or secured, although you will pay a higher interest rate on an unsecured loan. With this loan, the bank will probably require detailed proof that the money is being spent on the home itself and not for your vacation to Rio.

SECOND MORTGAGE

If you've been living in your home for awhile, chances are you have built up a large equity. This money can be tapped by placing a second mortgage on your property. Your home is the security for the loan. The property does not have to be your home to qualify, although you usually will get a better rate if it is. The bank doesn't watch what you do with the money on a loan like this.

HOME EQUITY LOANS

If you are borrowing on your principal residence, a more flexible version of the second mortgage is now out. It is called a home equity line of credit. Being marketed aggressively by banks, savings and loans, brokerage houses, and consumer finance companies, home equity loans make it easier than ever to tap into your home's equity and to take out the money for anything you want, whether it be renovating your house, renovating another house, or even making the down payment on a third house.

The credit is relatively cheap, and extremely flexible—you only pay for the money you've actually removed for the time you have it. This contrasts with a traditional second mortgage loan, where you pay interest on the entire loan, even though you may not need to use part of it right now. Also, the tax laws allow you to deduct the interest payments on your home equity line if it's used for home improvements.

But realize that all mortgage borrowing is a two-edged sword, because your home is the collateral and if you overextend yourself, it is possible you could lose your home. Watch your limit. With a home equity line remember to follow these four suggestions:

Set a reasonable limit on borrowing

Shop around for best rates

Beware of teaser rates

Set up a repayment schedule

REFINANCING MORTGAGES

Instead of taking out a second mortgage, you may find it is cheaper to refinance your existing first mortgage. This is especially true if you're in an environment where rates have dropped since you took out your first loan. If you take out a new variable loan, the starter rate may be very low relative to your previous loan. Beware of points and other fees that can add significantly to the cost of your borrowed money.

PERSONAL LINE OF CREDIT

Many banks will make secured or unsecured personal loans to borrowers with sufficient net worth or established credit. This can be at a cheaper rate than a second mortgage and is worth investigating.

Special and Government Programs and Loans

FHA TITLE 1 LOANS

There is a special loan program from the federal government called the FHA Title 1 home improvement loan program. It allows you to borrow up to $17,500 on your home whether there is equity in it or not. To find out where to get one, contact your regional office of the Federal Housing Administration. You can find this in the phone book under the government listings. Many banks do Title 1 programs, but beware of the sharks who will charge excessive points and fees for these desirable loans.

LIFE INSURANCE LOANS

Many policies will allow you to borrow money against the cash value of your policy. These are typically fixed loans at a low interest rate. Beware of lowering the value of your life insurance policy should something happen.

STOCK AND BOND LOANS

Most brokerages allow you to borrow on margin against your account. These loans are usually at reasonable interest rates. Beware of the illiquidity of doing this. If the value of your stocks falls and you get called, you will have to sell your stocks if you can't produce the cash.

LOCAL CITY AND REGIONAL LOANS

Some of the best loans are available from city housing authorities. These loans are funded by community block grants and local bond issues. Programs such as the rental rehabilitation program provide loans with interest as low as 6 percent to owners whose buildings fall within certain boundaries. These are not necessarily the bad parts of town. Many middle-class communities fall under block grant designations.

FMHA 504 LOANS

If you live in a rural area and qualify as a low-income family, the government will make loans available to you at 1 percent interest under this program. The purpose of this loan is to bring properties up to present building code requirements.

SECTION 312 REHABILITATION LOANS

The purpose of the Section 312 program is to encourage rehabilitation of properties in areas targeted by the federal government by providing low-interest-rate loans. The primary objective of these loans is to preserve the existing housing stock in neighborhoods where it might otherwise decline further. Many of these neighborhoods are currently making comebacks.

WEATHERIZATION PROGRAMS

Utility companies and government agencies will sometimes provide loans or grants to insulate a house. This can be a low-cost way of doing a vital renovation.

OTHER LOW-INCOME LOANS

If your income is below the median for the area, you may qualify for special low-interest-rate loans offered through your city or state. Contact your local department of economic development to find out what opportunities may be available to you.

Private Lenders and Loan Sharks

In every city, there are people that lend money. The rates can range from reasonable to exorbitant. If you are going to borrow from one of these people, make sure you will make enough to make this type of lending worthwhile.

You don't want to lose your home because you couldn't make 25 percent interest payments.

How to Get Bank Loans

In getting a renovation loan or a new purchase loan for a fixer-upper, knowing the right banker can make or break the deal. Many people will spend months searching for the right property, make careful inspections, determine potential increased value, and then throw it away by going with any bank just because they had the lowest rates or were the most convenient.

A good working relationship with a bank and a banker within that bank can be one of your most valuable assets when dealing in renovations for profit. Just as you would seek out a good accountant or lawyer, a good banker can be invaluable to you. Be aggressive, find the right banker. Note that many banks now do all their loans from a central loan department and the influence of the banker is nil. These are not the banks you want to work with unless you have a large net worth. Since most people initially may not have much more to go on than their character, a bank that recognizes people and doesn't process its loan applications like tax returns can be an invaluable asset.

Once you've found a bank that works with people, get to know several officers at the bank. There are inevitable personnel changes all the time and you don't want to get stuck because your banker is now at a branch 100 miles away.

Remember, banks are in the business of making loans. It's the only way they make their money. So go in as a potential customer of the bank, not like you're being greeted by the inquisition.

Banks are not the only place to get loans. Instead, try a mortgage broker. They can be your best money source. Most of us don't have time to keep up on what banks have the best rates and which ones are doing the type of loan we need. This is the job of the mortgage broker. With his extensive contacts in the banking industry, he can usually find you a loan that meets your needs. Although sometimes this may cost you a little more (the mortgage broker charges a fee), many times you actually end up paying less because of the better terms of the loan.

If you don't qualify for a loan, don't give up. There is always a way. I would caution, though, that if five banks turn down your project, you should double-check your original calculations before proceeding. Find out why the banks have rejected it. If you find their judgment to be unsound or too conservative, then resume your search for funds.

Getting Good Appraisals

If you are borrowing money from a bank or institutional source, the property is going to be the security for the loan. Since most loans are made at a predetermined loan-to-value ratio, the higher a value your appraisal states the property has, the higher a loan you can receive.

When you meet the appraiser at the property, you want to be prepared. You need to be a salesperson showing your home in the best light possible. Appraisal is more an art than a science, and as in any art, there is a lot of room for subjective judgment.

You need to develop rapport with the appraiser. If she feels like you're trying to give her a snow job, hiding flaws and defects in the property, she'll look extra carefully for them and your home may not qualify for the loan you are seeking.

It is recommended that you have a sheet of recent sales in the area handy for the appraiser. You will save her the problem of looking for comps, and you can choose ones that put your home in a favorable light. Just don't go to extremes. Remember, these people have seen a lot more property than you and will know when something seems too out of line.

It is your job to point out the good aspects of the house or area the appraiser might not know or notice, just as you would do for someone who is looking to buy the house.

Appraisers look at a neighborhood as you would, assessing its overall quality. However, they tend to go by designated borders. For example, if your home is on the border of two neighborhoods, you want to know what criteria is causing it to be considered part of the worse neighborhood and what criteria will allow it to be part of the better. Your job is to convince the appraiser it's part of the better neighborhood.

Appraisers also want to see if the neighborhood is hot or not. Do things sell quickly? Or have most homes languished on the market for over three months?

The following are some of the items appraisers consider.

Most Americans prefer quiet streets to noisy ones. We value our privacy. In any given town, values tend to be higher on the quiet streets. In suburbs, these are cul de sacs. Downtown, they may be side streets.

It is preferable to be out of sight of a commercial use.

Is your lot abnormally large or small for the area?

What is the sales price per square foot of living area?

What is the condition and apparent age of your home?

The three biggest contributors of value are bedrooms, bathrooms, and total living area.

To be listed as a bedroom, a room must have a closet and meet minimum dimensions. This is currently 8 feet by 10 feet.

Is the neighborhood stable, going up, or going down?

What is the property's relation to public amenities (local mom-and-pop groceries) or problems (schools or housing projects)?

What is the zoning of your lot and adjacent lots? If the lot next door is zoned industrial, even if there's a house on it and your real estate agent swears they'll never build a factory there, beware.

As you can see, it's an eclectic list. In order to get good appraisals, one must be aware of what the appraiser is looking for. In a nutshell, he wants to know if your house is functional, desirable, and what it's worth.

One of the twelve basic principles of property value is conformity. A house that conforms with the neighbors is worth more than one that sticks out. When we say conform, we mean a reasonable degree of architectural homogeneity, not necessarily identical look-alikes as in many suburbs. Those actually have lower value, as people want some identity to their homes.

To prepare for the building inspection, the appraiser gathers background information on the property. Zoning and building codes are looked at. Buildings are rated on their quality, condition, and functional utility. Good materials, proper construction techniques, and a high degree of workmanship all contribute to the appraiser's definition of quality. Condition is obvious. The reason it is a concern for appraisers is it helps them determine the remaining useful life of the structure or item. Functional utility is the ability of a room or a structure to perform its intended function under today's market conditions. Stairs that are too steep, old plumbing, and other items we talked about all register on an appraiser's form.

The building's deficiencies in terms of size, style, layout, and traffic patterns are all noted and affect value. A superadequacy is a building component that exceeds market standards. An overimprovement is an improvement that does not represent the most profitable use of the site because its cost or size precludes the optimization of value.

Refinancing Mortgages

When you go to sell, having an assumable loan in place makes it easy for a new buyer to purchase your property. Banks tend to be more lenient on someone assuming a loan than on a new purchase. Many people who could not otherwise qualify will now be able to purchase your property. Of course, there is a cost for this in terms of loan fees and time, but if you want to get top dollar and/or your property is top of the line for its type of buyer, refinancing now might just be the way to swing the deal.

Financing can make or break a sale of your property. There are many books on how you can structure a creative deal. If you offer someone a low down payment option, you can usually get more for the home because more buyers can afford to pay a low down payment. Conversely, if you demand 20 percent down and all cash, your price will be adjusted by the market accordingly.

Is It Worth Doing?

Remember, you must think about sales price when you buy so that you can work backward, and calculate your gain. You must allow for unseen contingencies in the renovation and budget for extra carrying costs if the property does not sell right away.

The costs to be aware of in determining how much cash you need and how much margin you have are as follows.

Original cost of purchase

Loan fees and closing costs

Renovation costs

Carrying costs while renovating

Carrying costs during sales period

Commissions and sales costs at closing

Utility bills and other service charges

Taxes and insurance

The more of your costs you can finance, the less cash of your own that is at risk, especially if you have non-recourse financing. One of the best purposes of going through the loan process is to determine if this deal is really the best for you—will it make you the money you expect and are you capable of dealing with downside risks? Using other people's money always makes it easier. If you can keep your cash used to a minimum, it allows you to breathe easier and live on your savings.

CHAPTER TWENTY-TWO

Checklist Before Your Sale

YOUR HOME SHOULD LOOK its best when being shown to prospective buyers. Remember, first impressions last. It is your goal to make the buyer feel so at home that she wants to buy the house right then and there.

The following lists are some final items that should be checked before showing the home in order to maximize its appeal.

General Exterior

Wash all painted surfaces as needed, particularly areas with mildew.

Pay special attention to the front entry.

Scrape, spot prime, and repaint any areas that won't clean in the front of the house.

Make sure the house numbers are clearly readable from the street. Polish any brass numbers, door knobs, and rails.

Landscaping

Mow the lawn. Edge the borders. Make your lawn as well manicured as possible.

Remove any objects from the yard that might be offensive or that pertain only to your style of living such as "little black boy" figurines.

Put out lawn chairs, a patio table, and/or a barbecue so people can envision themselves out in the yard relaxing.

Water and fertilize all shrubs to keep them looking healthy.

Remove any dead or sickly-looking plants. Fill in gaps with new plants.

Prune bushes and trees to help define their shapes and give the yard a more cared-for feeling.

Remove garden tools, hoses, and children's toys from the yard, especially the front yard. This only clutters up the look of your home and can actually be dangerous.

Make sure all walkways are cleared of leaves and ice.

Make sure flower and planter beds are all neat.

Entry

Make sure the front area feels warm and inviting.

Clean off the front steps. Make sure all dirt and plant matter are removed. This is not the place for last year's Christmas tree. Firewood should be moved to another location.

Make sure the doorbell works, the doorknob is on firmly and is polished, and if your front door has glass in it, that it is clean.

Make sure the front door light fixture is working.

General Interior

Clean all soiled walls, doors, and moldings of dirt and fingerprints.

Check all walls and ceilings for cracks. Patch and paint if necessary. Seal, prime, and paint any ceiling stains.

Clean all light fixtures.

Clean and polish the floors.

If necessary, sand hardwood floors and refinish with polyurethane

Remove any offensive or overly political or religious articles from view.

Make sure the house is clean and tidy.

Open the curtains to let in the sunlight and warm the house.

Brighten the lights with higher wattage bulbs.

Make sure all windows are clean inside and out.

Make sure doors open easily, doorknobs feel solid, and all windows are unstuck.

Remove excess pictures and posters to allow for more free-flowing expanses of wall.

Clean furnace, boiler, hot water heater, etc.

Straighten and organize all closets.

Make sure all light switches work.

Kitchen

Wash walls, floors, and countertops in kitchen.

Unclutter the countertops by storing small appliances.

Make sure the ventilation system is clean and operating. Replace the old, greasy filter in the stove hood.

Repair any dripping faucets.

Clean below sink area.

Set the table with your best china. Use folded cloth napkins and place a vase of flowers on the table.

Clear out kitchen cabinets and shelves and scrub. Replace only what you actually use. Cluttered cabinets make the kitchen look like it has inadequate storage space.

Wash and refinish cabinet fronts as needed.

Clean the inside and outside surfaces of appliances, especially the refrigerator, stove, and oven.

Bath

Clean all surfaces, especially the toilet, the tub, and shower walls.

Fix or replace any chipped tiles.

Remove any personal items from bathroom countertops or floor.

Repair leaky faucets.

Make sure toilet is set firmly and working well.

Place a vase with fresh-cut flowers on the vanity if there is room.

Stack some lush folded towels in view.

Replace shower curtain with a new one—they're almost impossible to clean.

Fireplace

Check fireplace screen.

Remove spent ashes and restock fireplace with wood.

Make sure damper and flue are working properly.

Dining Room

Set the table with pretty china and silver. Stimulate the buyer's imagination. This is a simple item that can transform an ordinary dining room into a warm and welcoming place.

Make sure the china cabinet is not crammed with items. You want a clean and tidy look. Clean the glass.

Clear sideboards and serving counters. Place a bowl filled with fruit or a vase of flowers on top.

Windows

Clean all windows inside and out so that they glisten.

Make sure the windows move freely up and down. Check for warpage.

Repair any cracked panes of glass or holes in screens.

Keep window sashes, storm windows, and screens at the same position in front of the house. The easiest way to do this is keep them all closed.

Repair any broken storm windows and screens.

Lower all shades and blinds to an equal level within a room. Make them also match from the front of the house.

Remove distracting objects that buyers will see as they approach your home. Time to hide grandma's giant yellow table lamp or to take out the air conditioner (unless it's the only way to make your home comfortable).

Little Techniques

In the fall or winter, have a fire going in the fireplace.

Play relaxing music softly in the background. Turn off the television.

Perhaps have wine or cheese out to cause prospective buyers to linger.

Be aware of smells. Freshly-baked cookies emanating from the kitchen bring warm memories to buyer's hearts.

Index